D0761860

Lawless World

Philippe Sands QC has been Professor of Law at University College London since 2002, and has also taught at Boston College School of Law, Cambridge University and New York University Law School. He is the author and editor of several books on international law and participated in the negotiation of the 1992 Climate Change Convention and the 1998 Rome Statute of the International Criminal Court. He is also a practising barrister at Matrix Chambers and has been involved in leading cases before English and international courts, including those concerning Senator Augusto Pinochet and the Guantánamo and Belmarsh detainees. He lives in London with his wife and three children.

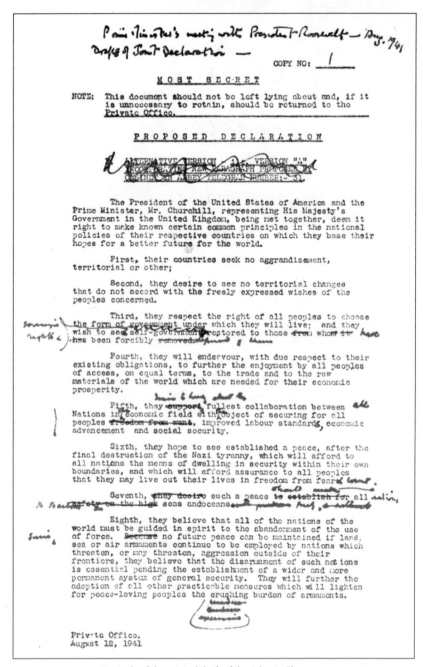

Facsimile of the original draft of the Atlantic Charter,
showing Mr Churchill's corrections by hand.

PHILIPPE SANDS

Lawless World

America and the Making and Breaking of Global Rules

ALLEN LANE

an imprint of

PENGUIN BOOKS

ALLEN LANE

Published by the Penguin Group
Penguin Books Ltd, 80 Strand, London WC2R ORL, England
Penguin Group (USA) Inc., 375 Hudson Street, New York, New York 10014, USA
Penguin Group (Canada), 10 Alcorn Avenue, Toronto, Ontario, Canada M4V 3B2
(a division of Pearson Penguin Canada Inc.)
Penguin Ireland, 25 St Stephen's Green, Dublin 2, Ireland (a division of Penguin Books Ltd)
Penguin Group (Australia), 250 Camberwell Road,
Camberwell, Victoria 3124, Australia (a division of Pearson Australia Group Pty Ltd)
Penguin Books India Pvt Ltd, 11 Community Centre,
Panchsheel Park, New Delhi – 110 017, India
Penguin Group (NZ), cnr Airborne and Rosedale Roads, Albany,
Auckland 1310, New Zealand (a division of Pearson New Zealand Ltd)
Penguin Books (South Africa) (Pty) Ltd, 24 Sturdee Avenue,
Rosebank 2196, South Africa

Penguin Books Ltd, Registered Offices: 80 Strand, London WC2R ORL, England

www.penguin.com

First published 2005
1

Copyright © Philippe Sands, 2005

The moral right of the author has been asserted

All rights reserved. Without limiting the rights under copyright
reserved above, no part of this publication may be reproduced, stored in
or introduced into a retrieval system, or transmitted, in any form or by any
means (electronic, mechanical, photocopying, recording or otherwise),
without the prior written permission of both the copyright owner
and the above publisher of this book

Set in 10.5/14 pt Linotype Sabon
Typeset by Palimpsest Book Production Limited, Polmont, Stirlingshire
Printed in Great Britain by Clays Ltd, St Ives plc

A CIP catalogue record for this book is available from the British Library

ISBN 0-713-99792-3

For Natalia,
and for all my students
of international law.

Les lois sont des toiles d'araignées à travers lesquelles passent les grosses mouches et où restent les petites.

(*Laws, like the spider's webs, catch the small flies and let the large ones go free.*)

Honoré de Balzac,
La Maison Nucingen

Contents

CONTENTS

Preface

In the 1940s the United States and Britain led efforts to replace a world of chaos and conflict with a new, rules-based system. Although their views were not exactly identical – one had an empire to protect and the other did not, one had a constitutional order promoting individual rights and the other did not – they hoped to make the world a better place, free from fear or want. They proposed new international rules to place limits on the use of force, promote the protection of fundamental human rights, and enshrine free trade and international economic liberalization. They created a coalition under the banner of a United Nations. Together with many other countries, their project was premised on a belief that the rules would create opportunities and promote values which were widely shared.

Over the next fifty years the mission to deepen and develop international law was, broadly speaking, successful. By the 1990s the Cold War had been won, the United States was the most powerful nation on earth, and Britain was punching above its weight. But it may have been too successful a mission. The rules which were intended to constrain others became constraining of their creators. Human rights norms took on a life of their own. They came to be applied in ways which were politically inconvenient, as the Pinochet case showed. Economic obligations began to undermine domestic decision-making on jobs and the environment. And the rules prohibiting the use of force came to be seen as insufficiently flexible to allow intervention when thought necessary, as Kosovo proved.

At the opening of the twenty-first century the world was a very different place from the one restructured by Franklin Roosevelt and Winston Churchill half a century earlier. International law had wrought a revolution, with rules reaching into the nooks and crannies of everyday life. But it had been a silent revolution. Most people were unaware of the great extent to which their daily lives were being touched by the new global rules. And the relationship between the US and Britain had changed, with a distinct reversal of positions. The US was more powerful, and increasingly antagonistic towards some of the rules which went too far in undermining sovereignty and vital interests. Britain was less powerful and more comfortable with its international commitments, although there were growing concerns in some quarters that the regional rules of the European Community and the European Convention on Human Rights might be changing the national identity for ever.

With the election of George W. Bush in November 2000, a US Administration took office that was outspoken in its determination to challenge global rules. Soon it turned into a full-scale assault, a war on law. This began even before 9/11, although that day's appalling events provided an added spur with the argument that international rules were somehow not up to the new challenges which the world now faced. I disagree fundamentally with that argument, and in this book I explain why. I trace the efforts of the first George W. Bush Administration to remake the system of global rules, from the abandonment of the Rome Statute on the International Criminal Court and the Kyoto Protocol on global warming, through the attempt to disapply the Geneva Conventions and other human rights norms at Guantánamo and other places, to the virtual disavowal of the United Nations' prescriptions prohibiting the use of force. Even when it comes to the international economic rules on free trade and the protection of foreign investments, which the Administration claims to support, there are signs of new thinking. Faced with this onslaught the British government was often silent or, in certain respects, a willing handmaiden to some of the worst violations of international law. Together, the two countries were trying to remake the global rules. But they were doing so without a proper script. Rather like the scenario for post-Saddam Iraq, no thought seemed to have been given to the question: what do we replace them with?

*

At the most personal level I could say that the roots of my interest in this subject go back to the decimation of my mother's family in the 1930s, in the pre-modern international law world which allowed massacre with impunity. Or it may have been my first teacher of international law, Robbie Jennings, a Yorkshireman with so much common sense that even the most ardent disbelievers could be brought to heel. But probably the catalyst was an execution in Virginia, well before George W. Bush took office. In the middle of Bill Clinton's second term of office, I spent a week in Richmond, Virginia, teaching a short course on the resolution of international disputes. The Commonwealth of Virginia is America's most important tobacco state, and fiercely insistent on its right to regulate its own affairs free from external interference. That means both federal and international interference. The message I brought – that international rules which the federal government could sign up to might constrain the actions of a state like Virginia – was going against the grain in that part of the world. It has parallels in the powerful national sentiment against the growing incursions of the European Community into British sovereignty, only at a far greater level of intensity.

The students at the T. C. Williams School of Law were smart, but sceptical about the themes which ran through my seminars. The idea that the influence of global rules was expanding rapidly and that this was, in itself, not necessarily a bad thing, was not a line they were used to hearing. During my week in Virginia a case reached the fifteen judges of the International Court of Justice in The Hague (a body that is sometimes referred to as the World Court). It concerned Virginia's right to execute a man who had brutally murdered a woman in Arlington, Virginia, not too far from Richmond. The coincidence was remarkable because the World Court hears so few cases (only two or three a year) and also because the issues before the Court touched so directly on the subject of my seminars. What is the effect of international laws on domestic actions? How do global rules impinge on sovereignty? Who makes the global rules, and how democratic are they? Should the International Court of Justice defer to the US, or to Virginia, and how?

These are familiar issues to British and other European lawyers, because we are used to the everyday impact of European Community rules and the law of the separate European Convention on Human Rights. But most Americans, even the well-travelled lawyers amongst them, are uncomfortable with the idea that foreign judges in a far-away international court, in a country they may never have visited (or even heard of) could halt an execution in Virginia, even temporarily.

'International law is for others, not for us' was the way an irate caller put it on a local radio phone-in programme.

The man to be executed was a Paraguayan called Angel Breard. He had been convicted of raping and murdering Ruth Dickie. Originally he had denied guilt, but eventually he confessed, believing that if he did so he would be spared the death penalty. 'I acted under a satanic curse' was his improbable defence.[1] He had been given access to defence lawyers, but was not put in contact with Paraguayan consular officials, and they were not informed of his arrest. Only after he had been convicted and sentenced did he and his lawyers learn about an obscure international treaty – the 1963 Vienna Convention on Consular Relations – which obliged the US to ensure that he was informed immediately of his right to have access to a consular official. By then it was much too late. Federal and state laws meant he could no longer raise procedural rights of consular access in new appeals to the Virginia courts, or to the US federal courts. The Clinton Administration admitted that in Breard's case it had violated the international rules. It offered an apology. It promised to do better next time. But it was not willing to suspend Breard's execution in the face of the claim that he might have argued his criminal defence differently – for example, by pleading guilty from the outset.

So Paraguay brought a case to the International Court. It argued that the US had violated its obligations under the 1963 Convention and that the execution should be suspended. On 9 April 1998, just five days before Breard was due to be executed, the International Court ordered the US to take steps to ensure that Breard was not executed before the Court had given its final decision in the case. This was an injunction, an order to suspend the execution.[2] A spokesman for Senator Jesse Helms, the then Chairman of the Senate Foreign Relations Committee, and one of the US Senate's most reactionary members, declared that the Court's order was 'an appalling intrusion by the United Nations into the affairs of the state of Virginia'.[3]

From my cosy European perspective it was unimaginable that the law-abiding authorities in Virginia and the United States could not find some way to respect the International Court's injunction, and stop the execution, at least temporarily. 'The governor, I take it, is a pretty reasonable chap,' I naively told a reporter from the *Richmond Times Dispatch*. 'He's not going to want to do anything that would bring

Virginia into disrepute.'[4] But the International Court's order cut no ice with the US Supreme Court (to which Breard and Paraguay had appealed) or the Governor of Virginia. The Clinton Administration fudged. It was caught between a desire to respect the international rules and American constitutional constraints on federal interference in Virginia's actions. Clinton offered Secretary of State Madeleine Albright to urge Virginia's Governor James Gilmore III to suspend the execution until the World Court had given its final ruling. But simultaneously he sent his Solicitor General to the US Supreme Court to argue that it could and should ignore the Court's order.

On the day the Supreme Court heard the case I returned to London. That same evening, by a 6–3 decision, the Supreme Court declined to give effect to the International Court's order. It ruled that Breard's argument that he might have run his case differently if he had had access to Paraguayan consular officials was not plausible. It concluded that this was an area in which Virginia retained full authority, unfettered by restrictions under the US Constitution or international law. As a matter of American law, Virginia was free to execute. Virginia's Governor refused to exercise clemency. Even before my plane had landed at Heathrow airport, Breard had been executed. There was global outrage. The BBC ran the story as a lead. Even CNN asked: 'Paraguayan Execution: Do Americans detained overseas face new dangers?'

I was shocked by the failure to suspend Breard's execution. The same treaty which Jimmy Carter had invoked to secure the release of the Tehran hostages, back in 1979, now produced a two-fingered response to the judges at the International Court.[5] An article I wrote for the Los Angeles Times produced a welter of aggressive emails, as well as the accusation (on the letters pages of the LA Times) that my arguments seeking respect for international law made me a 'Third World loyalist trying to set international precedent to undermine U.S. sovereignty'.[6] The story continued to niggle away at a number of levels. How could it be that a country as profoundly attached to the rule of law and principles of constitutionality as the United States could have so little regard for international law? Why was the country that led the negotiations of the 1963 Vienna Convention, and which brought fundamental human rights into international law, able to show such disdain for international rules and for the International

Court? And what of my own European prejudices, favouring rules and international law, were they preventing me from taking a more realistic approach to the limits of international law? Why were my friends and colleagues in American academe not agitating? And would it have been any different in Britain?

Within a year we had an answer to the last question. In March 1999, the Privy Council in London (as the highest court of appeal for Trinidad and Tobago) ordered the execution of two Trinidadians to be suspended until their cases before the Inter-American Commission of Human Rights had been decided.[7] These judges in London were willing to allow international law arguments to halt a government from riding roughshod over international legal proceedings. How can the difference in attitude to international law be explained? Is it political or cultural? Or a result of the fact that most American law schools do not teach international law, and those that do tend to treat it more as a poor relation of political science, international relations or social theory, with the result that its normative value is diminished?

*

Over the past few years I have seen these issues both from an academic perspective and also first-hand as a practising barrister, working on many of the international cases and negotiations that are touched on in the chapters of this book. I have discovered that things look rather different from the inside, that the international law that I was taught bears little relation to how the system works in practice. Most states take most rules seriously, most of the time. Governments, legal advisers and judges pay considerable attention to the rules of international law. The media focuses on the exceptions. That is not to say that law and politics are not intimately connected. Plainly they are, both at the national and international levels. The stories in this book may be understood as conflicts, between political values and legal rules, between competing conceptions as to the hierarchy of moral choices, between different interpretations of what the rules require.

What is striking is how little is known by the public at large of the transformation of international relations that has taken place over the past fifty years. Notions of sovereignty have changed with growing interdependence. To claim that states are as sovereign today as they were fifty years ago is to ignore reality. The extent of interdependence caused by the avalanche of international laws means that states are constrained by international obligations over an increasingly wide range of actions. And the rules, once adopted, take on a logic and a life of their own. They do not stay within the neat boundaries that states thought they were creating when they were negotiated. You can see that most clearly in the rules on free trade and foreign investment. What began in Europe as a discrete effort with the Treaty of Rome in 1957 to create a European Economic Community – a common market – has morphed into a system of rules regulating everything from the requirement that European fishermen wear hairnets to the harmonization of Value Added Tax. The same tendency is seen with the North American Free Trade Agreement, with inevitable impacts on non-economic issues, including standards on labour, health and the environment. The new European Constitution, signed in the autumn of 2004, does not mean the end of sovereignty, or the end of Britain as an independent European state. But it does inevitably mean even more limits on sovereign freedoms. Anyone who says otherwise is deluding themselves, or being dishonest. Every international treaty has a constraining effect. If it did not it would not be doing its job. No international treaty is ever just a 'tidying up exercise'.

The emergence of a new body of international law – more extensive rules, more detail, greater enforceability – has a profound impact for democratic governance and accountability. In Britain, as in most countries, the great majority of treaties are not scrutinized or debated by the national parliament; there is no parliamentary committee which oversees Britain's treaty negotiations, or a decision on whether or not to ratify a particular treaty. This is a startling gap, especially as the European Community increasingly signs up to treaties on behalf of its members. This democratic deficit is made all the more significant by the fact that new rules are often accompanied by new international courts and tribunals to ensure that obligations are complied with. The emergence of an independent and increasingly powerful international judiciary, deciding on issues from human rights to trade, from environmental protection to foreign investment, raises vital questions. Who are the judges? How are they appointed? Why should they be taking decisions with profound consequences for life at the grass roots?

One main purpose of this book, then, is to shed some light on international law, to explain in a little more detail what the rules are, how they are made, and how they are argued when contentious issues come up. It is not intended as an academic work. It is a practical book based on the personal experiences of a pragmatic Anglo-Saxon who is not seeking to apply Cartesian logic or develop some overarching international legal theory which can explain where we are and where we may be heading. I am conscious that by focusing on the US and Britain there may be an assumption that other countries have not played equally important roles. That would be wrong, and is certainly not my intention.

But the book has another and more central purpose. It makes the case for international rules. In this globalizing, interdependent world it is impossible to conceive of a return to nature, to a pre-regulatory planet in which each state is free to act as it wishes, unfettered by international obligations. This is wishful thinking, as the US and Britain have learnt in Iraq and in their 'war on terrorism'. Imperfect as the rules of international law may be, they are necessary and they reflect minimum standards of acceptable behaviour. They provide a standard for judging the legitimacy of international actions. They are in place and they need to be complied with if actions are to be treated as legitimate. That is not to say that the rules do not need regular re-evaluation. The system of international law faces a great many challenges, including challenges to the assumptions which Roosevelt and Churchill and other leaders may have had in the 1940s. The world legal order is no longer monopolized by states. Not all states are fully functioning entities; some have failed altogether, and a new breed of non-state actors has emerged of a less amenable kind, such as terrorist organizations which are not based within a single state, and which do not respect the rules.

In the face of these changes there is a temptation to argue that the international laws do not work, that they need to be changed. President Bush has made the argument. So has Prime Minister Tony Blair, in an elegant but confused speech in his parliamentary constituency in March 2004. I disagree with this approach, at least as a general proposition. There are good reasons why most international laws have been adopted. For the most part they work reasonably well. They reflect common values, to the extent that these can be ascertained. I do not believe that idealized notions of the sovereign state, or 9/11, or events in Iraq, have fundamentally changed the basic assumptions or created new paradigms.

In the 1940s the United States and Britain reconceived their notions of a world legal order. Faced with constraints on the exercise of its sovereignty, the US has sought to sidestep those rules, particularly where they provide no direct economic benefits. In recent years Britain has tended to turn a blind eye, or even to collude. In its first term the Bush Administration embarked on a course which threatens significant damage to the rules-based system which was put in place after the Second World War, but without making the world a safer or a fairer place. It proposed no viable alternative. And it undermined its own long-term interest by alienating many of its allies and delegitimating its own actions. In all of this it has been assisted by an idealistic and compliant British prime minister. Whilst he may have been well-intentioned, his principal role has been to legitimate much that is not defensible. At a time of great challenge, the rules – and respect for them – are more important than ever. The politics of international law may have changed. But, with all the will in the world, the rules cannot be wished or blown away.

The chapters which follow are illustrative of some general trends. Rules of international law become richer and deeper, and even more connected to daily political issues, and moral choices. As this has happened, more invasive rules have become more constraining on political choices. This in turn has emboldened the voices calling for a return to an earlier era. I begin in Chapter 1 with a short history of the period between the end of the Second World War and recent times, and the factors that have transformed the world in which a new legal order was constructed. Chapter 2 focuses on the Pinochet case and the end of presidential immunity and impunity, a high point in the dismantling of a system which classically gave states unfettered powers over their citizens. Chapter 3 looks at the circumstances in which the international community finally created an International Criminal Court, part of the same 'Pinochet moment'. Both these chapters show that the forces driving the neo-conservative approach of the Bush Administration were already emerging in the late 1990s. Chapter 4 is concerned with the environment, and the abandonment by the US of the complex mechanisms of the Kyoto Protocol to combat global warming. Chapters 5 and 6 examine two areas in which the US maintains – for the time being at least – a stronger commitment to international law, namely the rules to increase global free trade and safeguard overseas investments. Chapters 7, 8 and 9 deal with the post 9/11 disgraces of Guantánamo, Iraq and Abu Ghraib, when the constraints of international law were wilfully abandoned in the name of national interests and security. In the concluding chapter I piece together the threads which link these seemingly disparate and apparently self-contained stories, which show that international law is, at the end of the day, about people and politics. The views expressed in these chapters are mine alone, as is the responsibility for any errors which might have crept in.

December 2004

Faculty of Laws
University College London

Acknowledgements

This book is the product of a collective experience over many years, even if the responsibility for errors, omissions and opinions is mine alone. If I were to mention all the friends, colleagues and opponents who have contributed – directly or indirectly – the list would be a long one indeed. To those whom I have not expressly named, and in particular the numerous journalists, diplomats, civil servants and politicians who cannot be singled out, or mentioned, my warmest thanks also.

Gratitude begins with the teachers who introduced me to the subject of international law, at a point about halfway between the end of the Second World War and the so-called 'war on terrorism'. Although some of my teachers might not be pleased to see where I have ended up (on some topics at least), the ends we seek are shared. I could not have had a better introduction to the world of international law than the one received from Robbie Jennings, Eli Lauterpacht, Derek Bowett and Chris Greenwood, each of whom has become a friend. Alongside this classical cadre stood Philip Allott, who showed that it was possible to look at things differently and thereby opened up a whole range of other possibilities, not least the fact that it was appropriate to talk about international law in the same breath as politics, psychology, religion, culture, sex and the myriad of other topics that people around the world care about. Philip will be horrified and thrilled that I have written a book which might cause taxi drivers to talk about international law, but that is the point. Spending a year as a visitor at Harvard in the early 1980s was a formative moment in my educational experience, and for making that possible and opening my eyes to a wholly different world I am inestimably grateful to David Kennedy, who continues to try to slaughter all my sacred cows and constantly and rightly reminds me that my efforts have a darker side too.

From the world of legal practice I owe a real debt of gratitude to James Crawford. At a vitally difficult moment for me he had the confidence to introduce me to international litigation, and has been willing to provide insight and support ever since, at all times of day and night and wherever he may be in the world. I owe a similar debt to Pierre-Marie Dupuy, who provided the best possible introduction to a Frenchman's sense of Cartesian logic as well as the proper balance between work and family.

Several chapters of this book draw on direct experiences, whether in relation to litigation or negotiation. In each case I have been able to participate as part of a team, so that my experience and learning is a product of team effort. The Pinochet case would have been a remarkable experience under any conditions, but working with Reed Brody and Richard Stein, as well as Presiley Baxendale, Helen Duffy, Ed Fitzgerald, Jonathan Marks, Nigel Pleming and Geoffrey Robertson, made it especially memorable. For giving me the opportunity to participate in the final negotiations of the Rome Statute of the International Criminal Court I am enormously grateful to Rex Horoi and Neroni Slade. For entrusting me with the responsibility of protecting the interests of some of the most vulnerable countries in the world from the effects of global warming and participating in the negotiations of the Climate Change Convention I am especially indebted to Angela Cropper, Charles Flemming, Janet Maughan, Naresh Singh, Cletus Springer and Robert Van Lierop. For enabling me to understand the inner workings of the trade and investment world from Albanian and other novel perspectives I appreciate especially the efforts of Charlie Brower, Abby Cohen Smutny, Fatos Djini, Rezarta Gaba, Nadine Khamis, Peter-Jan Kuijper, Edwin Laurent, Darryl Lew, Aiman Odeh, Antonio Parra and Margarete Stevens.

Numerous friends and colleagues and even family members have had the kindness to comment on or assist with individual chapters or passages, or help with other things. Special thanks to Abigail Asher, Erin Cramer, Agnès Desarthe, Adriana Fabra and Nick Hornby for their detailed comments on individual chapters. Thanks also to Daniel Alexander, Doak Bishop, Bart Brown, Laurence Boisson de Chazournes, Deborah Cass, Kevin Childs, Andrew Clapham,

Jonathan Cooper, Anthony Dworkin, Hakan Friman, Noreena Hertz, Pierre Klein, Jesse Norman, David Rakoff, Catherine Redgewell, Marc Sands, Anya Schiffrin, Gerry Simpson, Dick Stewart and Chris Thomas (also for directing me to Nelson Mandela's autobiography). To those of you who were part of the global consultation and voting on the book's title, in particular those who had the misfortune to be on holiday with us last summer, Dante Desarthe, Orlando Figes and Stephanie Palmer, thank you.

The international law community is one of collegiality and tolerance. I have had the benefit of insights from friends as well as colleagues at universities, parliamentary libraries, law offices and barristers' chambers and courts across the world. I want to thank in particular Georges Abi Saab, Michael Anderson, Vicki Been, Nathaniel Berman, Roberto Flores Bermudes, Daniel Bethlehem, Roz Campion, Ed Carroll, Christine Chinkin, Warren Cooke, Matt Craven, Dan Danielsen, Anthony Dworkin, Tom Franck, Richard Gardiner, Gavan Griffith, Rosalyn Higgins, Erik Jayme, John Jackson, Ivo Josipovic, Helena Kennedy, Ben Kingsbury, Martti Koskenniemi, Karen Knop, Charlotte Ku, Anthony Lester, Cynthia Lichtenstein, Carlos Lopez Contreras, Vaughan Lowe, Andy Lowenfeld, Campbell McLachlan, Tom Mensah, Parry Mitchell, Ed Mortimer, Boldizsar Nagy, Matar al Neyadi, Francisco Orrego Vicuna, Alain Pellet, Radu Popa, Faisal Rahman, Sonny Ramphal, Dane Ratliff, Paul Reichler, Julio Rendon, Ricky Revesz, Bette Shifman, Linda Silberman, Bruno Simma, Marion Simmons, Ivan Simonovic, Gerry Simpson, Ian Sinclair, Anne-Marie Slaughter, Christopher Stone, Tullio Treves, Brian Urquhart, Eduardo Valencia Ospina, Tjaco van den Hout, Paul Walegur, Christopher Weeramantry, Ralph Wilde, Elizabeth Wilmshurst and Michael Wood.

At the Faculty of Law at University College London I am deeply grateful for the support shown by all my colleagues, in particular former Dean Jeffrey Jowell, and Michael Bridge and Ian Dennis. A number of colleagues along my corridor and elsewhere have put up with my obsessions and irritations, in particular Lizzie Barnes, Cathy Brown, Ian Fletcher, Michael Freeman, Sylvia Lough, Richard Macrory and Riz Mokal. In earlier years, colleagues and staff at the School of Oriental and African Studies and at New York University Law School provided tremendous encouragement for the various mini-projects which led to this one: thanks especially to Norman

Dorsen, Andrew Harding, Iqbal Ishar and John Sexton. At all three of these universities I have learnt a great deal every year from all of my students, who represent all corners of the earth and who have taught me that if international law is to make a difference it must be *international*, not British, or European, or American.

During the years in which the stories that form the backbone of this book occurred I was associated with two first-class non-governmental organizations, the Foundation for International Environmental Law and Development (FIELD) and the Project on International Courts and Tribunals (PICT). My colleagues at both displayed great tolerance of my peripatetic ways and were always available to have their brains picked. A big thank you to Beatrice Chaytor, Carolina Diaz Larsen, Shep Forman, Thordis Ingadottir, Ruth Khalastchi, Jurgen Lefevre, Ruth Mackenzie, Louise Rands, Cesare Romano, Greg Rose, Jake Werksman and Farhana Yamin.

Over the same period I have been associated with two barristers' chambers, both of which have been tremendously supportive. I am grateful to Paul Cooklin and other colleagues at 3 Verulam Buildings. At Matrix Chambers I discovered that barristers doing 'real law' might be willing to take international law seriously. I have learnt enormously from the colleagues with whom I have had the opportunity to work closely as we approach the fifth anniversary of Matrix Chambers, and never cease to be amazed by the fact that so many of them manage on so many occasions to persuade English judges to take international law seriously. Special thanks to Clare Montgomery and Hugh Tomlinson for their advice and comments, and thanks to all my colleagues, past and present, in particular to Alex Baillin, David Bean, Nick Blake, Cherie Booth, Dan Brennan, Kate Cook, Ben Emmerson, Danny Friedman, Conor Gearty, Murray Hunt, Raza Husain, Janet Kentridge, Charlotte Kilroy, Julian Knowles, Alison Macdonald, Ken Macdonald, Jonathan Marks, Karon Monaghan, Helen Mountfield, Tim Owen, Heather Rogers, Maurice Sheridan, Rabinder Singh, Rhodri Thomson and Anthony White. On the practice management side I want to thank in particular Sarah Davenport, Andy Hall, Kevin Hooper, Jane Fitzpatrick, Katy Forbes, Amanda Illing, Nick Martin, Zoe Mellor, Linda McGivern, Deborah Nicol, Carla Owen and Dan Waller.

A number of younger lawyers and students have provided

invaluable research assistance in the preparation of this book. I am particularly indebted to Anjolie Singh, who somehow manages to keep her cool and deliver quality on time in the midst of Balkan riots or Central American breakdowns. Thanks also to Sasha Blackmore for a fine job in reference-checking and to Karla Charles, Natasha Jehangir, Ivana Radacic and Ernest Titanji for their enthusiasm, energy and attentiveness as research assistants. My appreciation also to Gill Coleridge for her assistance in the home stretch, to Jane Robertson for her meticulous copy-editing, and to Anne Rowe at the *Hampstead and Highgate Express* for digging up archive material.

This book would not have come into being without the individual contribution of eight people. I am deeply grateful to six of them. Bruce Hyman enthusiastically took up the idea of a BBC radio series on America and international law, which Julia Hobsbawm then catalysed into a book. Felicity Rubinstein taught me things about contracts, the world of publishing and how to ignore my own instincts. Kate Barber took my scrawl and turned it into grammar, words and pages. James Cameron did what best friends are supposed to do. And Margaret Bluman, my editor, put her money where her mouth is and persuaded Penguin to take a punt, instilling confidence, a rigorous timetable and the perfect blend of criticism and encouragement. The two other people whose contribution made this book possible are George W. Bush and Tony Blair. I am not sure that thanks would be appropriate.

Finally, I have to thank my family for putting up with all this, again and again and again. Leo's Café Dimanche provided regular sustenance (and I could listen to your version of 'Yesterday' for ever). Lara's willingness to answer my phone at all times, and make up stories about who was on the other end, provided constant anxiety and relief. And Katya was just wonderful Katya, especially the greeting after nursery. Natalia, I won't mention the things you don't want me to, but I will say the biggest possible thank you for keeping my feet on the ground, for reading each and every word (more than once) and editing the whole, and for being title-adviser and general reality checker.

List of abbreviations

ANC	African National Congress
AOSIS	Alliance of Small Island States
CARICOM	Caribbean Community
COMPASS	Committee to Preserve American Security and Sovereignty
CPS	Crown Prosecution Service
DINA	Dirección Nacional de Inteligencia (Spain's National Intelligence Directorate)
ECHR	European Convention on Human Rights
EURATOM	European Atomic Energy Community
FDI	foreign direct investment
GATS	General Agreement on Trade in Services
GATT	General Agreement on Tariffs and Trade
GMOs	genetically modified organisms
IAEA	International Atomic Energy Agency
IBRD	International Bank for Reconstruction and Development
ICC	International Criminal Court
ICJ	International Court of Justice
ICRC	International Committee of the Red Cross
ICSID	International Centre for Settlement of Investment Disputes
ICTY	International Criminal Tribunal for the Former Yugoslavia
IFC	International Finance Corporation
ILC	International Law Commission
IMF	International Monetary Fund
IP	intellectual property

IPCC	Intergovernmental Panel on Climate Change
ITO	International Trade Organization
MAI	Multilateral Agreement on Investment
MIT	Massachusetts Institute of Technology
MMT	methylcyclopentadienyl manganese tricarbonyl
NAFTA	North American Free Trade Agreement
NATO	North Atlantic Treaty Organization
NGO	non-governmental organization
OECD	Organization for Economic Cooperation and Development
OPEC	Organization of the Petroleum Exporting Countries
SIAC	Special Immigration Appeals Commission
TED	turtle excluder device
TRIPs	Agreement on the Trade-related Aspects of Intellectual Property Rights
UNMOVIC	United Nations Monitoring, Verification and Inspection Committee
WMD	weapons of mass destruction
WTO	World Trade Organization

I

International Law:
a Short and Recent History

'The best defence of our security lies in the spread of our values. But we cannot advance these values except within a framework that recognizes their universality. If it is a global threat, it needs a global response, based on global rules.'

Tony Blair, 5 March 2004[1]

Although international law has a long history, it is only in recent years that it has emerged as a more regular feature of modern political life. Diplomatic immunities, genocide and other international crimes, trade wars, global warming, the detainees held at Guantánamo Bay, the war in Iraq, the abuses at Abu Ghraib prison have brought the politics of international law into everyday life. This is particularly so in Britain, a middle-ranking power which relies on respect for international laws. In the weeks before the Iraq War in March 2003, British Prime Minister Tony Blair pledged his adherence to international rules: British troops would only be committed to a war in Iraq if international law allowed, and the conditions of any occupation would respect global rules. Blair had little option. He faced festering public disquiet about the treatment of British detainees at Guantánamo, the lack of respect for the Geneva Conventions, and his government's silence.

Tony Blair's public commitment was a necessary response to a growing concern that Britain was on the verge of a second Suez, using force with little international support and dubious legality. In 1956 Prime Minister Anthony Eden did not bother to seek an official opinion from his Attorney General and overrode the objections of Sir Gerald Fitzmaurice, the Senior Legal Adviser at the Foreign Office.

Eden chose instead to rely on the more supportive views of Professor Arthur Goodhart, former Professor of Jurisprudence at Oxford and Master of University College, which had been set out in a letter to *The Times*.[2] Blair at least did consult with his Attorney General, Lord Goldsmith QC, on several occasions, although it is not clear that he got the same advice on each occasion.

In March 2003 the government took the unprecedented step of publishing the Attorney General's late-formed view that the use of military force did not require an explicit Security Council mandate. This unusual step was needed for political reasons: to address public and media concerns, to encourage wavering Labour MPs to vote for war, and to persuade Britain's Chief of Defence to commit troops. It may have succeeded on the latter two counts, but it failed in the court of public opinion: letters appeared in the press, and notable public figures weighed in on the illegality of the war. The Attorney General's argument continues to be the subject of almost unprecedented media and parliamentary attention. Lord Alexander, a conservative and highly respected former head of the Bar Council of England and Wales, thought the Attorney's advice 'risible' and said so publicly. Issues concerning the legality of the Iraq War will dog the reputation of the Prime Minister and his Attorney General for years to come. Peter Hennessy, the British political commentator, described the issue as 'the great faultline beneath the Blair premiership', which 'syringed the trust out of the Prime Minister's office'.[3]

By December 2004 more than 600 detainees were still held at Guantánamo Bay, including four Britons. Only a small number of these individuals had been charged before military commissions. Until the US Supreme Court intervened in June 2004 to declare their right of access to US federal courts, for more than two and a half years they had no access to legal representation, nor to any court of law or tribunal. Lord Steyn, a serving judge in Britain's highest court, the House of Lords, described detention under these conditions as a 'stain on American justice', wholly contrary to international law. Steyn also called on the British government to do more to protect the international rights of its citizens. His intervention was unparalleled, a reflection of concern at the very highest levels of the British legal establishment. A few months later, in December 2004, the Judicial Committee of the House of Lords ruled that a law enacted after 9/11 permitting the indefinite detention without charge of non-nationals alleged to be involved in international terrorism was in clear violation of Britain's international treaty obligations.

In the United States there had been less public interest in the finer detail of the legality of the Iraq War, or the conditions of detention at Guantánamo. That changed dramatically in March 2004, when the western world's attention was focused on international rules by the publication of photographs depicting graphically the abuse of Iraqi and other Muslim detainees at Abu Ghraib prison in Baghdad. The Geneva Conventions became the subject of angry exchanges at hearings in the US Senate. There followed the publication of a leaked Pentagon memorandum which appeared to authorize the use of torture, contrary to America's obligations under the 1984 Convention against Torture and Other Cruel, Inhuman or Degrading Treatment or Punishment. Actions taken in the aftermath of 9/11 were now raising serious questions about American commitment to basic rules of international law, including human rights and the treatment of detainees. Do those events signal the abandonment by Britain and the United States of their commitment to the post-Second World War legal and institutional arrangements which they, more than any other countries, put in place? What does this say about the future of international law in the twenty-first century?

*

The British public has become accustomed to issues of international law affecting political discourse. This flows from membership of the European Community and obligations under the European Convention on Human Rights. Both international conventions have had a significant effect on British life. In the view of a sizeable minority of the population that effect gives rise to calls for withdrawal and the reclaiming of British sovereignty. But these international rules are seen as being in some way special, and not a part of the general rules of international law which have emerged since the Second World War.

The change in British public interest in international law dates back to October 1998, when I was at the University of London's School of Oriental and African Studies. My areas of focus included the environment – still a relatively new subject – and international courts and tribunals. International courts had been a very specialized topic but then began attracting greater attention with the impact of human rights courts (including the European Court of Human Rights) and the World Trade Organization's new system for resolving trade disputes. In July 1998 agreement had been reached on the creation of a permanent International Criminal Court. This attracted great attention in the media. I was maintaining a discrete practice as a barrister, specializing in international law. The field was of little practical interest to most of my colleagues in my barristers' chambers, many of whom maintained a polite but distant bemusement regarding this area of the law. Occasionally an international legal issue would break into public consciousness. There would be debate, for example, on sovereignty and whether or not some new EC treaty amendments should be ratified, or whether the new Labour government's proposal to incorporate the European Convention on Human Rights into English law would change Britain's constitutional order and further diminish its sovereignty. But the vast majority of the many developments in international law which had occurred since the 1940s were ignored. They were not subject to any real public scrutiny, either in Parliament or in the media.

Important international treaties were not even being discussed in Cabinet: I remember watching *Question Time* on television one autumn evening in 1997, and being struck by the fact that Jack Straw, who was the Home Secretary at the time, had no knowledge of the controversial intergovernmental negotiations for a proposed new treaty which would regulate global investments (the so-called Multilateral Agreement on Investment, which collapsed later in 1998 in the face of objections from a coalition of governments and non-governmental organizations (NGOs)). A Cabinet minister later confirmed that this treaty, like most, was never discussed or even mentioned. International law was a tightly guarded secret, monopolized by a small elite of foreign offices and civil servants, a handful of transnational corporations and NGOs such as Amnesty International and Greenpeace, a small number of academics, and an even smaller number of lawyers in private practice.

Judging by media attention and dinner party chat, that situation has changed significantly over the past few years. To pinpoint a precise date for the change I would say the sixteenth of October 1998. This was the day on which the former President of Chile, Senator Augusto Pinochet, was arrested while recuperating in a private London clinic from back surgery. His arrest followed a request by Judge Baltasar Garzón, an independent Spanish criminal prosecutor, who was seeking Pinochet's extradition to Spain to face criminal charges for violating international laws between 11 September 1973, when he seized power from Salvador Allende in a *coup d'état*, and March 1990, when he relinquished Chile's presidency. The arrest was to raise a fundamental question of international law: was Pinochet entitled to claim immunity from the jurisdiction of the English courts on the grounds that the alleged crimes were committed whilst he was Chile's head of state? Politically, the question was of vital importance because it signalled a move away from the old international legal order, which was essentially dedicated to the protection of good relations between states. During the legal proceedings which were held before various English courts over the next two years, obscure rules of international law moved into the mainstream of political and public debate. The rules, the judges and the lawyers were scrutinized and discussed in the press, and the debate became a global one. From London to Santiago, from Kingston to Reykjavik, the media covered the case in the minutest detail. The courtrooms were packed with local and international journalists, and they had many questions. What rules of international law permitted Britain to exercise jurisdiction over a Chilean at the request of Spain? Where did the rules of international law come from? How were they enforced? How were they to be interpreted? What if different countries applied them differently? How did international law balance the interest of a sovereign state not to have its former head of state subjected to the indignity of criminal proceedings abroad with the interests of victims and the need to end impunity for the most serious international crimes?

The House of Lords' first judgment, on 25 November 1998, was broadcast live on the BBC and CNN and transmitted on radio broadcasts around the world, the first time this had ever happened. The following day the judgment led the front pages of virtually every newspaper in the world. It was a landmark day: under international law the former head of state of one country could not claim immunity from the jurisdiction of the courts of another country to avoid facing charges that he had committed the international crime of torture. In the end the decision of the House of Lords was based on a single treaty, the little known (but now mightily important) 1984

Convention against Torture. The case gave rise to copycat litigation, new constraints on the actions of governments, and an unparalleled interest in international law. The 1984 Convention became significant five years later in the controversies over the detention camps at Guantánamo Bay and Abu Ghraib prison in Iraq.

The Pinochet case was significant for another reason. It coincided with increased attention to other rules of international law which had been put in place over the past fifty years, and which increasingly (but silently) impacted on people's daily lives. Rules of international law which had been adopted since the end of the Second World War have provided the foundations for globalization. By the late 1990s there had been a sustained period of economic liberalization, and this was now marked by large demonstrations in Seattle and elsewhere against globalization and the rules of the new World Trade Organization. These, it was said, would prevent countries from applying their own health, environmental and labour standards. They were a new form of colonialism. During the 1990s, following the collapse of the Soviet bloc and the end of the Cold War, the international community created a new International Criminal Court (after fifty years of discussion) to end impunity for the most serious international crimes, including genocide and war crimes. It was during this period, in 1999, that President Milošević of the Federal Republic of Yugoslavia became the first serving head of state to be indicted by an international criminal tribunal, in The Hague. But it was also a time when sharp disagreements emerged between states as to how far the rules of international law should go. Negotiations for a global agreement on foreign investments collapsed. The United States withdrew from the negotiations to prevent global warming, as well as from other international treaties and negotiations. In the aftermath of the 9/11 attacks on the World Trade Center and the Pentagon attention was focused on the rules of international law to combat terrorism, as well as on the conditions of detention of prisoners at Guantánamo Bay and other camps in Afghanistan and Iraq. Throughout this period there was also sustained public debate on the continued validity and effectiveness of the rules prohibiting the use of armed force, which had been forged in the aftermath of the Second World War. The events in the Balkans in 1992, in Rwanda in 1994, the Great Lakes region in Africa since 1997, Kosovo in 1999, Afghanistan in 2001 and, most bitterly, in the spring of 2003 in Iraq, raised serious questions about the adequacy of international rules to protect fundamental human rights and to use force in self-defence or under the aegis of the United Nations Security Council.

International rules are now frequently seen as providing an independent benchmark against which to assess the justification of behaviour – and in particular the behaviour of states – which is politically or morally contentious. When I first studied the subject in the early 1980s, taught by a diminutive and remarkable Yorkshireman called Robbie Jennings, who went on to become a judge at the International Court of Justice, international law was presented as a topic which only one or two of the 300 students attending the international law lectures at Cambridge would ever come across in real life. We were taught that international law governs relations between states at the international level with little, if any, impact on citizens or on local issues.

Before the Second World War international rules had been minimal in content, and addressed only a small number of areas of human activity.[4] The two main sources of international legal obligation were – and continue to be – treaties and customary law. But there were very few treaties, and the practice of states which gave rise to customary law was difficult to discern.[5] Beyond the League of Nations and the International Labor Organization – both established in 1919 by the Treaty of Versailles, which brought the First World War to an end – there were almost no international organizations. Apart from the Central American Court of Justice, created in 1908, the first truly international court was the Permanent Court of International Justice in The Hague, related to the League of Nations. In 1927, in a dispute between France and Turkey, the Court declared, without pause or embarrassment, that states were basically free to do anything that was not expressly prohibited by international law.[6] This was a world of sovereign freedom, with few international rules to constrain the behaviour of governments.

However, there were rules of international law protecting the rights of minorities in certain parts of Europe, and emerging rules on the employment of women (particularly if they were pregnant or engaged as night workers) and of children. There were rules governing the treatment of foreigners and their property, including the investments of corporations abroad. But there were no rules of international law protecting fundamental human rights. International law did not prohibit the wholesale slaughter or elimination of groups of people on grounds of religion or ethnicity or political belief – as had happened in Nazi Germany, the Soviet Union and many other parts of the world. Nor were there restraints on territorial domination or the creation of colonies. The idea that a group of people had a right to self-determination was a distant dream. Piracy and slavery were outlawed, but discrimination, racism, apartheid and colonial domination and exploitation were not.

Nor was there any general prohibition on the use of force. In 1928 the United States, Britain, France and Germany, amongst others, had agreed in the Kellogg–Briand Pact to condemn war and renounce it as an instrument of national policy 'in their relations with one another'. There were rules on how warfare could be conducted, including how prisoners of war should be treated and the types of weapons which could not be used, but these were extremely limited in scope. No global free trade rules existed, although a small number of bilateral trade rules had been adopted and preferences existed, for example in the British Empire. There were no rules of general international law committing states to conserve nature and protect the environment. In short, the world of international law was premised on the principle that sovereign and independent states could do more or less what they wanted, except where they had expressly agreed otherwise. Since very little was prohibited, their freedom to act was virtually unlimited.

A little more than half a century ago, this permissive legal landscape became the subject of an ambitious and sustained effort by various countries to build a rules-based system. From 1941 onwards the United States and Britain, with their allies (known as the United Nations), adopted a blueprint for a series of new institutions and laws to serve as the foundation for a rules-based approach to the international order. The Atlantic Charter was the starting point. On 14 August 1941, meeting aboard the US flagship *Augusta* in Ship Harbor, Newfoundland, American President Franklin Delano Roosevelt and British Prime Minister Winston Churchill adopted a charter declaring 'certain common principles in the national policies of their respective countries on which they base their hopes for a better future for the world'. The Atlantic Charter, as it was known, committed America and Britain to a new order based on a few key principles: an end to territorial aggrandizement or territorial changes; respect for self-government; social security; peace and freedom from fear or want; high seas freedoms; and restraints on the use of force.

These principles served as the guidelines for a new world order and were later enshrined in the United Nations Charter. The Roosevelt/Churchill scheme can be reduced even further to three simple pillars, which have remained in place for the last sixty years: a general obligation on states to refrain from the use of force in their international relations, except under strict conditions of self-defence or where authorized by the international community acting through the Security Council or a regional body; a new commitment to maintain the 'inherent dignity' and the 'equal and inalienable rights' of all members of the human family, through the adoption of international instruments which would protect human rights by the rule of law; and an undertaking to promote economic liberalization through the adoption of free trade rules and related international obligations in the fields of foreign investment and intellectual property.

The Atlantic Charter inspired actions by states and also by individuals. Writing in his autobiography, Nelson Mandela saw the Charter as reaffirming his faith in the dignity of each human being and propagating a host of democratic principles:

Some in the West saw the charter as empty promises, but not those of us in Africa. Inspired by the Atlantic Charter and the fight of the Allies against tyranny and aggression, the ANC created its own charter, called African Claims, which called for full citizenship for all Africans, the right to buy land and the repeal of all discriminating legislation.[7]

The Atlantic Charter captured the public imagination. A few months after it was adopted, on 1 January 1942, America and Britain expanded their partnership to include the USSR, China and twenty-two other countries, joining together in the United Nations declaration. Within weeks of the end of the Second World War a series of international conferences had been convened to create a world order based on common values and minimum international rules, around the three pillars which Roosevelt and Churchill had agreed on.

In April 1945 delegates from fifty countries met in San Francisco to negotiate a Charter for the United Nations to replace the defunct

League of Nations. In his opening speech President Truman set out America's strong commitment to international law, sweeping aside the opposition from hard-core Republicans in the US Senate. The UN Charter was signed on 26 June 1945 and came into force four months later. Its stated objectives included the development of international law, in particular to protect human rights, prevent war and promote economic and social progress. This was the starting point for the system of modern global rules. Although the US had never joined the League of Nations, it did become a party to the UN Charter.

Within a decade a totally new system of international law and organizations had been created. By the 1950s there existed an embryonic global constitutional order, with rules that remain in place – albeit rather shakily in some cases – to this day. The system which emerged largely reflected an effort to export Anglo-American values, and was motivated in part to distinguish the values of the West from those of the Soviet bloc, which had become entrenched behind the Iron Curtain which divided Europe. The development of the global rules was to become a major battleground for the Cold War.

In the field of human rights and humanitarian law an important first step was the agreement to prosecute Nazi war criminals. The Charter for the Nuremberg Military Tribunal was agreed on 8 August 1945 by Britain, America, France and the Soviet Union. This radical and far-reaching document aimed to codify the rules of international law on war crimes and crimes against humanity. The head of the American delegation was Robert Jackson, a Justice of the United States Supreme Court, who went on to be the Chief Prosecutor at Nuremberg. In his memoirs he described how British officials wanted to dispose of the six or seven leading Nazis without trial, fearing that an open trial would provide a sounding board for Nazi propaganda. But Roosevelt disagreed: according to Jackson he 'was determined that a speedy but fair trial should be accorded to war criminals . . . the President insisted that there be a documentation of their crimes'.[8]

A few weeks later, a Commission on Human Rights was established at the United Nations. The American delegation was led by Eleanor Roosevelt, the recently widowed First Lady. Over the next few years she led efforts to negotiate what became the Universal Declaration of Human Rights, adopted in December 1948 by the UN

General Assembly. It is arguably the single most important international instrument ever negotiated. She considered this text to be her finest accomplishment for its promotion of the values reflected in the US Constitution:

We wanted as many nations as possible to accept the fact that men, for one reason or another, were born free and equal in dignity and rights, that they were endowed with reason and conscience, and should act towards one another in a spirit of brotherhood. The way to do that was to find words that everyone would accept.[9]

The Declaration set out the first ever code of basic human rights which would give effect to the United Nations' determination that 'human rights should be protected by the rule of law'. It was a non-binding instrument, but it led directly to binding obligations and new instruments in Europe, the Americas and Africa. In 1966 many of its provisions were incorporated into two legally binding instruments of potentially global application, the International Covenant on Civil and Political Rights and the International Covenant on Economic and Social Rights.

The day before the Universal Declaration was adopted, on 9 December 1948, the world's first global human rights treaty was agreed: forty-one countries signed the Convention on the Prevention and Punishment of Genocide in Paris. The treaty characterized genocide as 'a crime under international law', and committed the parties to prevent and punish genocide. The United States did not become a party for another forty years. When it did so, however, in signing the implementing legislation President Ronald Reagan declared that he was fulfilling 'the promise made earlier by Harry Truman to all the peoples of the world', and rejected the argument that the Convention somehow infringed American sovereignty.[10] A year after the Genocide Convention, on 12 August 1949, forty-three countries adopted the four Geneva Conventions for the Protection of War Victims, including treaties on the treatment of prisoners of war (Geneva III) and the protection of civilians (Geneva IV). These instruments criminalized various acts, and made individuals – as well as governments – responsible. These are the international instruments which President George W. Bush sought to circumvent half a century later.

New international agreements were pursued equally vigorously on economic matters. On 27 December 1945, after just three weeks of negotiations, the Bretton Woods Agreements were concluded, named after the vacation resort in New Hampshire where they were negotiated by forty-four countries. The agreements created the World Bank and the International Monetary Fund (IMF), the basic framework for international financial relations which was considered indispensable to post-war economic reconstruction and development, as well as longer term banking and currency stability. The vision of economist John Maynard Keynes was central to these two agreements, inspired by the same theories which had influenced Roosevelt's New Deal. Two years later, on 30 October 1947, twenty-three countries adopted the General Agreement on Tariffs and Trade (GATT), the global framework rules committing parties to remove barriers to international trade in goods. GATT did not, however, include any formal institutional structures. That was left to a third organization, which was intended to exist alongside the IMF and the World Bank. The Statute of the International Trade Organization (ITO) was adopted in Havana in March 1948, and was supposed to provide the institutional framework for the GATT free trade rules, as well as new rules to encourage overseas investments and end monopoly and other restrictive business practices. This seems to have been a treaty too far, at least for the US Congress, reflecting its distrust of global government. Under pressure, President Truman announced that he would not seek congressional approval for ratification of the ITO. It was effectively killed off until the mid-1990s, when the World Trade Organization (WTO) was created, ironically with strong American support. The failure of the ITO was an early sign that American endorsement for these new rules and institutions was not a foregone conclusion.

Nevertheless, by the 1950s the foundations of a new international legal order had been created, and the vision of Churchill and Roosevelt largely accomplished. Over the next fifty years a growing body of international rules was put in place, largely in the form of treaties, most of which have received widespread support. During this period of decolonization the number of states multiplied and the membership of the United Nations expanded rapidly. It reached 100 in 1961 and now stands at 191. Important arms control agreements were negotiated in the 1960s, with the treaty banning atmospheric nuclear tests (1960) and the treaty on nuclear non-proliferation (1968) attracting considerable public attention. In the early 1970s a systematic effort began – with the strong support of President Richard Nixon – to put in place rules for the protection of the global environment, including those relating to biodiversity, the ozone layer and the climate system. And beyond the global instruments were an even more extensive raft of regional treaties, aiming to protect fundamental human rights and creating economic unions and other regional trading and financial arrangements in Europe, Latin America and Africa, as well as in the Islamic world and with the western group of members of the Organization for Economic Cooperation and Development (OECD).

By the early 1990s, after the Cold War had ended and the Berlin Wall had been torn down, the liberal Anglo-American vision of a rules-based international system appeared to be becoming a reality, albeit an imperfect one. Civil society and the private sector became actively interested in international rules, which also became the subject of increased media attention. That is not to say that during this period global order had been established and the rules were always complied with. Vietnam, the overthrow of Salvador Allende, Pol Pot, Idi Amin, the Balkans and Rwanda are merely the tip of a half-century of violence and abuse. But the new international rules provided a framework for judging individual behaviour and government acts and, in theory at least, an end to impunity. It could no longer be said that international law allowed such atrocities.

The United States and Britain had provided leadership and lent their support because they saw rules as a means of bringing stability. But this was not altruism at play: a rules-based system would promote Anglo-American values, create markets and protect established economic and social interests. It would also provide an instrument around which to build support against the Soviet bloc, and gain influence over a decolonized developing world. The rules created opportunities. Also in the 1980s and the 1990s a different voice emerged, reflecting an American and British approach which was considerably more sceptical about international rules and multilateralism. In the United States Ronald Reagan was elected into office, aiming to protect American sovereignty and an American way of life seen to be threatened by international law. With the rise of neo-conservatism in the United States, many of the rules were seen as making unjustified encroachments on

American power. Reagan, Margaret Thatcher and Helmut Kohl of Germany walked away from the Law of the Sea Convention after fifteen years of negotiations, refusing to sign a treaty which, they claimed, undermined entrepreneurship and deregulation. In the context of the Iran Contra scandal and the conflict in Nicaragua and other parts of Central America, the United States withdrew its acceptance of the jurisdiction of the International Court of Justice (Britain did not follow suit, and to this day remains the only UN Permanent Member to accept that Court's general jurisdiction, albeit with important and recently added caveats).

Well before 9/11 the United States had turned against many of the international rules which lay outside the economic domain, including some which had attracted very broad support. Whereas President Jimmy Carter had invoked the rules of consular protection in the Iran hostages crisis, in 1979, twenty years later President Bill Clinton had no compunction in instructing his Solicitor General to tell the US Supreme Court that his Administration would not object if the Supreme Court ignored the International Court of Justice's order that the execution of Angel Breard be temporarily suspended. Treaties were negotiated, but not signed. Many that were signed were not ratified. So the United States became one of just two countries, with Somalia, not to join the Convention on the Rights of the Child, because it outlawed the death penalty for juvenile criminals. The 1997 Kyoto Protocol (aimed at combating global warming) was demonized as a unique threat to the economy and American lifestyle (gas guzzlers in particular). And the 1998 Statute of the International Criminal Court was treated as though it was a great threat to American power, constraining military activity and subjecting American soldiers and leaders to the risk of politically motivated prosecution by an independent international prosecutor.

The United States was entirely free to choose not to become a party to these or other treaties, but its reasons for not doing so marked a dramatic change of perspective. There emerged a presumption against international rules: they no longer created opportunities, but were seen as imposing significant constraints. This was a return to American exceptionalism, an attitude which had periodically – and powerfully – dominated its thinking earlier in the century. We are different, said the neo-conservatives, the rules cannot apply to us. We need to create an international order which is friendly to America's security, prosperity and principles, proclaimed the sponsors of the Project for the New American Century in 1997, including Dick Cheney, Donald Rumsfeld and Paul Wolfowitz, the architects of the post-9/11 'war on terrorism'. Ironically, the retreat from the established international order coincided with the United States' ever-greater dependence on the global economy, one area where respect for the rules was seen as vital.

And as this new approach emerged, Britain too found itself pulled in different directions. On the one hand, as a declining power with no empire to protect, it was more committed than ever to the international rule of law. On the other hand, it did not wish to alienate its great friend and ally.

*

In the meantime public perceptions of international law have been transformed. At some point in the 1990s these arcane rules moved out of the corridors of foreign ministries and into the boardrooms of businesses, the lobbying newsletters of non-governmental organizations (NGOs), and the front pages of our newspapers. International law went public. The monopoly which states held over the rules began to crumble. How did this happen?

The conditions under which the changes have occurred are complex, and already the subject of a body of literature and ideas to which I will not add. Against the background of changes which took place in the 1980s and 1990s – the end of the Cold War, the economic and social integration of Europe, the rise of religious fundamentalism – four factors have emerged to transform perceptions about the function and nature of international laws.

The first of these is 'globalization', a concept which caught on in the 1990s but which is, in reality, premised on a rules-based system of international relations, and international economic relations in particular. There would be no globalization without international law. Professor Anthony Giddens has depicted globalization as a 'stretching process', in which connections are made between different social contexts and regions, which then become networked across the earth as a whole. This creates the perception that there exists a connection between the interests of different countries and communities. What one country does to the environment, or to the human rights of its citizens, may be of legitimate interest to another community outside that country. The Pinochet case is a simple example of legal globalization in action: the British courts entertain a request from Spain to extradite to that country a Chilean for acts he is alleged to have carried out in Chile and Argentina, and then deny Pinochet's claim to immunity on the basis of an international convention to which the three countries are parties and which treats the acts in question as international crimes. Without the treaty the case collapses: Spain would not have had a legal interest to which the English courts were able to accede. Chile would lose its entitlement to claim immunity for the acts of Pinochet while head of state. In a globalizing world international law recognizes the competing interests of different communities and finds ways to prioritize them.

By providing a minimum set of rules international law underpins globalization. It encourages and eases air transport, trade and telecommunications, the factors necessary for economic globalization to occur. Activities which were previously limited to the local or national levels are internationalized, requiring law-making beyond the single state. Ironically, this in turn contributes to the very conditions which give rise to manifest feelings of disempowerment – citizens feel they have had no role in the development of the new international rules which disempower them. This feeling generated the anti-WTO demonstrations in Seattle in November 1999. So international law provides the foundations for globalization and, at the same time, becomes the object of discontent. And perhaps even more curiously, other international rules – promoting human rights and protecting the environment – become a source of transformative power to attack some of the harsher economic and social consequences of globalization.

International rules alone are not responsible for globalization, which is catalysed by technological innovation, the second factor in the change in perception of the international legal order. It is not only the nature of the changes which prompt interest and action, but also their extent. We are only now becoming aware of the tremendous capacity for new technologies to produce harmful effects over extended geographic distances. The accident at the Chernobyl nuclear power plant in April 1986 illustrated the permeability of national boundaries in a manner which was not previously understood: hill farmers in Cumbria had their pasturing lands polluted and their livelihood destroyed by restrictions on sheep-grazing, and the British government continues to compensate them for pastures which remain off-limits nearly twenty years later. The depletion of the ozone layer and the onset of global warming reveal a greater understanding of the impact which new technologies may have over time and distance. We now know that releasing the contents of an aerosol spray in one country can ultimately harm the environment and citizens of another. A Londoner's hairstyle may be an Australian's cancer. The legal fiction of the sovereign state crumbles in the face of natural realities and economic impulses. Regulating an ever-broader range of activities necessarily becomes an international task.

New technologies also transform the means of communication, with significant consequences for access to the products and processes of international law. Telephones, faxes, email and the internet have hugely increased the global exchange of information, and the speed at which it is communicated. These technologies have made generally accessible the documentation which forms part of international negotiations and decision-making processes. When I first studied international law, many of the most important United Nations' documents– such as Security Council resolutions – were not available in the libraries of major universities until several years after they had been adopted. Security Council resolutions are now available to every person in the world with internet access, within minutes of their adoption. Security Council resolution 1546, which addressed the conditions of Iraqi governance after 30 June 2004, was instantly available once it had been adopted. People could read it and form their own views, and many did.

Similarly, judgments of international courts can be downloaded from their websites on the very same day that they are presented to the parties. In June 1999 I sat with an Albanian government minister in Tirana viewing the website of the International Court of Justice as that body refused to order a halt to the bombing of Yugoslavia by NATO, in the actions taken to protect Kosovan Albanians. On the day the Court gave its judgment in that case I am told that there were almost one million hits on the Court's website. An even greater number accessed the Court's website in July 2004, to read the Advisory Opinion that Israel's construction of a wall in the Occupied Palestinian Territory, including in and around East Jerusalem, was contrary to international law and should cease forthwith.[11]

There is a third factor for change, which is gradually weaving its way into international legal consciousness. This is the notion of 'democratization', which Professor Thomas Franck of New York University Law School has described as 'becoming a global entitlement'.[12] Democracy reflects the emergence of a universal expectation that those who seek a validation of their empowerment – the governors – should govern with the consent of the governed. Democracy has invariably been addressed as a national issue, giving rise to principles of self-determination, freedom of expression and the emergence of a normative entitlement to participate in electoral and other decision-making processes. Increasingly it is seen as encompassing rights of access to information, and to administrative and judicial remedies to challenge administrative acts which wrongly interfere with rights. Democratic claims too are being internationalized. If participatory democracy is relevant to the national levels of governments then why should it not also apply at the international level, where so many decisions which affect people's lives are now being taken?

There is ample evidence that access to information, decision-making and remedies is now being sought in relation to the activities of international organizations, such as the World Trade Organization. You need look no further than the powerful claims concerning the 'democratic deficit' in the European Community to see the extent to which issues of democratic governance challenge international decision-making and provoke powerful grass-roots opinions. With the internet people now have a great deal more information than before, and with that information corporations and NGOs – whose interests are at issue – are increasingly keen to influence governmental decisions. This has led to radical changes even within such conservative bodies as the World Bank; a decade ago it would have been unimaginable that private groups would be able to challenge some of the Bank's lending decisions. But that is precisely what has happened with the creation of the World Bank Inspection Panel in 1993, a radical initiative which was taken as a result of efforts by disenchanted citizens. Against this background the exclusion of civil society from access to the WTO and other international bodies is hard to justify. Rules of international law which perpetuate feelings of exclusion will generate public disquiet and anger. International laws and organizations exist to serve people, not governments.

Finally, the trend towards deregulation and the enhancement of the role of private enterprise and ownership as a dominant feature of modern, post-industrial society is the fourth factor in increasing public interest in international law. If the frontiers of the state are to be pushed back at the national level, as Margaret Thatcher famously declared in 1977 before she became prime minister, then why should they not also be pushed back at the international level? Deregulating international capital flows, promoting private investments overseas and increasing global trade have greatly extended the international role of the private and corporate sectors. Not surprisingly, these players are not content with a backseat role in the making and applying of international law. They want to influence the content of the rules and contribute to their enforcement. They do so by pressuring governments and, increasingly, participating directly in international treaty negotiations. The result is that governmental and commercial interests act together at the international level, so that international laws accommodate changing requirements and provide for an increased role for the private sectors in the design of those rules. One example is the Kyoto Protocol on global warming. This commits developed countries to cut their emissions of carbon dioxide and other greenhouse gases. With Russia's ratificaton on 18 November 2004, the Kyoto Protocol came into force on 16 February 2005. As it enters into force it will create an international market for trading in the right to emit greenhouse gases, with a direct role for the private sector.

Global free trade rules are another area where corporate interests are directly affected. If the private sector is to have rights and obligations under international instruments, on what basis can they be excluded from the law-making process, or the traditional inter-governmental arrangements for dispute settlement? These issues coalesce around a new reality: as the activities of the private sector are directly affected by international laws they can legitimately expect to play a greater role in international affairs, and in international law-making.

Globalization, advanced technologies, democratization, privatization and deregulation were not part of the traditional, state-centred background against which the United States and Britain made their visionary proposals in the 1940s. The four factors described above not only pose challenges to the established system, they help to transform it. By the 1990s the basic norms of international law were broadly established and accepted. As decolonization was followed by the fall of the Berlin Wall and the collapse of the Soviet bloc, Francis Fukuyama famously (and prematurely) declared the 'end of history'. The world seemed to be poised on the verge of a new global order, reflecting shared values, commitments and rules.

Or so we were led to believe. During the Clinton Administration a powerful group of neo-conservatives plotted to remake the international legal order. Their plan was set out in various manifestos, such as the Statement of Principles and other documents associated with the Project for the New American Century. The main targets included the rules which had allowed the detention of Pinochet, the new International Criminal Court, and the Kyoto Protocol on global warming. It was said that these threatened American national security. In November 2000 George W. Bush was elected into office, bringing with him many of the signatories of the Committee for the New American Century. John Bolton became one of President Bush's senior foreign policy advisers and was appointed Under Secretary for Arms Control and International Security at the US State Department. In 1997, as Senior Vice President of the American Enterprise Institute in Washington, DC, he declared that treaties were simply political 'and not legally binding'.[13] Richard Haass, Director of Policy Planning at the US State Department and now President of the prestigious US Council on Foreign Relations, declared the Bush Administration's commitment to 'à la carte multilateralism';[14] in other words, the US could pick and choose those rules which it wished to follow, and in other areas dispense with multilateral rules and proceed according to its own interests.

Then came 9/11, and the wars in Afghanistan and Iraq. Shortly after the end of the war in Iraq in April 2003, Richard Perle, an architect of the neo-conservative agenda in the United States, went even further, declaring publicly that the war in Iraq provided an opportunity to refashion international law and undermine the United Nations. Such actions began to look like part of a systematic neo-conservative effort to refashion the international legal order in the light of new priorities and values. British Prime Minister Tony Blair seemed sympathetic to the call. After Iraq, in a speech at his constituency in Sedgefield, in the north-east of England, he too argued for a new international law:

It may well be that under international law as presently constituted, a regime can systematically brutalize and oppress its people and there is nothing anyone can do, when dialogue, diplomacy and even sanctions fail, unless it comes within the definition of a humanitarian catastrophe. [. . .] This may be the law, but should it be?[15]

*

I am not starry-eyed about international law. I recognize that, on occasion, it has failed millions around the world, and will continue to do so. But do recent events justify a wholesale change of approach? In the aftermath of 9/11, the 'war on terrorism' has been used to justify an assault on established international legal rules. One has to be clear that 9/11 did not require the rules to be suspended, or even abandoned altogether. Even before that day George W. Bush's Administration had walked away from new international rules tackling global warming and biological weapons, and had been taking active steps to undermine the International Criminal Court. Even so, it is not the case that the United States has turned its back on the entire body of international law, or even most of it: the US is broadly committed to international free trade rules, for example those of the World Trade Organization and the North American Free Trade Agreement. It is seeking to adopt new rules in Central and South America and elsewhere in the world. It is strongly committed to the use of international laws to protect the rights of American investors overseas, and to rules protecting intellectual property rights. But do we want an international legal order which is essentially limited to the economic side of globalization? Or do we want international rules which promote other values and interests, as the US and Britain originally conceived?

While the events of 11 September 2001 became a catalyst for the systematic disregard of established international rules on human rights, the treatment of combatant prisoners and the use of military force around the world, I would maintain that this is not the moment to abandon the vision set out in the Atlantic Charter. Quite the contrary. International law at the beginning of the twenty-first century is more important than ever. The role of the United States in trying to remake global rules needs to be seen for what it is, namely an abandonment of values that are more vital than ever. In large part, the

British government has colluded or turned a blind eye, and has much diminished its ability to have a positive influence on the essential debate about the function of those international rules. Meanwhile public emotions are provoked by governments' failures to abide by these rules. Sixty years after the Atlantic Charter was adopted, two key questions need to be addressed. Do we need new global rules, as the British Prime Minister has proclaimed? Or do we need fewer rules, as the Bush Administration proposes?

2

Pinochet in London

'[T]he idea that such a brutal dictator as Pinochet should be claiming diplomatic immunity, I think, for most people in this country, will be pretty gut-wrenching stuff.'
Peter Mandelson, British Cabinet Minister, 18 October 1998[1]

'Where were you when Pinochet was arrested?' In the select world of international law the sixteenth of October 1998 is the closest you will get to a JFK or a John Lennon moment. The date marked the beginning of a legal process which transformed the international legal order, and brought arcane points of international law to the front pages of our newspapers and on to our television screens.

Pinochet had come to power on an earlier 11 September, in 1973, heading a coup which overturned the democratically elected Marxist government of Salvador Allende. During the fifteen or so years over which Pinochet ruled Chile more than 3,000 people were murdered or disappeared. Fifteen years after he had left office more than 1,500 of those who had disappeared had still not been accounted for. Much of the terror was directed by the Chilean Directorate of National Intelligence, the DINA, headed by one of Pinochet's former pupils, Colonel Manuel Contreras Sepúlveda.[2] Contreras explained his mission in an interview he gave in 2002:

[We] were ordered to repress subversions and terrorism that existed in Chile in that epoch . . . We were ordered to do that, and we accomplished that, and Chile was the first country in the world that succeeded in eliminating terrorism from its territory. We eliminated the terrorists from Chile, throwing them out of the country, detaining them in Chile, putting them on trial, with the result that we produced very few dead compared with other countries, which still have terrorism.[3]

The Colonel had previously confirmed that he had served 'as the delegate of the President'. He reported directly to Pinochet 'without any intermediary'. His orders always came from Pinochet himself.[4]

The 'elimination of terrorists' was not an internal matter, limited to the territory of Chile. In November 1975, Pinochet's Chile had proposed an operation to eliminate enemies all over the world, known as 'Operation Condor', bringing together military leaders from Argentina, Bolivia, Chile, Paraguay and Uruguay. A delegation from Brazil joined in 1976.[5] In September 1976, Orlando Letelier, a former Chilean ambassador to the United States, was murdered. Over the next five years the 'Condor' victims included a former president, a dissident military chief and various democratic political leaders. Amongst the victims in Chile were British and Spanish nationals. Many questions remain unanswered, including the role of the United States in the coup of 11 September 1973 and in 'Operation Condor', and the part played by Henry Kissinger, Richard Nixon's Secretary of State in the run-up to the coup and in the first months of 'Operation Condor'.

Pinochet left office in March 1990, but was appointed a Senator-for-Life. He continued to have a role in the Chilean government, advising on arms purchases. He visited Britain frequently, travelling on a diplomatic passport. On 22 September 1998 he arrived in London for a private visit, to undergo surgery for a herniated disc. Three weeks later, Chile's former head of state and a personal friend of Margaret Thatcher was arrested while recuperating at the London Clinic, just off Harley Street. On the evening of Friday, 16 October, around 9 p.m., Nicholas Evans, an English magistrate, signed a provisional arrest warrant following a request from Spain. The warrant called on 'each and all of the Constables of the Metropolitan Police Force' to arrest Pinochet, on the grounds that between 11 September 1973 and 1 December 1983 he 'did murder Spanish citizens in Chile'. Over the following days the arrest made the headlines all over the world. This was the first time that a former head of state had been arrested in Britain. It signalled a new commitment to international human rights law, a further step towards ending impunity.

Pinochet's arrest made international news because it reflected a fundamental shift in the balance of international priorities, and a commitment to the rule of law. Until October 1998 it was generally thought that a head of state – even a former head of state – had the right to enjoy complete immunity from the criminal jurisdiction of the courts of any other country for acts which might have been carried out in office. The rationale was a traditional and long-established rule of international law: a head of state is treated as the incarnation of the state itself – '*l'état c'est moi*'. This means that any restraint on the individual amounts to an interference with the independence and sovereignty of the state itself. To arrest Pinochet was to impugn the honour and sovereignty of Chile itself.

Pinochet had travelled to the United Kingdom in the belief that his status protected him from being investigated there for allegations concerning violations of fundamental human rights while he had been head of state. Shortly before he left Santiago he gave an interesting interview for the *New Yorker* magazine. This remarkably ill-advised contribution provided titbits of information on everything from his regular teas with Mrs Thatcher to his abiding commitment to the rule of law: 'Human rights! I say there has to be human rights for both sides.'[6] But the '*aspirante* dictator', as he styled himself, was let down by his advisers. They had not considered the effects of new international human rights laws. In particular, they had not accounted for the 1984 UN Convention against Torture, which required states to prosecute or extradite any alleged torturer, or anyone who had been complicit in torture. Curiously, at the tail end of his presidency, in October 1988, Pinochet had personally taken the decision that Chile should ratify this Convention, presumably as a way of signalling his regime's new-found commitment to fundamental rights. The decision would come back to haunt him.

Along with other conventions outlawing genocide, terrorism and discrimination, the 1984 Convention made torture an international crime for which individuals could be responsible. During the afternoon of 16 October 1998, a Spanish magistrate, Judge Baltasar Garzón, issued an order for Pinochet's detention for crimes of genocide and terrorism. Through Interpol he circulated an international warrant for Pinochet's arrest.[7] Garzón's actions were part of a broader effort by independent prosecutors in other countries, including Spain, France, Belgium and Switzerland. Each subsequently made their own extradition requests. Garzón's order was based on allegations that Pinochet had carried out criminal activities in co-ordination with the Argentine military authorities between 1976 and 1983, and had ordered the elimination of several individuals and the torture, kidnapping and disappearance of others. The warrant alleged that these activities had been carried out through the operations of the DINA, as part of 'Operation Condor'.

News of Pinochet's arrest emerged by the morning of Sunday, 18 October. It led to an animated discussion in our household. 'Look at the implications,' I said to my wife. 'You wouldn't be so thrilled if it was Mandela who was being arrested in the US for killing a bunch of white kids in some ANC attack in the 1980s,' I argued. I was articulating the classical international law approach, largely premised on the fear that all hell will break loose if you start playing around with the sacred rules. But this time Natalia was lined up with Peter Mandelson, the British Cabinet Minister who took to the airwaves to welcome the arrest of a 'brutal dictator'.[8] They were both right. Pinochet's arrest posed a real test for the international legal order, which aims to reconcile two objectives that can come into conflict: on the one hand, the need to respect the sovereign equality of states from external interference, and, on the other, the commitment to take active steps to safeguard fundamental human rights by ending the impunity of leaders from criminal process and prosecution. Did international law serve the interests of states and sovereigns, or was it intended to provide justice for the victims of the most serious international crimes?

By most accounts the traditional arguments against exercising criminal jurisdiction against a former head of state were certain to prevail. The classical position was well established in the practice of courts around the world and there were no exceptions. An early example was the decision of a New York court in 1876, in the case of *Hatch v. Baez*.[9] Davis Hatch was an American who claimed to have been injured while visiting the Dominican Republic. He blamed Buenaventura Baez, the country's President. When Baez subsequently visited New York, after he had left office, Hatch brought his claim to the New York court. The court accepted that since former President Baez was physically present in New York it could, in principle, exercise jurisdiction over him. But Baez claimed immunity from the court, on the grounds that the acts which Hatch complained of had occurred while he was President. The New York court decided that Baez was immune from its jurisdiction. His acts were 'official acts' of a foreign and friendly government, which was sovereign. Immunity was necessary 'to preserve the peace and harmony of nations', and that objective trumped all other values. The Baez principle had been applied in proceedings before national courts ever since, except where the state concerned had waived its immunity (one example of that concerned the cases brought in the United States against former President Marcos, where the Philippines waived immunity). There was also an emerging exception to the blanket immunity rule for cases which were before international courts. Article 227 of the Versailles Peace Treaty of 1919 had proposed the prosecution of the German Kaiser for 'a supreme offence against international morality and the sanctity of treaties'. This is shorthand for aggression or illegal warfare. Similarly, the proceedings before the International Military Tribunal at Nuremberg did not allow any of the defendants to claim immunity on the basis of their official positions. But Pinochet was before the English courts, not an international criminal tribunal.

Pinochet's lawyers adopted the same approach as Baez had in the New York courts more than a century earlier. They argued that an English court had no right to exercise criminal or civil jurisdiction over a former head of state in relation to any acts done by him as a sovereign, and they came very close to succeeding. The argument was based on two English Acts of Parliament which, they claimed, reflected a general rule of absolute immunity. Pinochet was the former head of state of a friendly country, and even if the acts alleged had occurred at all they were official and presidential in character. The preservation of peace and harmony between Chile and the United Kingdom required that he be granted immunity.

Within two weeks of his arrest the case was before a court comprising three judges, presided over by the Lord Chief Justice of England and Wales, Lord Bingham, the second most senior judge in the country. Shortly before the hearing opened I gave a news interview on the BBC World Service. Asked about the likely outcome, I expressed a view that was shared by most independent observers:

established international law favoured Pinochet, there were no precedents which went the other way. But as a postscript I ventured the perspective that international law was changing, that new developments in human rights suggested a different outcome, and that there was no particularly compelling policy reason why any person's status should, as such, put them above the law. I could quite see why a serving head of state should not be indicted before the courts of another country: in practice the only indicted presidents or prime ministers would be those of less powerful states before the courts of more powerful states. But there was no reason of principle why a former leader such as Pinochet should not be judged for serious crimes committed while in office. The principle should apply across the board – to Margaret Thatcher, Tony Blair or George W. Bush.

The hearings before the Divisional Court were brief, lasting just two days. The lawyers had only a short time to prepare their arguments, and none of the barristers who appeared had a strong background in international law. In any case the international law arguments did not get much of an airing. Pinochet was seeking judicial reviews of the arrest warrants issued by two magistrates, and was applying for habeas corpus (a right to liberty) against the Commissioner of the Metropolitan Police. The Crown Prosecution Service (CPS) opposed the applications. The role of the CPS was to represent the interests of Spain, which had made the request for extradition to the UK on behalf of Judge Garzón. Even though the Spanish government objected to Garzón's actions, he was independent and Spain was required to transmit the request. None of the three governments most directly affected – those of Spain, Chile or Britain – involved themselves formally in the case, at least at that stage. On 28 October 1998 the Divisional Court ruled unanimously in favour of Pinochet. Following the Baez principle, the three judges ruled that he was entitled to his claim to immunity by virtue of his office: Pinochet was absolutely immune while head of state; thereafter immunity was limited to acts which were done in the exercise of his functions as head of state. For these judges the case therefore turned on the question of whether the acts had been carried out by Pinochet in an official capacity: putting it another way, did he murder or torture or maim in a private capacity or in a public capacity? That this question can even be asked is incomprehensible to most sensible people. It confirms their view that the law in general – and international law in particular – is disconnected from common sense. Murder is murder, after all, and it is counter-intuitive to imagine that the same act carried out in two different contexts could lead to a different decision as to whether a court should be entitled to try someone. It is equally difficult for many people to digest the idea that an internationally outlawed act – such as torture or genocide – could ever be said to be carried out in an official capacity. If international law prohibits such acts, how can a government or a head of state be allowed to claim immunity where it is alleged they have been carried out?

On behalf of Spain, the Crown Prosecution Service argued precisely this: it could never be the proper exercise of governmental functions to commit international crimes as allegedly committed by Pinochet. But the court did not accept the logic of that argument. Mr Justice Andrew Collins explained: 'Unfortunately, history shows that it has indeed on occasions been state policy to exterminate or to oppress particular groups. One does not have to look very far back in history to see examples of that sort of thing having happened.'[10] He recognized that where the matters were as serious as those alleged in Pinochet's case, there was bound to be a temptation to bend the law to the facts, and to rule that if the defendant was responsible he should pay for the terrible crimes that had been committed. But Mr Justice Collins concluded that the law was clear, and that it could not – and should not – be twisted to meet the needs of any individual case.

The Crown Prosecution Service appealed against the judgment to the Judicial Committee of the House of Lords, Britain's highest court. This time there was a little more time for preparation. The points of international law were decisive and were fully argued. The hearings began on 4 November and ran for two weeks. A number of interested parties, who had not been involved in the first hearings, were given permission by the Law Lords to appear in the appeal: one group was led by Amnesty International and the Medical Foundation for the Victims of Torture, the other by the New York-based Human Rights Watch, who asked me to join their team of lawyers. I therefore had an opportunity to observe first-hand one of the most important international law cases ever decided.

The English legal tradition values oral argument, unlike the continental approach which places a greater premium on written pleading. This contributes greatly to the sense of drama, especially in this instance, since the case concerned real torture, real victims and a real president. Oral arguments in cases before the Judicial Committee are heard in an ordinary committee room on the upper floors of the House of Lords at the Palace of Westminster, under the shadow of Big Ben. It is perhaps not quite fair to describe the rooms as 'drab', as Reed Brody of Human Rights Watch has done. But certainly they are not glamorous, or high-tech, or even well appointed with decent chairs and tables. Every day the room was crammed – standing room only – with scores of journalists and observers, including a very large contingent from Chile and other parts of the world. The support was not one-sided, however, and both Pinochet and his victims were represented; some not-so-discreet note-takers could be observed apparently attending on behalf of a range of American interests, including the government and, according to some of the wilder rumours, Henry Kissinger. The cramped conditions meant that the many participants did not have the luxury of being separated by much space. For most of the hearings I sat next to Pinochet's principal human rights adviser during the first phase of his presidency. It was he who had advised Pinochet, towards the end of his presidency in the late 1980s, to commit Chile to join the 1984 Convention against Torture. The irony was not lost on him. For these visitors, indeed for all of us, it was a uniquely curious bonding experience because the stakes were so high. We were packed intimately close into a small room in the House of Lords, hearing arguments brought by a Spanish prosecutor about events which had occurred thousands of miles away, in a different country, more than twenty years earlier, which had had little direct connection with the United Kingdom or the British government (although there had been a number of British victims, including Dr Sheila Cassidy, who had operated on the knee of one of the DINA's most wanted targets, Nelson Gutiérrez, and was subsequently arrested and tortured by the DINA).

There are twelve Law Lords (the first lady, Brenda Hale, was only appointed in 2004). Five were selected to sit on this case. As the most senior member of the panel Lord Slynn presided over the case, one of the few Law Lords with a strong background in international law. At the time of the hearings he was Chair of the International Law Association, and had previously served as an Advocate General at the European Court of Justice in Luxembourg. (Two months earlier Gordon Slynn and I had sat together in New York at a symposium on 'Strengthening Democracy in the Global Economy', which had been chaired by Bill Clinton, with Tony Blair as a leading attraction. Clinton had particularly impressed us, not least because this was the very day on which his four-hour video testimony to Kenneth Starr in the Monica Lewinsky matter had been broadcast publicly.)[11] He sat with Lord Lloyd, Lord Nicholls, Lord Steyn and Lord Hoffmann, the last two South Africans by birth who had studied in Britain as Rhodes Scholars. They were assisted by a formally attired clerk to the Judicial Committee, whose outfit made a great impression on the overseas visitors. In the first row before their Lordships were the principal QCs and junior barristers for the main parties. From where the Law Lords sat, on the left-hand side were counsel for the Crown Prosecution Service, in the front row. To their right, counsel for Senator Pinochet. Immediately behind were the solicitors for these two parties, and also the *amicus curiae* (friend of the court), appointed by the Court to assist the judges on the comparative aspects of international law. Then in the third row were the NGOs who had been allowed to intervene. And behind them the public seats, occupied by journalists, observers and interested citizens from around the world. This public area included vociferous supporters of Pinochet, as well as leading activists and opponents of his regime. Isabel Allende, the daughter of Salvador Allende, sat through some of the proceedings. So did Francisco Letelier, the son of Orlando Letelier, who had been assassinated on Pinochet's orders in 1976 as part of 'Operation Condor'.

The hearings were concerned with the question of Pinochet's right to claim immunity under English law, and in particular the correct interpretation to be given to the State Immunity Act of 1978, which set out the basic rules. But the Act was not entirely clear on the immunity of a former head of state, so arguments were directed to the rules of international law. The governing principle was that English law had to be applied consistently with international law. If the English law was ambiguous, then international law would fill the gaps. This assumed, of course, that the rules of international law were clear, which they were not. Both sides and all the interveners devoted a great deal of attention, as did the judges in their questions, to the international law issues, which were given serious and careful consideration. There was no sense of scepticism in the Lords Committee Room, or any feeling that international law should be treated differently, or that it did not merit the judges' attention. Here was a clear difference from the US Supreme Court, the majority of whose Justices treat international law as a great irrelevance.

The case focused largely on arguments over whether international law had, or had not, been transformed since the Second World War. Had the raft of new international agreements requiring states to prosecute or extradite alleged perpetrators of international crimes crystallized into rules of customary international law which limited, or removed, the immunity which a former head of state was traditionally entitled to claim? On behalf of Spain and Judge Garzón, the Crown Prosecution Service painstakingly took the judges through the major developments which had taken place since the Second World War: the UN Charter, the Nuremberg and Tokyo war crimes trials, the ratification by the General Assembly of the United Nations of the Nuremberg Principles, the 1948 Convention prohibiting genocide, the 1979 Convention prohibiting hostage-taking, and finally the 1984 Convention prohibiting torture. All of these instruments, it was argued, outlawed a series of heinous acts and made it illegal for any state or its officials – including a President – to engage in them in a public capacity. The claim to immunity, the CPS argued, was inconsistent with these new developments in international law, which were directed towards punishment of perpetrators and an end to impunity. The argument was summarized by the Crown Prosecution Service: 'the United Kingdom is under no obligation to Chile, as a matter of international law, to accord immunity in respect of the acts of which [Senator Pinochet] is accused. On the contrary, international law rejects the concept of immunity for such acts. This means that, as a matter of international law, a former Head of State cannot plead immunity to a charge of crimes against humanity or indeed *a fortiori* genocide.'[12] These arguments were supported by the non-governmental organizations which intervened in the case. They argued in favour of a rule of customary international law which would mean that torture and related acts could never be treated as official acts and so could not, under any circumstances, generate a right to claim immunity.

These arguments were forcefully resisted by Senator Pinochet's lawyers, who argued for respect for the traditional rules. The principle of immunity was well established in international law. To show that the immunity rule had been changed, the CPS had to point to a positive act by the international community which removed, or limited, such immunity. They could not do so, it was argued, as there was no such act. Nor, it was said, was there any applicable treaty which said in express terms that a head of state, or a former head of state, could not claim immunity in respect of the most serious international crimes: 'it is submitted that the Appellants can point to no crystallized principle of customary international law to the effect that sovereign immunity does not apply as a matter of domestic law in respect of acts which are . . . "tainted by criminality or other forms of wrongdoing"'.[13]

The judgment of the House of Lords was anxiously awaited in the ten days that followed the hearings. At issue were two competing conceptions of the international legal order: the traditional approach, giving primacy to the interests of the state, and the emerging modern approach which pointed to the interests of victims and an end to impunity. The arguments were finely balanced. I found it impossible to predict the outcome.

The House of Lords gave its judgment on 25 November 1998. The convention is that each of the five Law Lords gives his decision in turn. The result may therefore not be known until the fifth has spoken. The judgments were delivered in the main chamber of the House of Lords, and were broadcast live on BBC radio and, for the first time, also on CNN television. Lord Slynn spoke first. He explained the basis for his conclusion that Senator Pinochet was entitled to immunity: 'if States wish to exclude the long-established immunity of former heads of state in respect of allegations of specific crimes, or generally, then they must do so in clear terms. They should not leave it to national courts to do so because of the appalling nature of the crimes concerned.'[14] Lord Lloyd spoke next, agreeing that the traditional rule of immunity had not been displaced by more recent developments, and in particular the creation of various international criminal tribunals. The setting up of these tribunals showed that international crimes committed by heads of state or other responsible government officials cannot be tried in the ordinary courts of other states, he said, since if they could 'there would be little need for the international tribunal'.[15] So far the score was 2–0 for Pinochet, with three judges still to declare. Lord Nicholls concluded that the acts which Pinochet was alleged to have carried out were not to be regarded by international law as a function of the state and were not to be treated as acceptable conduct on the part of anyone. Accordingly, no claim to immunity could be made by a former head of state in respect of them. Lord Steyn agreed: a former head of state is only entitled to claim immunity for acts performed in the exercise of functions as a head of state. The alternative approach – which had been adopted by the Divisional Court at first instance – would lead inexorably to the conclusion that when Hitler ordered the 'final solution' his act would have to be regarded as an official act deriving from the exercise of his functions as a head of state, and that he would be entitled to immunity. That, said Lord Steyn, was an unacceptable conclusion: 'the development of international law since the Second World War justifies the conclusion that by the time of the 1973 *coup d'état* [in Chile], and certainly ever since, international law condemned genocide, torture, hostage-taking and crimes against humanity (during an armed conflict or in peacetime) as international crimes deserving of punishment. Given this state of international law, it seems to me difficult to maintain that the commission of such high crimes may amount to acts performed in the exercise of the functions of a head of state.'[16]

This left only Lord Hoffmann. Of the five he had been the only one during the hearings who had appeared sympathetic to the 'no immunity' argument, and he concurred with Lord Nicholls. When he spoke, the whole Chamber gasped (a sound that is audible on the BBC archive for anyone interested in dramatic historical moments),[17] although he gave no further reasons for allowing the appeal and finding against Senator Pinochet. The upshot was clear: the very nature of the international legal order appeared to have shifted. The interests of victims were not trumped by the interests of sovereigns and their states.

That evening, news broadcasts around the world led with the story. A common theme was the transformation of the international legal order. The *Financial Times* described the case as 'a landmark in human rights law'.[18] For Salvador Allende's daughter, Isabel, the decision was 'marvellous, a truly great satisfaction'.[19] Pinochet's son Augusto struggled with his anger: 'My father has received a sadistic and cruel blow on his birthday that goes beyond the rights of mankind.'[20] It was, wrote columnist Hugo Young in *The Guardian*, 'a singularly unflinching statement from the judicial majority'. Although couched in legalities, it was 'bold and principled, taking a stand on behalf of the globalization of fundamental human rights which will be seen as a milestone'.[21] European leaders generally welcomed the ruling, while the response in the US was 'muted'.[22]

As the case unfolded, the Clinton Administration was caught between the Chilean government, which opposed Pinochet's extradition, and those who supported Judge Garzón's actions. Shortly after the House of Lords judgment, a State Department spokesman announced that the Administration was reviewing documents relating to the period in its possession and would declassify and make public as much material as it could, consistent with American laws and national security.[23] (A first batch of 5,800 documents was released in June 1999, providing valuable new information on what America knew, as well as its efforts to support the coup.)

But the case was not over. That evening we watched *Newsnight*, the BBC news programme, which was devoted almost entirely to the historic judgment. One of the participants was a Chilean senator and Pinochet-supporter who referred to Lord Hoffmann's connections with Amnesty International, and in particular the fact that Lady Hoffmann was a volunteer working for Amnesty. This, she said, indicated that the House of Lords was not impartial. The comment was swatted away by the presenter, Jeremy Paxman, as an irrelevance. But how wrong he was. In the following days the British press began to focus on the precise nature of Lord Hoffmann's relationship with Amnesty International, which had been one of the NGOs to intervene in the case. This raised squarely the issue of whether the decisive judgment had been given by a judge who might be seen as having a personal interest in the case. In its report of the judgment, *The Guardian* described him as 'probably the cleverest of the law lords, asking questions which cut away at the verbiage and . . . impatient with waffling QCs'.[24] I have already noted my impression that, of the judges who had heard the case, he was the only one who appeared to be sympathetic to our side. On the other hand, he had a background in commercial law, rather than human rights, and recent judgments he had given on the application of the death penalty in the Caribbean – where he had rejected Amnesty's arguments – suggested that he would not have had any sort of predisposition, one way or the other.

Despite the growing furore over the issue, on 9 December Home Secretary Jack Straw, acting under his statutory duties, authorized the courts to proceed to consider Pinochet's extradition to Spain, now that the immunity issue had been decided. This was a brave decision, since he could have ended the proceedings then and there. The next day Pinochet's lawyers applied to the House of Lords to set aside its earlier judgment, on the grounds that Lord Hoffmann's links with Amnesty International – the fact that his wife worked at the International Secretariat and that he was a member and chairman of Amnesty International Charity Ltd (AICL) – gave rise to the appearance of a possible bias. This too was an unprecedented challenge. There was no higher court than the House of Lords. So Pinochet was asking it to annul its own judgment, an audacious application if ever there was one.

Within a week the Judicial Committee of the House of Lords had set aside its landmark judgment. It concluded that Lord Hoffmann should not have sat on the case since he was a member and chairman of Amnesty International Charity Ltd, a body which carried out Amnesty's charitable purposes. The circumstances in which he had decided to sit – had the other Law Lords known of his connections? – remain unclear, although he recently gave an interview to our obscure local newspaper, the *Hampstead & Highgate Express*, in which he admitted to a misjudgement.[25] The Law Lords directed a full re-hearing of the appeal, over three weeks, beginning at the end of January 1999.

It was a surreal experience to sit through the same case again, in the very same room, so shortly after the first hearing. More or less the same participants were involved, although this time the government of Chile formally intervened on the side of Pinochet, without making exactly the same arguments. This time a panel of seven Law Lords was assembled, under the presidency of Lord Browne-Wilkinson. The great moment of the case cast a shadow over the proceedings.

The British legal and political establishment had been rocked by the unprecedented annulment of the first judgment in the most keenly watched case the House of Lords had ever decided. There was great concern that a different judgment would bring permanent damage to its authority. Could the House of Lords abandon its earlier decision and reach an entirely different conclusion?

The case did follow a different path, proving that the law is not something which is mechanically applied, and leaves a great deal to personality and disposition. Again the Law Lords examined international law in fine detail, but this time they focused more closely on a single treaty, the 1984 Convention against Torture and Other Cruel, Inhuman or Degrading Treatment or Punishment. It was apparent from their questions that this panel of judges was not convinced by the argument that the rules of customary international law entitled Pinochet to claim immunity. Apart from treaties, customary law is the main source of international legal obligation. Proving a rule of customary law is difficult. Unless you can identify a decision of some international court which has already decided the point, you have to persuade the court that there is state practice, that it has been consistent over time, and that the practice is compelled by a belief that it is required by international law.[26] Establishing a customary rule gave rise to understandable perplexity on the part of the judges. How do you get into the mind of a state? Lord Browne-Wilkinson asked a barrister for the Crown Prosecution Service how one should identify a rule of customary international law. Having heard the answer, he exclaimed: 'Ah, I think I understand. If we say it is customary international law then it is. If we say it's not, then it is not.' The burden is a heavy one for any judge. In this case it was all the greater.

Second time round it turned out to be far easier to focus on the crimes which Pinochet was charged with, and specifically the accusation of torture. Perhaps this was because, with a little more time available, the specific facts of the allegations could be considered more carefully. By six votes to one, on 24 March 1999, the House of Lords ruled again and decisively that Pinochet was not entitled to claim immunity from the jurisdiction of the English courts. A *New York Times* editorial described this as 'sovereignty's worst day in memory'. (It happened to be the same day that NATO had begun its bombing campaign in Serbia, ostensibly to protect the fundamental human rights of Kosovan Albanians from their own government.)[27] But Pinochet's loss of immunity was limited to acts which had occurred after 28 October 1998. Why that date? Because that was the day on which the 1984 Convention against Torture came into force for the three states affected by Judge Garzón's extradition request: Chile, Spain and Britain.

The 1984 Convention was central to the decision of the House of Lords. It required all state parties to prosecute any person who is alleged to have committed the crime of torture anywhere in the world; alternatively to extradite such a person to a country where he or she would be prosecuted. But the Convention was completely silent on the question of immunity. So the question had to be answered: what did the drafters of the Convention intend? The majority of the House of Lords concluded that it would be incompatible with the aims of the Convention to allow someone charged with torture to escape punishment by reason of the office which he held at a particular time. Lord Browne-Wilkinson summarized his conclusions in the following way:

[T]he Torture Convention did provide what was missing: a worldwide universal jurisdiction. Further, it required all member states to ban and outlaw torture: Article 2. How can it be for international law purposes an official function to do something which international law itself prohibits and criminalizes. [. . .] Under the Convention the international crime of torture can only be committed by an official or someone in an official capacity. [Under the traditional approach] they would all be entitled to immunity. It would follow that there can be no case outside Chile in which a successful prosecution for torture can be brought unless the State of Chile is prepared to waive its right to its officials' immunity. Therefore the whole elaborate structure of universal jurisdiction over torture committed by officials is rendered abortive and one of the main objectives of the Torture Convention – to provide a system under which there is no safe haven for torturers – will have been frustrated. In my judgement all these factors together demonstrate that the notion of continued immunity for ex-heads of state is inconsistent with the provisions of the Torture Convention.[28]

By this legal logic, Pinochet's loss of immunity resulted from the implied consequences of a treaty which Chile, Spain, the United Kingdom and 110 other states had signed. But there was nothing in the treaty itself which expressly addressed the question of immunity.

In preparing for the case Human Rights Watch had carried out an exhaustive review of the entire five-year history of negotiations for the Torture Convention, with the assistance of a marvellous group of students at Yale Law School's Orvill Schell Center for International Human Rights. This showed that the subject of immunity had never been discussed at all. The solitary dissenting judgment of Lord Goff focused on this point. 'How extraordinary it would be,' he mused, 'and indeed what a trap would be created for the unwary, if state immunity could be waived by a treaty *sub silentio*.' For Lord Goff, one of only two seasoned international lawyers who had sat on the second case, and Chairman of the British Institute of International and Comparative Law, common sense, principle and authority pointed to only one conclusion: that over one hundred states could not have intended to agree to the exclusion of state immunity silently and accidentally.

The difference of approach in the majority and dissenting judgments illustrates the ambiguities which are inherent in any treaty. Philip Allott, one of my law school teachers and a former UK Foreign Office legal adviser, had taught us that treaties were 'just agreements to disagree, reduced into writing'. Why had immunity never been raised in the negotiations? Probably there would have been a majority view against immunity, but they would have been fearful of raising an issue in which a powerful minority would put their opposition on the record. And the minority might have been concerned that they would be overruled. Or, possibly, no one had thought about the immunity point, although I think that is unlikely.

In any event, Lord Goff's traditional approach did not carry the day. The judgment confirmed that where states have legislated internationally – by treaty – to criminalize certain acts, then there will be no immunity for a former head of state before the national courts of countries which are parties to that treaty. This is a more restrictive approach than the earlier judgment of the House of Lords, but I think the second judgment will turn out to be more acceptable to states, since it is not based on the somewhat amorphous concept of customary law. Nevertheless it provides decisive and strong support for an emerging new international legal order, which reflects human rights concerns and the interests of victims over other interests.

The second judgment of the House of Lords did not end the case in the English courts, however. Having determined that Pinochet was not entitled to immunity from the jurisdiction of the English courts, Pinochet was then subject to the ordinary proceedings for his extradition to Spain. These required, amongst other things, the Home Secretary once again to decide whether to authorize the extradition to proceed. He did this, in April 1999. Again, it was a brave decision. In the summer of 1999 Pinochet made his first appearance in the dock at Bow Street Magistrates Court, where the indictment was read out to him. It was a singularly dramatic day in Chile, where the country remained divided by the prospect of its former head of state facing justice overseas. But even as these proceedings were under way, the political cogs were turning. Although the law had been allowed to run its course, as the British, Chilean and Spanish governments had indicated it should, the conclusion was unexpected and caused tremendous problems for all three governments. It looked as though obscure rules of international law were causing them to lose control. In September 1999 Jack Straw announced that he had received information that Pinochet's health was failing, and that he should be subject to medical examinations to determine whether he was fit enough to stand trial. *The Observer* newspaper reported that during the summer of 1999 there had been a concerted effort by the three governments to find alternative ways to bring to an end the protracted legal proceedings which were leading inexorably – and surprisingly – towards Pinochet's extradition to Spain.[29] What happened exactly is not clear. But news reports claimed that Tony Blair and his then Foreign Secretary, Robin Cook, hatched a plan with Eduardo Frei, the President of Chile, and José Maria Aznar, the Prime Minister of Spain, and his Foreign Minister, Abel Matutes, to stop Pinochet's extradition. They would rely on an apparent discretion in Britain's Extradition Act to allow an early return, on 'humanitarian grounds'.

In October 1999 the Chilean Embassy in London submitted medical reports which suggested that Pinochet's condition had deteriorated and that he might not be fit to stand trial. In January 2000, at Jack Straw's request, Pinochet underwent an independent medical examination by three medical practitioners and a consultant neuropsychologist. According to Straw, the examination concluded that Pinochet's health had deteriorated in September and October 1999, that he was unfit to stand trial, and that no improvement to his condition was expected. The Home Secretary reported that he was 'minded' to take the view that no purpose would be served by continuing the extradition proceedings and that he should therefore bring them to an early close, and allow Pinochet to return to Chile. By now, prosecutors from four states were requesting extradition: Spain, France, Belgium and Switzerland. They were invited to make representations, as were Amnesty International, Human Rights Watch and the other non-governmental organizations which had been involved in the legal proceedings.

Prosecutors from France, Switzerland and Belgium asked to see the medical report to form their own view. Jack Straw refused, on grounds of confidentiality. If a deal had been agreed by Britain, Spain and Chile, they had forgotten to tell the Belgian government about it. Along with other barristers, I was hired by the Belgian government to prepare a legal challenge in the English courts to Straw's refusal to give the Belgian government's prosecutor access to the medical report, despite its request. The press reported that Belgium was considering bringing a case against the United Kingdom to the International Court of Justice in The Hague. Belgium decided to proceed before the English courts. On 15 February 2000 the Court of Appeal upheld Belgium's appeal and ordered disclosure to all four requesting states. 'Does fairness require disclosure of this [medical] report to the requesting states?' asked Lord Justice Simon Brown, the presiding judge. Yes, he said, because of 'the very great moment of the case'. If Pinochet was sent back to Chile the consequence would be that, accused of the most terrible crimes, he would be untriable anywhere in the world, and he would not be extradited to Spain, Belgium or anywhere else. The requesting states would have the opportunity to comment on the medical report, justice would be seen to be done, minds would be set at rest, there would be little in the way of delay, and 'a uniquely controversial case would have been decided according to the fairest possible procedures'.

I left the court immediately after the judgment and went directly to Heathrow to catch a flight to New York. By the time I arrived at JFK airport, just a few hours later, Pinochet's medical records were available on the worldwide web. I do not know who posted them. The question to ask is: who had the greatest interest in making that type of confidential information so widely and publicly available? The publication of the detailed medical records engendered some sympathy for

Pinochet. Judge Garzón commissioned an independent report from eight Spanish doctors. They were not persuaded that the reports established his unfitness to stand trial. 'Mr Pinochet presents both a physical and mental condition sufficiently normal to face any uncomfortable situation, such as presence at a trial,' they considered.[30] The Spanish doctors also referred to a 'subterfuge' and bemoaned the significant and negative jurisprudential consequences of relying on the report so as to allow Pinochet to avoid his date with justice.

On 2 March 2000 Jack Straw announced the termination of extradition proceedings. But one potential barrier remained. Another international treaty, the 1957 European Convention on Extradition, on which Spain and Belgium had relied and based their requests for extradition, did not include medical unfitness as a reason for a refusal to extradite. A decision to return Pinochet to Chile on medical grounds would arguably violate that Convention. Straw dealt with the problem head-on: although 'the [1957] Convention does not allow for the refusal of extradition on the ground that the accused is and will remain unfit to stand trial in the requesting state', [31] the Convention had not been incorporated into English law, which meant that it could not be relied upon in any challenge to his decision before the English courts. By expressly contemplating a violation of the 1957 Extradition Convention, Straw had established a complete defence in English law to the argument that he had failed to take into account Britain's international legal obligations. As the Home Secretary put it, he 'attaches great importance to the international obligations of the United Kingdom', but in this case they were outweighed by other compelling considerations. That same day Pinochet left the United Kingdom for Chile. As he waited at a military airfield to leave Britain, Margaret Thatcher arranged for him to be presented with a silver Armada platter. This was, she said, a token of her personal esteem after the 'great injustice' of his detention, 'which should never have taken place'.[32]

*

The story surrounding Pinochet's last visit to Britain began and ended with alleged violations of international law, from the coup of 11 September 1973 and the international crimes which followed, to Jack Straw's decision to ignore the European Convention on Extradition. But the sixteen months that Pinochet spent in the United Kingdom immeasurably strengthened the perception that international law had 'bite'. In the five years following his return to Chile, he has been constantly hounded by criminal prosecutors and he has recently lost his immunity from process before the Chilean courts. The House of Lords had confirmed the importance of international laws and treaties, not once but twice. Internationally, every head of state now knows that he or she may be accountable for the consequences of acts which massively and systematically violate fundamental human rights laws and international criminal laws. Despots and dictators, indeed anyone who might be accused of committing international crimes, will now travel abroad with a great deal more trepidation. Some choose not to travel at all, and then will do so only after obtaining considered legal advice on the possibility that they too may face arrest and charges. Pinochet's bubble of personal invincibility was burst. For the victims of international crimes these treaties may be seen as having more enforceability than was previously thought to be the case.

Pinochet's detention has not met with universal approval, however. There has been something of a minor backlash against the House of Lords judgment. In February 2003 the International Court of Justice gave a rather traditional ruling, which has been interpreted by some as an attempt to reverse the Pinochet judgment, although I do not now believe that to have been the intention, at least of all the judges.[33] A year later, the Special Court for Sierra Leone rejected a claim of immunity from Charles Taylor, the former president of Liberia, basing its decision partly on the Pinochet case.[34] Henry Kissinger has been one of the more powerful critics of the House of Lords judgment, a fact which may not be entirely unconnected with his own alleged involvement with Pinochet's coup and 'Operation Condor'. He has written that the House of Lords could have decided that a Chilean court, or an international criminal tribunal specifically established for crimes committed in Chile, was the appropriate forum for proceedings, not the courts of England or Spain:

The unprecedented and sweeping interpretation of international law in *Ex parte Pinochet* would arm any magistrate, anywhere in the world, with the unilateral power to invoke a supranational conception of justice; to substitute his own judgment for the reconciliation procedures of even incontestably democratic societies where the alleged violations of human rights occurred;

and to subject the accused to the criminal procedures of the magistrate's country, with whose legal system the defendant may be unfamiliar and which forces him to bring evidence and witnesses from long distances.[35]

Mr Kissinger would seemingly have good reason to be concerned. In a recently released transcript of a telephone conversation, five days after Pinochet's coup, he told President Nixon that 'we helped them'.[36] In the same conversation he complains about the 'unbelievable filthy hypocrisy' of those who were objecting to American involvement in Chile. He is quite right, of course, to point out that foreign courts, located at a great distance from the place of the crime, are not well placed to consider evidence and witnesses. But he misses the real point, and misunderstands the changing nature of international law. The 'supranational conception of justice' has not been plucked out of thin air, by judges or lawyers who substitute legal analysis with political views. It derives from international law, from the 1984 Convention against Torture, which the United States and the majority of other states have voluntarily undertaken to comply with. International law commits states to prosecute torturers, or extradite them to countries which will prosecute them. International law does not encourage or permit magistrates or judges to do anything which governments have not accepted they may, or in some cases must, do. I agree that prosecutorial discretion has to be exercised with care, and that the 'fairest possible procedures' have to be followed. Pinochet had fair procedures, and he had his day in court, unlike his victims.

What Henry Kissinger really objects to – although he cannot quite bring himself to say it in so many words – is the loss of sovereign and executive power, and its subjection to the limits of the rule of law by an independent judiciary. His complaint is that ultimately foreign policy cannot be constrained by rules of international law. He is echoing earlier concerns. George Kennan, the distinguished US diplomat in the Department of State, once said that the most serious fault in past American policy formulation was 'the legalistic-moralistic approach to international problems'.[37] This is a theme which has been given fuller expression by the Administration of George W. Bush, which took office on 20 January 2001 and which has done more to curtail fundamental human rights than any US government in living memory.

One of its first targets, even before the opportunities engendered by 9/11, was the concept of the new International Criminal Court which, it claimed, was a product of the same mindset that delivered the Pinochet judgment.

3

A New International Court

'There is a thing called the International Criminal Court . . .'
Donald Rumsfeld, 21 June 2002[1]

Fifty years after Nuremberg and Tokyo, 121 states, meeting in Rome, agreed to create a new international criminal court. The International Criminal Court (ICC) is now up and running in The Hague. Under the Rome Statute of 1998 it has jurisdiction over the three most serious categories of international crimes: genocide, war crimes and crimes against humanity. The crimes include widespread or systematic attacks against civilians, such as murder, torture and rape, and would cover the kinds of charges laid against Pinochet by Judge Garzón.

Some of the House of Lords judges expressed concern about an English court hearing Pinochet's case, and wondered whether it would not have been better for the case to have been dealt with in Chile, or before an international court. These judges, like most people around the world who have looked at the Statute, seem to welcome the ICC. But not everyone does. Not George W. Bush or Donald Rumsfeld or Henry Kissinger, although some of their statements have been so off the mark that I wonder sometimes if they are talking about the same Statute.

*

The Pinochet case put the spotlight on the emerging system of international criminal justice. But it also raised a great number of other issues, not least how to avoid abusive or capricious prosecutions. One question that is frequently asked is this: if courts are to play a role in dealing with international crimes, then which ones – national or international – are best suited to punish the crimes against humanity and war crimes, which have been outlawed by international law since the late 1940s? This is a particularly pertinent question in relation to the decision to subject Saddam Hussein to an exclusively Iraqi trial.

The question assumes that the criminal law dispensed through courts is a proper way – although not the only way – of dealing with the most serious international crimes. Not everyone shares that assumption. I have no illusions about the effectiveness of internationalizing the criminal law. It will not be a panacea for all the ills of the world. It will not eradicate gross violations of fundamental human rights. But it may be the least bad option for dealing with the gravest crimes, or at least some of them. The other options are not especially attractive, or always workable. One option used to be extra-judicial summary justice, executing the perpetrators, but that is no longer favoured. International crimes can be ignored, as most were until the second half of the twentieth century. Or they can be dealt with by national amnesties, as happened in Chile, with the result that many victims were left aggrieved and feeling that justice had not been done, that there had been no 'closure'. Or they can be addressed through processes of 'truth and reconciliation', as has happened in South Africa after the end of the apartheid regime. Or they can be the subject of diplomatic deals between governments.

These options are not mutually exclusive. But since the Second World War the international community has decided that the perpetrators of the gravest crimes should be tried before courts of law, and that their actions are thereby criminalized. The arguments in favour of court trials include deterrence, punishment and 'seeking the truth'. These gained the upper hand once and for all, we thought, with the adoption of the Rome Statute. Britain's Labour government, newly elected in May 1997, played an important role in making agreement possible, reversing the policy of the previous Conservative government, which had allied itself with sceptics, including the United States, who favoured a more anaemic version of the international court, which could be controlled politically. Britain is now one of the strongest supporters of the Court, so that on this issue the United States and Britain are miles apart. Given the similarities of their values, how can this be explained?

Although Bill Clinton signed the Statute, the Bush Administration, since it came into office in January 2001, has been running an aggressive, mendacious and ill-informed campaign to undermine the ICC. Its approach to the ICC is symptomatic of a more generalized opposition to international rules and to multilateralism, and reduces the effectiveness of raising legitimate concerns. Such an attitude is surprising when seen in historical context: the United States once played a key role in establishing international criminal courts. Further, it contradicts the Administration's view on the suitability of international criminal courts for others, for non-Americans. The 'special relationship' between Britain and the United States has not yet made any discernible difference to America's approach.

Under international law the signature of a treaty does not create binding legal obligations. That comes later, with national ratification or accession. But Clinton's signature did oblige the United States not to do anything that would frustrate the functioning of the ICC.[2] Even this was a step too far for many American commentators, and not just the neo-conservatives who treat the Court as a symbol for everything that is wrong with international laws that constrain sovereignty or the naked exercise of power. I have attended academic conferences in the United States where the subject of the ICC can turn normally placid and respected scholars into Rottweilers. US Secretary of Defense Donald Rumsfeld summarized the reasons behind the more general objections to the Court:

The lack of adequate checks and balances on powers of the ICC prosecutors and judges; the dilution of the UN Security Council's authority over international criminal prosecutions; and the lack of an effective mechanism to prevent politicized prosecutions of American service members and officials.[3]

What he really means is that the rules will not allow the United States or other countries to use political power to control the proceedings. And 9/11 has provided a further rationale. As Rumsfeld put it, his concerns become even more troubling 'in the midst of a difficult, dangerous war on terrorism', with the risk that the ICC could attempt to assert jurisdiction over American service members and civilians involved in counter-terrorist and other military operations. Quite why this should not cause a problem for Britain, America's closest ally in the 'war on terrorism', has never been explained. In May 2002 the Administration announced it would 'unsign' the Rome Statute, declaring that the United States would not be a party to the

ICC Statute. 'Unsigning' was seen as a way of freeing the United States to engage in a ferocious campaign against the Court. The Bush Administration committed itself to a policy of extinguishing all possibility that any American could ever be tried in a case before the ICC's judges. The attacks have been carried out on several fronts. President Bush published a new National Security Strategy in September 2002. Amongst the commitments is this:

We will take the actions necessary to ensure that our efforts to meet our global security commitments and protect Americans are not impaired by the potential for investigations, inquiry, or prosecution by the International Criminal Court (ICC), whose jurisdiction does not extend to Americans and which we do not accept.[4]

Bush's campaign against the ICC has caused concern around the globe, and is frequently picked up by the press. Such bullying causes tremendous resentment. So does the double standard, which says that international criminal courts are good enough for your citizens, but not for ours. A state is entirely free to decide whether or not it will join an international agreement. China and Russia, for example, have not joined the ICC, and are adopting a reasonable 'wait and see' attitude. The American campaign of vilification, on the other hand, raises serious questions as to the Administration's approach to international law more generally. What is it about the International Criminal Court that has generated such ferocity? Are the attacks reasonable? And what changed to justify the abandonment of earlier support for global justice?

*

The attitude to the ICC contrasts with America's historical support for international criminal courts for non-Americans. After the First World War, President Woodrow Wilson's Administration prepared the first draft of Article 227 of the Versailles Treaty, opening the way to the indictment of Kaiser Wilhelm II of Germany.[5] Even though the Kaiser was never tried, having taken refuge in Holland, that treaty obligation was historically important in signalling a first step towards individual criminal responsibility for war crimes, even for leaders. Towards the end of the Second World War this commitment took another important step forward. President Franklin D. Roosevelt overrode Winston Churchill's proposal to execute German war criminals. He persuaded the British government to accept the principle of an international military tribunal to try the most senior Nazi officials. Roosevelt appointed Robert Jackson, a serving US Supreme Court Justice, to head the American team negotiating the Nuremberg Statute. In time Jackson became Chief Prosecutor at the Nuremberg international military tribunal. The Nuremberg judgments were a landmark in asserting individual criminal responsibility under international law. They provided the foundation for other United Nations efforts to enshrine the idea of individual responsibility for crimes, reflected as early as 1948 in the Genocide Convention.

On the first anniversary of Roosevelt's death, Jackson explained why the President had supported Nuremberg. He believed that

the war criminals who had overrun [Czechoslovakia] and other countries and inflicted such barbaric treatment on the inhabitants should be identified and punished – not because of mere vengeance, but chiefly because he felt that punishment was one way that repetition of this sort of thing could be prevented or made less likely.[6]

In the 1950s the United States led initiatives within the United Nations to create a permanent international criminal court. The task was eventually passed over to the UN's International Law Commission, which produced a draft Statute for an International Criminal Court many years later, in 1994. The Clinton Administration welcomed the draft, which coincided with the atrocities in Yugoslavia and Rwanda. Indeed, Clinton's Secretary of State, Madeleine Albright, had led efforts within the United Nations Security Council to create the first international criminal tribunals after Nuremberg and Tokyo. In 1993 the Security Council established the International Criminal Tribunal for the former Yugoslavia, which was charged with prosecuting 'persons responsible for serious violations of international humanitarian law committed in the territory of the former Yugoslavia since 1991'.[7] The following year a second international tribunal was created, the International Criminal Tribunal for Rwanda, which had jurisdiction for the most serious international crimes committed on the territory of Rwanda. These international tribunals were created as organs of the UN Security Council, which meant that the permanent members of the Security Council – including the United States – could wield considerable control over important decisions, such as the appointment of the Prosecutor, the election of the judges and the budget. The Yugoslav and Rwanda tribunals were important and positive steps in constructing an international criminal justice system. It is too cynical to dismiss them as afterthoughts, substitutes for the failure to take military action sooner to prevent gross violations of fundamental rights in the Balkans, and the genocide in Bosnia.

The United States continues to play a leading role in the operation of both international tribunals and has been the single largest contributor of funds. Neither would have come into being without American support or creativity, and it is certain that some of the most notorious defendants – Slobodan Milošević in particular – would never have been delivered to The Hague without American pressure. It was widely reported that the Bush Administration was threatening to withhold up to US$100 million in financial aid if the new Yugoslav government did not deliver Milošević to the tribunal.[8] So it is clear that there is no objection in principle to the idea of international criminal courts. If there is an objection it is to the exercise of international criminal jurisdiction over Americans.

These reactive international efforts spanning nearly fifty years – at Nuremberg, Tokyo, The Hague, Arusha (Tanzania) – reflect a broad recognition that in some cases national courts will not be able – or willing – to prosecute the most serious international crimes. The Pinochet case showed the potential role for national courts, as well as the pitfalls. History has shown that national courts will only rarely try their own nationals for war crimes, and even more rarely for crimes against humanity or genocide, even when a new government comes to power. National courts would often have to deal with crimes taking place far from where the court is based, where the only real connection with the facts may be the temporary presence of the defendant within the territory of the state. The English courts were only able to exercise jurisdiction over Pinochet because he happened to visit Britain. The courts of Senegal were only able to proceed with a case against Hissène Habré, the former leader of Chad, because he was living in exile in that country.[9] In some cases, criminal indictments have been issued when the accused is not even present in the jurisdiction: one notorious example was the indictment by a Belgian prosecutor of Israeli Prime Minister Ariel Sharon, which led the United States to threaten not to attend NATO meetings at that organization's headquarters in

Brussels. Other examples include a Belgian prosecutor's indictment of a serving foreign minister of the Democratic Republic of Congo, a French prosecutor issuing proceedings against Libyan President Qaddafi, and a Serbian court indicting Tony Blair. Prosecutions such as these will always be seen as politically motivated, having dubious international legitimacy and no prospect of success.

However, the creation of international criminal courts has not been the only initiative aimed at plugging the justice gaps where national courts fail. In the 1990s the United Nations established 'internation-alized' criminal courts in Bosnia and in Kosovo. These courts include local and international judges, and they apply a mix of local and international criminal law. In 2000 an international Special Court for Sierra Leone was created by treaty between the United Nations and Sierra Leone, to try leaders bearing the greatest responsibility for serious violations of international and Sierra Leonean law. And in 2003 the United Nations finally reached agreement in principle with the government of Cambodia to create a special section of the Cambodian courts system to try senior leaders of the Khmer Rouge most responsible for serious crimes between April 1975 and January 1979. The United States has not objected to any of these initiatives, or to the principle that the criminal law should be applied to the perpetrators of the most serious international crimes. In none of these cases has the US objected to jurisdiction being exercised over the most high-ranking political leaders and military personnel. On the contrary, US Secretary of State Colin Powell proclaimed that the United States is

the leader in the world with respect to bringing people to justice. We have supported a tribunal for Yugoslavia, the tribunal for Rwanda, trying to get the tribunal for Sierra Leone set up. We have the highest standards of accountability of any nation on the face of the earth.[10]

How then, when it comes to the ICC, can the American approach be explained, or justified?

*

The idea of a permanent international criminal court with a full-time panel of judges was first seriously proposed in 1946, in the context of Nuremberg. During the 1950s the issue was addressed by the International Law Commission (ILC), the UN body charged with codifying and developing the rules of international law. The ILC was asked by the UN General Assembly to study 'the desirability and possibility of establishing an international judicial organ for the trial of persons charged with genocide'. The ILC is not generally known for its speed, and it completed its deliberations in 1994, a reflection of the political and legal complexities which an international court of this kind engenders. It took the Yugoslav and Rwandan courts to break the deadlock. The proposal which emerged from the ILC was modest. Its thirty-five members – lawyers, academics and government advisers, serving in an individual capacity – did not envisage a fully-fledged international body which would apply its own distinct rules. They proposed a system of delegated powers: a country which was a party to an international criminal law convention (such as the 1948 Genocide Convention or the 1984 Convention against Torture), and which had custody and jurisdiction over an accused, could transfer him to the International Criminal Court.[11] The Court would then only act with the agreement of the relevant state. The key point was that the ICC would not have a prosecutor who could decide to charge any particular person. States themselves would maintain control over such decisions. More to the point, this system would allow powerful states to bring pressure to bear on smaller states not to refer a matter to this limited version of the present ICC.

The ILC's proposal was intended to pre-empt criticisms from countries that would object to anything more ambitious. The political context at the time was difficult, as one of the key drafters for the ILC group, Professor James Crawford of Cambridge University, made clear:

[T]he institutional problem in the 1990s was huge. There had been no experience of the international administration of criminal justice since [Nuremberg and Tokyo]. Attempts to establish an international criminal court had run into the sands and were widely seen as utopian. International criminal law had developed in a different direction, and the enforcement of crimes which were inherently international in character or context (genocide, war crimes) had been almost entirely ineffective.[12]

But the proposal emerged at the right moment. In the face of outrageous violations of fundamental human rights in Central Europe and Africa, powerful states and the Security Council had failed to prevent the horrors. They were compelled to turn their attentions to the creation of international criminal tribunals for Yugoslavia and Rwanda. At around the same time, non-governmental organizations, such as Amnesty International and Human Rights Watch, were reinventing their programmes for international criminal justice. In addition democratic political changes, particularly in Central and Eastern Europe, South Africa and South America, were focusing on individual accountability for systematic atrocities under apartheid and other regimes which had massively abused civil liberties and fundamental rights. These factors conspired to push the international community towards new ideas for delivering justice where the most serious international crimes had been committed. At the instigation of Trinidad and Tobago, the UN General Assembly first considered the ILC's proposal in 1995, and in 1996 decided to establish a court. A Preparatory Committee on the Establishment of an International Criminal Court met from 1996 to 1998.

*

When I attended the UN diplomatic conference in Rome, in the summer of 1998, the emerging draft of a Statute for an International Criminal Court had moved beyond the more modest ILC proposal. As the meeting opened it was clear that a very few participants (led by the US) favoured an approach which would allow states – or at least some of them – to control the Court. One of the key issues to dog the Rome conference was whether a state could block a prosecution. By now the United States could no longer count on Britain's support. The Labour government, elected in May 1997, was committed to a strong and independent international criminal court.

I participated in the negotiations in Rome, working with the delegation from the Solomon Islands, with my friend and colleague Andrew Clapham, who teaches international law in Geneva. We had been asked to help the Solomons, which wanted to contribute to this landmark development. We saw first-hand how the great majority of participating states, as well as the many NGOs which were present during the negotiations, sought to put in place new global rules to limit impunity for perpetrators and prevent future crimes. Under the direction of Ambassador Neroni Slade of Samoa, now a judge at the ICC, we were charged with completing the text of the preamble to the Rome Statute, which was considered to be non-contentious.

While other groups grappled with complex and important issues of criminal law, our biggest problem came from the prose suggested by the delegation of Andorra. They wanted to include language to the effect that international crimes would 'rip asunder the delicate tapestry' that keeps humankind together. Some of our colleagues thought the 'ripping' bit to be too suggestive. We were saved by the Japanese, who claimed that a tapestry was not a concept widely known in that country. And so 'ripping tapestries' were replaced by 'a delicate mosaic [which] may be shattered at any time'. Some thought 'mosaic' might be too Christian, but, since we were in Rome, it passed.

The preamble to any treaty is only hortatory. It does not create binding obligations. Nevertheless, the preamble to the Rome Statute was picked up by the House of Lords in the Pinochet case. In his judgment against immunity, Lord Hutton relied on the preamble's affirmation 'that the most serious crimes of concern to the international community as a whole must not go unpunished'. The ICC and Pinochet could thus both claim a share in the effort to develop new global rules.

The important issues were elsewhere, however: should prosecutions only proceed with the authorization of the Security Council? What mechanisms would be put in place to limit the independence of the Prosecutor, and to stop abusive prosecution? Should the Court be able to exercise jurisdiction over the crime of aggression, the illegal waging of war? Under what circumstances could the Court exercise jurisdiction over nationals of states which were not parties to the Statute of the Court? What would be the relationship between the Court and national criminal courts?

For five weeks during the summer of 1998 I was able to observe the way in which these and many other complex political and legal questions were resolved through a process of intense and often bitter negotiation. Actively participating in the negotiations were not only the representatives of 148 or so states and the International Committee of the Red Cross, but also hundreds of others belonging to delegations of non-governmental organizations from around the world. The NGOs provided vital assistance to the delegations of many of the smaller countries. They included groups like the American Bar Association, which argued for a strong and independent court. Many others were co-ordinated through the NGO Coalition for the

International Criminal Court, a remarkable initiative which linked disparate groups from north and south, east and west. There was almost non-stop press attention, reflecting public interest in the development of global rules. By the final days of the conference the negotiations were being covered almost on a daily basis, amidst frenzied speculation that the discussions would collapse altogether. That must have been the desire of some delegations, including the United States.

By the last day there was no consensus, and at the final hour of that final day the United States made a major strategic blunder: apparently on late instructions from Washington, David Scheffer, the head of the American delegation, called for a vote on the text. This may have been driven by the mistaken belief that the majority of states would not wish so important a decision to be taken without a consensus (there exists in diplomatic circles a strongly held view that if a treaty cannot be adopted by consensus its long-term prospects are crippled). Scheffer told me later that he counselled against calling for a vote. But a vote went ahead. The draft Statute received overwhelming support. Just seven of the 148 participating states voted against it. Bart Brown, an American academic serving on the delegation of Trinidad and Tobago, described it as 'a diplomatic defeat of epic proportions' for the United States.[13] Although the ballot was not open, the United States, China and Israel announced after the vote that they had voted against the draft. Other opponents are thought to have included Libya, Iraq and Yemen; as Scheffer has said to me, 'not a great group to find yourself in'. The Rome Statute entered into force four years later, on 1 July 2002, after sixty states had ratified. More than half the states of the world have now joined, including twenty-four of the European Union's twenty-five members (the Czech Republic is in the process of ratifying).

The final text was significantly different from earlier versions. The Statute creates an independent and permanent International Criminal Court with the power to exercise jurisdiction over persons for the most serious crimes of international concern. These crimes are separately defined in the Statute – genocide, crimes against humanity and war crimes – and are not tied to the various international criminal treaties which have been adopted since 1948. At some point in the future the Court will also have jurisdiction over the crime of aggres-

sion, but only after the parties to the Statute have agreed on a definition. That is unlikely to happen soon, since it requires the agreement
of some 90 per cent of the participating states, and it is probable that
NATO members would prevent agreement. The Court can exercise
jurisdiction over any person who is a national of a state party, or who
has committed a crime on the territory of a state party. It is quite clear
that if an American commits a crime against humanity on British soil
that person is, in principle, subject to the jurisdiction of the Court.

But for the Court to be able to exercise its jurisdiction several hurdles
have to be overcome. First, the Court only exercises a residual or 'complementary' function (in cricketing terms, it acts as a long-stop). The
Statute makes it clear that crimes are to be investigated and prosecuted
at the national level first and foremost. The International Criminal
Court will only act if national procedures have failed. Second, although
the ICC Prosecutor has some preliminary powers to act on his own initiative (or where a case has been referred to him by a state party or the
Security Council), he must still satisfy a number of conditions before
proceeding to a full-scale investigation. This means that the scope for
politically motivated prosecutions by a 'rogue prosecutor' is extremely
limited, if it exists at all. The Prosecutor can only proceed to investigate
if he can persuade three ICC judges to give the go-ahead. After that a
person can only be arrested or summoned to appear before the Court if
the Prosecutor can persuade the three judges from the Pre-Trial
Chamber that there are reasonable grounds to believe that the person
has committed an ICC crime. The Prosecutor will also have to persuade
the Pre-Trial Chamber that arrest is necessary to ensure the person's
appearance at the trial. So the Prosecutor's real independence is limited
and contingent. He has no power of his own to investigate or arrest:
that power is controlled by the judges. And, subject to one exception,
the Prosecutor cannot be compelled by states to act in a particular way.
The exception is in Article 16 of the Statute: if the UN Security Council
has requested the Court not to proceed, then there can be no investigation or prosecution against a person for twelve months. This was a
compromise: the United States had originally proposed that investigations and prosecutions could only be initiated *after* a positive decision
by the Security Council. This would have meant that a Permanent
Member of the Security Council could always veto a criminal investigation. Not surprisingly, the approach was unacceptable to the great

majority of states in Rome. They viewed the proposal as a way of subjecting the Court to political pressures, and the control of the Permanent Members of the UN Security Council, and thus undermining the independence of the Court and the Prosecutor. The American proposal would also allow political deals to be made, such as the one reported by *The Observer* newspaper between Chile, Spain and the UK, which led to Pinochet's early return to Chile.[14] Singapore's alternative was more attractive, and was the proposal ultimately adopted, although not without murmurings. The South Africans I sat next to during the Conference expressed genuine concerns. As one of them said to me privately, external political pressures – which had meant so much in South Africa at the end of the apartheid regime – would be harder to apply. How could the rest of the world stop the ICC investigating atrocities which were covered by a legitimate national amnesty, or reconciliation process? This will be one of the very real challenges to be faced by the ICC's judges in coming years. The Statute is silent on the question of national amnesties or processes of truth and reconciliation. The Court is bound to be faced with arguments that it should not interfere with a legitimate and effective national consensus which decides that criminal proceedings are not the right way to redress past wrongs.

In the circumstances, however, the American argument did not persuade the majority. A blocking veto for a Permanent Member was unacceptable. This caused fury within the American delegation in Rome. It has served to poison the Bush Administration's approach ever since it came into office, and explains much of the vitriol which has been heaped on the Court since January 2001. What appears to be a modest drafting detail masks a fundamental issue for international law: when can brute political power override the rule of law and legal processes? This is a big question, and the answer given by the Rome negotiations suggests a tilting of the balance against pure political considerations being allowed to prevail. The inability of the United States to impose its own views suggests that hegemonic power may be rather more limited than some commentators imagine, at least on paper.

*

The safeguards which have been built into the Rome Statute have proved to be acceptable to a great number of states, including the UK and France. Like the United States, they are Permanent Members of the Security Council. Like the United States, they regularly commit troops to UN peace-keeping efforts around the world. The UK and France ratified the Rome Statute and were amongst the founding members of the Court. Shortly before hostilities began in Iraq, in March 2003, commentators began to ask whether the UK's membership of the ICC would expose British soldiers to prosecution, particularly if the war was illegal. The British government's position has always been that its soldiers were not at risk, since they would not commit war crimes or other acts coming within the Court's jurisdiction. But even if they did, it was said, they would be subject to full investigation under British law. In this way the Court's jurisdiction would not come into play, under the principle of 'complementarity'. A number of British soldiers have since been prosecuted in the English courts for abusive behaviour in Iraq. There is no suggestion of any need to prosecute at the ICC.

The Court does not have jurisdiction over the legality of the Iraq War. There is therefore no possibility of the ICC Prosecutor bringing a case against the British Prime Minister, Attorney General and other political leaders who contributed to the decision to commit British troops. But disinformation abounds. An ill-informed editorial in Britain's right-wing *Sunday Telegraph* newspaper provocatively claimed that if 'a group of judges on the International [Criminal] Court decide that an action in which commissioned British troops were involved was "illegal under international law", those troops could end up being prosecuted for murder, even if their conduct was perfectly in accord with the highest standards of the Army'.[15] This is simply wrong: the editor of the *Sunday Telegraph* should read what the Statute actually says. The Court cannot prosecute the waging of an illegal war, known as the crime of aggression. Nevertheless, popular misconceptions seem to have concentrated even high-placed military minds, if news reports are correct. The very existence of the ICC reportedly prompted Sir Michael Boyce, the UK Chief of Defence Staff at the time of the Iraq War, to request from the British Attorney General a clear and unambiguous opinion that the war would not be illegal under international law.[16] The circumstances in which that opinion was provided, just two days before the war began, remains a festering political issue for the British government. But it has nothing to do with the ICC, whose jurisdiction is limited to the conduct of the war, not the decision to go to war.

If the ICC is good enough for the British and the French, then why not also for the US? The Bush Administration has relied on three main arguments to justify the unremitting assault on the Court. Whilst its concerns may have legs in an academic or theoretical sense, none comes close to justifying the near hysteria which mention of the Court generates in many parts of the American government, as well as amongst large numbers of academics who should know better. There is only one way to explain the reaction: the Court has become a useful stalking horse for a broader attack on international law and the constraints which it may place on hegemonic power. The targeting of the ICC in this way by President Bush in his presidential debate with Senator John Kerry in October 2004 was illustrative of this tendency. It was unnecessary and unfortunate. Far better, according to these voices, for international law to be enforceable only selectively, and not across the board.

Top of the list of American concerns is the independence of the Prosecutor. In June 2003 the parties to the Rome Statute unanimously elected Luis Moreno-Ocampo as the Court's first Prosecutor. An Argentinian, Ocampo's experience includes prosecuting members of the armed forces who were involved in Argentina's 'dirty war', and the disappearance of thousands of trade unionists, students and intellectual leaders, as well as the trial of Chilean secret police for the murder of General Carlos Prats, under Pinochet's regime. Everyone I have met who knows him from his days in Argentina attests to his integrity. The scheme adopted in Rome means that Mr Ocampo will be independent and cannot be controlled directly by the United States (or anyone else) acting through the UN Security Council. From this the conclusion is reached that Mr Ocampo cannot be stopped from bringing politically motivated and abusive prosecutions against American nationals, including military personnel and their political masters, and that he may do so.[17]

The way in which prosecutorial discretion is exercised is a live issue in all political and legal systems. It is also the subject of the highest degree of hypocrisy. Many of the people who criticized the independent Spanish criminal prosecutor Judge Garzón for his prosecution of Pinochet (which could not be prevented by the executive under the Spanish legal system) rejoiced at Kenneth Starr's investigations of Bill Clinton for matters which cannot, by any stretch, even in the Deep

South, be treated as crimes against humanity. Prosecutors have to be independent if there is to be any semblance of a rule of law. If national prosecutors should not be subject to political control then why should the situation be any different at the international level? The Prosecutor is accountable to the ICC judges and to the state parties to the Rome Statute. If he behaves contrary to his duties under the Statute he can be removed from office. It is vital that the Prosecutor should be allowed to act independently.

That does not mean that the Prosecutor should be able to act as he wishes. The Rome Statute strikes a balance. Ultimately, it places authority in the hands of the judges, not the Prosecutor. Only if he can persuade the judges will he be able to investigate and prosecute. The balance is acceptable to the 100 or more countries that are members of the Court, including several whose troops are actively engaged in military missions around the world, such as France and the UK. Yet the Bush Administration rails against what US Under Secretary of State John Bolton has called the Court's 'unaccountable Prosecutor and its unchecked judicial power'.[18] Such complaints ignore the fact that the limits on the ICC Prosecutor and judges are far greater than those for their counterparts on the Yugoslav and Rwandan criminal tribunals. What is good enough for the Serbs, Croats, Bosnians and Rwandans is not sufficient for Americans. This is an example of a gross double standard. The claim of exposure to abusive political prosecutions is overegged.

*

The Bush Administration has articulated a second key concern. It argues that the Court's jurisdiction over individuals is too broad, that the Court can prosecute and convict American nationals even though the United States is not a party to the Rome Statute. This is true: the Court has jurisdiction not only over nationals of party countries, but also over *any* person who commits an international crime on the territory of a state party. An American who commits war crimes or crimes against humanity in Afghanistan (which became a party to the Rome Statute in February 2003) can be tried by the Court. A CIA officer who conducted an abusive interrogation at Bhagram air base could be tried before the Court. According to the Bush Administration this merely serves to undermine 'the independence and flexibility that America needs to defend our national interests around the world'.[19] The flexibility to do what? The flexibility to commit war crimes? The flexibility to provide assistance to others in perpetrating crimes against humanity? The flexibility to turn a blind eye when your allies commit genocide? Let us be clear about what 'flexibility' means here: it means that no American should be tried by the ICC under any circumstances. As Donald Rumsfeld put it: the 'United States will regard as illegitimate any attempt by the court or state parties to the [Rome Statute] to assert the ICC's jurisdiction over American citizens'.[20] Why should this be so? Subject to the limits set out in the ICC Statute, if an American citizen is suspected of an international crime in an ICC member state, why should he or she not be investigated or prosecuted?

In May 2002 the Bush Administration announced that it would not ratify the Rome Statute. Three months later Congress passed the American Servicemembers' Protection Act.[21] According to Human Rights Watch, the Act is intended to intimidate countries which exercise their sovereign right to ratify the Rome Statute. It is difficult to disagree. The Act authorizes the American President 'to use all means necessary and appropriate' to release any American national who is 'being detained or imprisoned by, on behalf of, or at the request of' the ICC. The Act is sometimes referred to as 'The Hague Invasion Act'. It prohibits all American co-operation with the ICC (but not the Yugoslav and Rwandan tribunals), including the sharing of any intelligence. It prohibits the participation of American troops in UN peace-keeping operations unless they are granted complete immunity from the risk of prosecution before the ICC. Acting under this provision the Administration threatened to block the August 2003 UN peace-keeping operation in Liberia until it had obtained an exemption for personnel from non-state parties to the ICC from the ICC and from any other jurisdiction except that of the sending state.[22] Later that month it held up the adoption of a Security Council resolution condemning the attack of 19 August against the UN headquarters in Baghdad, until references to the ICC in the draft resolution had been removed.[23] Without bringing any real benefit, these acts merely serve to inflame opinion abroad.

The Act prohibits the United States from providing military assistance to the government of a country that is a party to the ICC, although an exception has been carved out for all NATO members, major non-NATO allies (such as Egypt, Israel and Jordan)[24] and Taiwan (which prompted a protest from China). In July 2003 President Bush announced a suspension of military aid to a number of other state parties to the ICC, although these are not set in stone. The President can waive prohibitions for specific countries on the grounds of 'national interest' or where the country concerned has entered into an agreement preventing the ICC from proceeding against US 'personnel' who are present in that country (on which see further below). Waivers have been adopted for more than thirty countries.

Since 'The Hague Invasion Act' came into force it has been used to persuade many states not to join the ICC. It has provoked an angry response across the globe, from countries large and small, in the Caribbean, South America, and Central and Eastern Europe. Having handed over Milošević to the International Criminal Tribunal for the Former Yugoslavia (ICTY), the government of Serbia and Montenegro had good reason to be scathing about America's double standards: one rule for Serbs and another for Americans. President Koštunica believes that the American approach will undermine the international legal order, and allow many criminals to sleep soundly and to continue committing crimes.[25]

In applying 'The Hague Invasion Act' the Bush Administration has embarked on an ambitious programme to persuade every country in the world – including its allies – to agree that they would not transfer to the ICC any American, under any circumstances. The effort is based on an obscure provision of the Rome Statute, Article 98(2). This prevents the Court from ordering a party to the Statute to surrender to it certain 'sent' persons who are protected by international agreements, unless the state which has 'sent' that person has agreed to his or her surrender to the Court. The drafters of Article 98(2) seem to have had in mind diplomats and military personnel, people who can truly be considered to have been 'sent' by one state to another to perform some sort of official function. Such protection was plainly intended to apply to persons who could claim privileges and immunities under diplomatic conventions[26] or international agreements on the stationing of troops.[27] The drafters did not envisage people whose travels were totally unconnected with the exercise of official state functions, such as tourists or businessmen, even if they were former government officials. Nationals who are not travelling on state business – such as Augusto Pinochet (who came to the UK in 1998 for medical reasons) or Henry Kissinger (who visited the UK in 2003 to publicize his new book) – should not be able to benefit from immunities under Article 98(2).

Donald Rumsfeld sees things differently, apparently motivated by the unfortunate circumstances in which Dr Kissinger's travel plans had to be curtailed following an attempt to serve a subpoena on him. This was 'for something that happened twenty-five years before in Chile, and something he was not aware of or knowledgeable about', Mr Rumsfeld complained. Without the right agreements immunizing them from the ICC, 'the United States and other countries wouldn't want to put their people on the ground where they could be subject to irresponsible and inaccurate challenges and lies'.[28]

Guaranteeing the foreign travel of Dr Kissinger and others has led to a huge and costly bureaucratic exercise. The United States has persuaded more than seventy-five countries to enter into agreements, purportedly under Article 98(2), including thirty-two states which are parties to the ICC. These states have undertaken not to surrender any American national to the ICC without the consent of the United States, under any circumstances. In return the United States gives no undertaking to investigate or prosecute any American who may have been involved in war crimes, crimes against humanity, or genocide. So it is not surprising that these bilateral agreements have come to be seen as bilateral immunity agreements.

Some forty-five countries have refused to sign these agreements. About half have lost American military aid as a result. The nations of the Caribbean Community have protested at the punitive actions taken by the United States against six of its members who are ICC members but who refused to sign immunity agreements.[29] They rightly point out that cutting military aid will only undermine regional efforts to stop drug trafficking.

The European Union has also come out very strongly against these immunity agreements, which it sees as undermining the integrity of the Rome Statute and the commitment to prosecute perpetrators of the gravest international crimes. That obligation is reflected in the preamble to the Rome Statute. The EU has also concluded that participation in these overly broad US immunity agreements is inconsistent with other international laws for the prevention and punishment of the most serious international crimes, such as the Torture and Genocide Conventions. The Community objects to the agreements on principle, including their application to nationals of parties to the ICC (the American agreements would seem to lead to the absurd situation that if the United States extradites a British national back to the UK that person cannot be sent on to the ICC, even if the British government has no objection). In response the Bush Administration has charged the European Union with undermining American efforts to shield Americans from prosecution by the ICC. It has warned that the impact on transatlantic relations will be 'very damaging' if the EU does not stop.[30] The United States has even questioned whether 'the preferences of the EU's legal experts . . . have undergone a thoroughgoing examination by political and policy practitioners, weighing their strategic implications'.[31] In other words, legal analysis is to be trumped by the overriding need to pacify the United States. Here, at least, is an insight into the approach the Bush Administration has taken to the role its own legal advisers should adopt in interpreting international agreements.

*

The bilateral immunity agreements go far beyond what the Rome Statute allows. In the autumn of 2003 the Lawyers Committee for Human Rights asked me and two colleagues to prepare an independent opinion on the legal issues.[32] We did not agree with the view of some NGOs that Article 98 prohibits ICC members from signing new bilateral immunity agreements with the United States. But we had little difficulty in concluding that the agreements which had been signed went too far, in particular in their intended application to all American nationals. We also concluded that insofar as the agreements went beyond what the Rome Statute allowed, they would not be enforceable before the ICC. In other words, a state party to the ICC would not be able to rely on such an agreement to refuse to give effect to an order by the ICC judges that an American national (who was not a 'sent' person) should be surrendered to the Court. A number of states have taken this view in refusing to sign overly broad agreements. At some point a case will come before the Court and the issue will be tested.

I also have little doubt that over time the Bush Administration's policy on the Rome Statute will be recognized for what it is: mendacious, ill-informed, misconceived in law, and ineptly executed. Kofi Annan has condemned the blanket exemption as being wrong and 'of dubious judicial value', adding that 'it would be unfortunate for one to press for such an exemption, given the prisoner abuse in Iraq'.[33]

The double standards which are in play were perfectly illustrated to me in October 2003. I was in Freetown, Sierra Leone, appearing before the Special Court for Sierra Leone in the case brought by that Court's Prosecutor against Charles Taylor, the former President of Liberia. He had been indicted for war crimes and crimes against humanity committed on the territory of Sierra Leone. A legal issue had arisen, because Taylor had been indicted while he was still head of state of Liberia. His lawyers invoked the House of Lords' judgment in the Pinochet case (obviously not having read it very carefully) to claim that he was entitled to immunity from the jurisdiction of the Court. I had been appointed by the Appeals Chamber as an *amicus curiae* (friend of the court) to provide independent advice to the Court on the rules of international law, specifically on the question of head-of-state immunity. Like the ICC, the Sierra Leone Court is an international court created by treaty – in this instance, between Sierra Leone and the United Nations. Liberia was not a party to the treaty. In principle, therefore, there was no difference in the relationship between Charles Taylor and the Sierra Leone Court, on the one hand, and George W. Bush and the ICC on the other: both were presidents of countries which were not parties to the treaty creating the international court. How could it be, then, that the United States could support the indictment of Charles Taylor? The United States had even offered a reward of US$2 million to anyone who would assist in Taylor's removal from Nigeria, where he had been granted political asylum, to Freetown, to face trial before the Sierra Leone Special Court. How could Donald Rumsfeld's objection to the ICC exercising jurisdiction over any American national – since the US was not a party and did not recognize the Court – be reconciled with his support for the Sierra Leone Court and Charles Taylor's indictment?

I put the question to the American Ambassador to Sierra Leone, Peter Chaveas, during a break in the hearings. He was not able to give me an answer, beyond indicating rather cheerfully that the issue had not been given any thought. This was curious, since Ambassador

Chaveas told me that one of his tasks in Freetown had been to negotiate an ICC bilateral immunity agreement with the government of
Sierra Leone and this he had done just a few months earlier, in March
2003. I also put the question to David Crane, the Prosecutor responsible for Charles Taylor's indictment. Before moving to Freetown he
had worked for the US Department of Defense, as an Inspector
General, and before that as Assistant General Counsel to the US
Defense Intelligence Agency. It is a testament to his independence that
he recognized the inconsistency in the US government's position on
the jurisdiction of the two courts. A more principled and sustainable
position would be for the United States to object to all international
criminal courts and tribunals. But that is not the position adopted.

*

And what of the United Kingdom? The Labour government has been
a strong supporter of the Court since its inception. It accepts that the
'complementarity' principle and the safeguards built into the Statute
are sufficient to protect British citizens and troops on active duty from
malicious or politically motivated prosecutions. I have not been able
to find any evidence that the UK has exerted a restraining influence
on the misguided excesses of the Bush Administration. On the
contrary, in March 2004 the press reported that the UK had signed a
new bilateral extradition treaty between the two countries, and given
the US an undertaking that any person extradited from the US to the
UK would not be surrendered to the ICC.[34] The agreement was
mentioned in a letter from David Blunkett, the British Home
Secretary, to John Ashcroft, the US Attorney General, which confirms
that the new bilateral extradition treaty precludes the onward
surrender to the ICC of a person extradited from the United States.
It then states: 'the UK would contest any request from the ICC for
such surrender, as being incompatible with Article 98(2) of the Statute
of the ICC'.[35] That undertaking is inconsistent with the EU guidelines which apply to Britain: Blunkett's undertaking to Ashcroft
covers British and other EU citizens, as well as nationals of other ICC
parties; it makes no provision for investigation or prosecution for the
crimes over which the ICC may seek jurisdiction; and it accepts an
excessively wide definition of who is to be considered a 'sent' person.
I have real doubts as to whether the UK could rely on Blunkett's
undertaking if the ICC ordered the UK to surrender a person to its

jurisdiction. More troubling still is the signal which Blunkett's letter gives to the rest of the world: in spite of its support for the ICC, the 'special relationship' with the United States compels Britain to submit to the pressure of the Bush Administration. In June 2004 the US proposed a new Security Council resolution to extend the immunity from the ICC of UN peace-keepers, which had first been agreed in 2002. One of the few Security Council members to support the United States publicly was Britain. 'We need to keep the American interests in mind,' said Bill Rammell, a British Foreign Office minister. After Abu Ghraib, however, and after Kofi Annan's criticism of the proposal, the United States and Britain were unable to muster sufficient support and the US dropped the proposal. A small victory perhaps, but does it mark a turning of the tide? Let us hope that the second Bush Administration pursues its concerns in a more constructive way.

4

Global Warming:
Throwing Precaution to the Wind

'I like George's directness. I like the way he has understood my political problems. Has he offered to ring seventy of my MPs, say he's going to end global warming, sign up to the Kyoto Accord and return America to an agrarian economy? No. Has he been as helpful as he can? Yes.'

Tony Blair, 16 March 2004[1]

Friday, 9 January 2004. London. 8.32 a.m. The *Today* programme, BBC Radio 4. 'There is now a convergence of scientific opinion, global warming is now clearly related to our use of fossil fuels and to deforestation, and it poses the biggest challenge to governments for this century.' Biggest challenge? Greater than international terrorism?

'We've seen very recent effects. The hottest ten years since 1991, on record. Twenty-one thousand estimated premature fatalities across Europe over the last year. What we need is global action to deal with a global problem.'

'And what exactly is your charge sheet against George Bush?'

'What we are seeking from the United States is to join with us in taking effective action to deal with this major threat and also to take a leadership role with us in seeking for international action.'

'Well, the Bush Administration pulled out of the Kyoto Protocol.'

'That's a problem of major concern to us.'

Not a spokesman for Greenpeace or Friends of the Earth, but Sir David King, Chief Scientific Adviser to the British government, before he was reined in by 10 Downing Street to maintain a harmonious Anglo-American front.[2]

I was directly involved in the efforts to negotiate the first global warming treaty in the early 1990s. So it was refreshing, at last, to hear a senior British civil servant off the leash and giving the American government the public tongue-lashing it deserved. It had been three years since Bush bailed out of the Kyoto Protocol. For that whole period I had heard nothing seriously critical from the British government. And most certainly the criticism was deserved. Why was the United States taking no hard action on global warming? 'I oppose the Kyoto Protocol because it exempts 80 percent of the world, including major population centers such as China and India, from compliance, and would cause serious harm to the U.S. economy,' was the way Bush put it to US Senators Helms, Hagel, Craig and Roberts in March 2001, two months after taking office. The private letter signalled America's abandonment of international co-operation to limit greenhouse gas emissions and prevent global warming. It over-turned his predecessor's signature of the Protocol, reversed an election pledge to treat carbon dioxide (the most significant greenhouse gas) as a pollutant, and marked a turn back towards actions motivated exclusively by domestic economic considerations. All without prior warning, even to the United States' closest allies. For Britain, which had bent over backwards to accommodate American interests in the 1992 UN Framework Convention on Climate Change and its 1997 Kyoto Protocol, the decision came out of the blue.

There is no rule of international law which requires a state to become a party to a treaty. Sovereignty means any country is free to decide whether or not to ratify the Kyoto Protocol, or any other inter-national instrument. And a decision not to ratify does not necessarily reflect a lack of commitment to international law. The United States has not joined the Law of the Sea Convention, but has gone out of its way to follow the rules it lays down. What raised hackles – and led to mass demonstrations during Bush's first visit to Europe in June 2001 – was the way in which the Administration felt able to discard a decade of international efforts to address a serious problem which, even President Bush recognized, could only be addressed by multilat-eral co-operation. The decision was seen as an arrogant step aimed at refashioning the global order, putting American lifestyles above foreign lives, American economic well-being above all other interests, and manifesting a refusal to be constrained by new international rules. The handling of the decision set the tone for a perception that has been hard to shake off, that this Administration has a selective and self-serving commitment to multilateralism and global rules.

More importantly, it reflected the Administration's failure to understand that international issues are interconnected. The decision meant that the Kyoto Protocol could only come into force if Russia ratified, since a majority of the largest industrialized polluters have to join before the Protocol becomes operational. So it strengthened Russia's hand on other issues, such as the membership it was seeking in the World Trade Organization, bringing that country closer to pro-Kyoto Europe. By committing Russia to ratifying Kyoto, in November 2004, President Putin took full advantage of this American gift.

The abdication of global environmental leadership also has to be seen in its broader historical context. Until the 1990s the United States was at the forefront of international efforts to promote global rules for environmental protection. No country took its international environmental obligations more seriously. What changed?

*

The modern rules of international environmental law have a short but rich pedigree. They can be traced back to the late nineteenth century, and an obscure spat between the United States and Britain. The world's first reported environmental dispute concerned the little-known fur seals found in the Pacific waters of the Bering Sea, between Alaska and Russia. George Steller identified the seals in 1742, after he had been shipwrecked. It took another forty years to find the seals' rookeries, on the Pribilof Islands, named after Gerassim Pribilof, a Russian mariner and employee of the Russian American Fur Company. This company had cemented Moscow's domination of Alaska, from the late eighteenth century until the territory was sold to the United States in 1867. The discovery of the fur seal rookeries reopened trade between Russia and China, which had collapsed in the face of stiff competition from Britain and Holland. The Chinese prized the seal's fur. It was they who had uncovered the mystery of plucking, dyeing and preserving the skins.[3]

The seals were born on the Pribilof Islands. They migrated across the Bering Sea to the United States. In May each year the bulls returned from Alaska to the islands, and a month or so later the females followed.[4] They had been doing this since time immemorial, without human interference. In the 1880s that changed. At that time international law allowed countries sovereignty over their land territory and a narrow band of water up to a maximum of three miles off their coasts.[5] Sovereignty meant total control. It included the right to regulate hunting of Pacific fur seals, an activity which the United States banned outright to maintain populations. But the United States could not impose its laws and regulations on fishing or hunting fur seals beyond its territorial waters, in the area known as the 'high seas', which is beyond any state's sovereignty. Under rules of international law dating back to antiquity and the Middle Ages, navigation on the high seas is free to all.[6] The principle had been formally articulated in 1609 by the Dutch scholar Grotius, whose book *Mare Liberum* argued that the open sea could not be state property and was by nature free from the sovereignty of any state. These ideas were initially opposed by seafaring nations, including Britain. King Charles I wanted Grotius to be punished for his audacity, which would limit British naval power. But by the nineteenth century Grotius's theories had achieved universal support. There was no greater proponent of the freedom of navigation than imperial Britain. This rule of international law provided a basis for empire and trade. It was a global rule which allowed commerce and modern globalization.

For the British, freedom of navigation on the high seas included the right to take all the fruits of the sea. Specifically, it allowed the hunting of fur seals whilst they were making their annual migration from Alaska to the Pribilof Islands each spring. As the Pacific fur seals left American waters they were intercepted by British fishing fleets, lying in wait for their valuable prey. Huge numbers of fur seals were captured, killed and skinned. Between 1868 and 1897 the reported catch of Pribilof seals on land was 2,440,213, with more than 650,000 being taken by pelagic sealing, although this number is almost certainly underestimated.[7] Many of these furs were sent back to London's East End, where they were turned into garments for an emerging middle class. This was a lucrative business: between 1867 and 1902 the fur-seal catch was estimated to be worth hundreds of millions of US dollars (at today's values). But it had a devastating impact on the seal population. The United States protested against the British actions. It tried to persuade the British government to stop the activities of the British vessels, but to no avail. So the United States turned to more direct actions to protect the seals, arresting several

British vessels on the high seas, beyond its own waters. The British objected that this was an illegal interference with their freedom of the high seas.

The two governments agreed to refer the dispute to an international arbitration, one of the first of its kind, which was presided over by the King of Norway and six other eminent arbitrators. The United States claimed a property right in the seals, as well as the right to protect them for the benefit of humankind. It argued these rights under international law, invoking the practice of nations, the laws of natural history and the common interests of mankind.[8] The United States said that it alone possessed the power to preserve the seals, as a trustee 'for the benefit of mankind'. More recent conflicts in the oil-rich Middle East come to mind in reading the United States' argument at the close of the nineteenth century:

The coffee of central America and Arabia is not the exclusive property of those two nations; the tea of China, the rubber of South America, are not the exclusive property of those nations where it is grown; they are, so far as not needed by the nations which enjoy the possession, the common property of mankind; and if nations which have custody of them withdraw them, they are failing in their trust, and other nations have a right to interfere and secure their share.[9]

The British defence was less convoluted and, as it turned out, more persuasive for the majority of the arbitrators. Britain claimed that the Bering Sea was an 'open sea' in which the right of all nations to fish could not be restricted by a unilateral act of the United States, unless a treaty between the two countries provided otherwise. We have a 'right to come and go upon the high sea without let or hindrance, and to take therefrom at will and pleasure the produce of the sea', it was argued. Taken to its logical extreme, the British claimed the right to hunt the fur seals to extinction.

In 1893 the arbitration tribunal gave its ruling. It found for Britain by five votes to two, ruling that high seas fishing freedoms trumped conservation. But all was not lost for the seals, or for new rules of international environmental law. Britain and the United States had agreed that if the US lost the case the arbitral tribunal should adopt new international rules to conserve the seals. So the arbitral tribunal adopted the first rules of modern international environmental law, regulating when and where seals could be captured. This first environmental case revealed an American desire to put conservation above economic interests. It also reflected a willingness on the part of both countries to restrict traditional sovereign freedoms with new rules of international law.

*

America's instinct for conservation has also been a longstanding domestic concern. International rules soon came to be seen as an instrument for exporting American values. In 1864 the US Congress had donated Yosemite Valley to California for preservation as a state park, the world's first. By the time President Woodrow Wilson established a National Parks Service, in 1916, there were twenty-one national parks under the authority of the US Interior Department. The system was extended in the 1930s by President Franklin D. Roosevelt, who personally endorsed efforts to internationalize this system. In 1940 the United States and seventeen other Central and South American states adopted the Western Hemisphere Convention. This committed them to establish a continent-wide system of national parks, as well as wilderness areas in which all commercial developments would be prohibited. In some areas the 'passage of motorized transportation' was to be prohibited altogether, early recognition of the impact which the automobile was to have on the environment. The 1940 Convention is still in force today, although under threat from other international rules, for example, those relating to foreign investments.

Thirty years later, on 1 January 1970, Richard Nixon signed into American law the National Environmental Policy Act. This was the world's first comprehensive environmental protection regime. Nixon's contribution to environmental protection is not widely appreciated, nor is the fact that his concerns extended beyond national boundaries. The United Nations Charter has no explicit environmental rules, and until 1972 no UN institution was dedicated to environmental matters. It was Nixon's Administration which joined efforts for an environmental programme within the United Nations, and supported the UN's first global conference on the protection of the environment, held in 1972 in Stockholm. In the run-up to that conference, Nixon proposed a new global instrument: 'It would be fitting by 1972 for the nations of the world to agree to the principle that there are certain areas of such unique worldwide value that they should be treated as part of the heritage of all mankind and accorded special recognition as part of a World Heritage Trust.'[10] The World Heritage Convention was adopted in 1972, and the United States was the first country to ratify. Today it protects more than 700 cultural and heritage sites around the world, from Kew Gardens in London to the Galapagos Islands 600 miles west of Ecuador. This was the treaty that saved the Croatian city of Dubrovnik, another World Heritage site, from bombardment in the Balkans conflict in the 1990s.

Throughout the 1970s and 1980s the United States stepped up global efforts to protect the environment. It joined a raft of new global instruments on endangered species, oceans and fisheries. Then a new environmental threat emerged, requiring a truly global response on a vast scale. The ozone layer is located high above the atmosphere. It protects us from cancer-causing ultraviolet and other hazardous rays. In 1979 scientists from the British Antarctic Survey discovered a hole in the ozone layer. They predicted that an increase in its size would cause great harm unless urgent steps were taken to limit emissions of ozone-depleting substances. The United States led international efforts to address the problem, and in 1985, after five years of tortuous negotiations, much delayed by sceptical Europeans, more than 130 countries adopted a global convention to protect the ozone layer. It was only a framework instrument, creating a forum within which international monitoring of the ozone hole and emissions of harmful substances could be co-ordinated and more concrete measures adopted. Before the ink was dry on the treaty, new scientific evidence had emerged of the growing threat to the ozone layer. Within two years the Montreal Protocol on Substances that Deplete the Ozone Layer was adopted, in 1987. It imposed unprecedented, stringent obligations to ban the production and use of many substances which were in widespread use around the world, from the propellants in hairsprays and deodorants to the chemicals in refrigerators. Then it was the European Community members who balked at the science and the economic and lifestyle consequences of international actions. The United States promoted a 'precautionary approach', promising action in the face of scientific uncertainty where there was a real threat that the consequences would be serious or irreversible. This was during the presidency of Ronald Reagan.

The 1987 Montreal Protocol imposed real constraints and real costs. It was quickly recognized that developing countries would be significantly disadvantaged by having to meet the additional economic costs of international obligations which required new products and technologies to be used. There was also an issue of fairness: why should developing countries be subject to limits which the industrialized countries had not faced at their equivalent stage of development? It became clear that few of the poorer nations would join unless they had an incentive to do so. Why should China and India join a treaty which would make it more difficult for their citizens to have refrigerators? Like global warming, the protection of the ozone layer required a global effort. What was needed were global rules which everyone could sign up to. A hairspray which contained chlorofluorocarbons (CFCs), used by enough people, was harmful to the ozone layer irrespective of whether it was used in New York or Nairobi. So in 1990 amendments to the Montreal Protocol were negotiated in London, to allow developing countries to join. The United States played a major role in brokering rules which would allow India and China to sign. They were given a ten-year grace period to meet the targets and timetables for phase-outs of production and use. They were to be compensated financially for the additional costs of meeting those targets and timetables.

The Montreal Protocol has now been ratified by almost every country in the world. It is eliminating the production and use of a whole raft of products which were thought to be safe but are now known to be harmful. There is evidence that the ozone hole is closing and that the problem will, over time, be resolved. The Montreal Protocol is frequently hailed as an international instrument which will be effective: American legal creativity and political muscle helped to make it a truly global instrument.

*

The adoption of the amendments to the Montreal Protocol coincided with the emergence of the first inklings of serious evidence of the threat of global warming. This too would require a global response, but the challenge would dwarf the relatively discrete and narrow issues raised by the hole in the ozone layer. In the summer of 1989, with my friend James Cameron and two American environmental lawyers, Wendy Dinner and Durwood Zaelke, we created a public interest law firm which would provide free legal assistance to developing countries on issues of environment and development. Shep Forman, Janet Maughan and Karel Vosskuhler at the Ford Foundation in New York gave us our first grant: $200,000 over two years to provide free legal assistance on global warming to a group of about forty small island states, mainly from the Pacific and the Caribbean. From our small office in the old Chelsea Art School, where the artist Graham Sutherland had once had his studio, we worked with the group of countries which eventually organized themselves into the Alliance of Small Island States (AOSIS). It included some of the poorest and most vulnerable countries in the world, but also some of the most able and effective international negotiators I have come across, in particular Angela Cropper at CARICOM, the regional organization for the Caribbean.

Each of these countries is particularly vulnerable to the consequences of global warming, in particular the threat of sea-level rise which is expected to engulf vast tracts of low-lying coastline. Some of the Alliance's members will, literally, disappear if, as a result of global warming, the seas rise by more than a metre or two. The Maldives in the Indian Ocean, the Marshall Islands in the Pacific, and many Caribbean islands are amongst the AOSIS countries which are most vulnerable. Other countries outside AOSIS, such as Bangladesh, are equally threatened. For all these countries global warming became a clear and present issue in August 1990, when the UN's Intergovernmental Panel on Climate Change (IPCC) published its first report.

The IPCC is an independent body of scientists from around the world. The single largest funder is the United States. Its first report provided compelling evidence that atmospheric concentrations of greenhouse gases, especially carbon dioxide, had increased significantly since the industrial age and were contributing to a detectable increase in climate temperatures. The report predicted that further increases would be likely to increase global temperatures, and this could in turn raise sea levels. Taking a 'business-as-usual' scenario (i.e. if no actions were taken to reduce emissions of carbon dioxide and other greenhouse gases) it was estimated that global temperatures would rise by about 0.3 °C per decade during the twenty-first century.[11] This could mean an increase in pre-industrial global mean temperatures of about 2 °C by 2025, and about 4 °C by 2100. The IPCC predicted increased global rainfall, a loss of sea ice and snow cover, and a rise in sea levels of 20 cm by 2030, and 65 cm by the end of the twenty-first century.[12] Although the IPCC report was tentative and largely based on theoretical analysis, it provided the basis for preliminary international actions. The problem was both economic and political: the principal source of greenhouse gases is the burning of fossil fuels – oil, coal and gas. Addressing global warming is intimately connected with everyday industrial activities, in particular the production of electricity and transportation. But the problem goes wider. Other contributory factors include deforestation, agricultural practices and livestock.

Shortly after the first IPCC report was published, a World Climate Conference was held in Geneva in September 1990. I attended as a legal adviser to the delegation of St Lucia, one of the small island states. I worked closely with a number of very able negotiators. The AOSIS group was led by Lincoln Myers, the Environment Minister of Trinidad and Tobago. The Climate Conference turned out to be the starting point for the international negotiations on global warming which continue to this day. During this process I learnt the importance of consensus in international law-making and the tremendous damage which can be wrought by the unreasonable objector. The starting point for any negotiation on a challenge like global warming is that it requires a global response: if the international community cannot come together on the need and the means to address such a problem then it is unlikely that it will be able to produce an effective international response. In September 1990 it was clear that there was no consensus on climate change – whether it was a real problem and if so what to do about it. The OPEC oil producers and the United States plainly did not want a convention. You did not need to be particularly well informed to spot the close links between oil-producing countries and the multinational oil companies. Early on this informal coalition understood that effective action on global warming would mean reducing carbon dioxide emissions, more efficient and less polluting factories and cars, and higher oil prices, reduced oil sales and a move to alternative sources of energy fuel supplies. The decision of these countries to oppose effective international rules on global warming was driven by short-term economic considerations, and at the cost of longer term risks.

The scientists at the Second World Climate Conference had little difficulty reaching a basic level of consensus. 'If the increase of greenhouse gas concentrations is not limited, the predicted climate change would place stresses on natural and social systems unprecedented in the last 10,000 years,' they stated. The scientists' meeting was followed by a two-day ministerial meeting. This was far more contentious. The tables had turned, as compared with ozone. The European Community wanted greenhouse gas emissions from industrialized countries to be no greater in 2000 than they were in 1990. AOSIS wanted cuts in emissions of up to 60 per cent. The US and OPEC members objected to any commitments of any sort on targets or timetables. At a decisive moment Lincoln Myers made an impassioned intervention, calling for the precautionary principle to be applied. 'We, the small islands, will not be treated like some codicil, like an afterthought. I want to have a country to go back to.' It was a vital intervention, and it worked in building some consensus. The result was a Ministerial Declaration which focused on limited actions by developed states, which were responsible for 75 per cent of the world's emissions of greenhouse gases. Although it was not legally binding, the Declaration called on the developed countries to take actions which would have a significant effect on limiting emissions of greenhouse gases. It gave the green light to negotiations for a global framework treaty on climate change to be adopted by June 1992, at the Earth Summit in Rio de Janeiro.

Where would these negotiations be conducted, and who would run them? Industrialized countries wanted the negotiations to be conducted by the United Nations Environment Programme in Nairobi. The reason was not stated openly, but it was plainly because fewer developing countries had diplomatic missions in Nairobi, so would be able to participate less fully or effectively in the negotiations. The developing countries wanted the negotiations at the United Nations headquarters in New York, where they were fully represented. This would enable them to participate effectively, but would mean that most of the negotiators would be generalist diplomats, with no particular experience on the issues which a climate change convention would have to address. The compromise was a travelling roadshow. It was agreed that there would be five negotiating sessions, each lasting two weeks, between January 1991 and May 1992. Ten weeks of formal negotiations would be shuttled between Washington, New York, Geneva and Nairobi.

In February 1991 President George H. Bush hosted the opening round of negotiations at a soulless convention centre at Chantilly, about forty miles outside Washington, DC. The location would keep the expected hordes of NGOs away. I need to say something about how an international agreement is negotiated, since the process is not generally understood. It does not resemble law-making in national bodies like France's Assemblée Nationale, India's Parliament, Britain's Houses of Parliament, or the US Congress. The first principle of international law is that all states are sovereign and, theoretically at least, equal. This means that each participates in international negotiations on an equal basis. The reality is very different, as neither the power of states nor their role in addressing global warming is equal. In these negotiations more than 150 states participated. Some, such as the Maldives, had tiny delegations of just one or two people. Mr Majid of the Maldives Meteorological Office was mostly on his own. Other countries have enormous delegations – fifty or more – including scientists of different disciplines, economists, lawyers, diplomats and so on. Numbers are important because the negotiations are disaggregated, and do not take a centralized form or occur in a single room. There are 'formal' meetings which take place in plenary sessions or in specialized working groups, with sessions meeting in parallel. I would frequently bump into Mr Majid shuttling between two sets of discussions. The real business is done at 'informal' meetings, which can take place in the corridors, in side rooms, at embassies and missions, or in bars and pubs, even in individual delegates' hotel rooms. They usually take place out of hours when there is no simultaneous translation into the six working languages of the UN. There are also 'quasi-formal informal' meetings which can address a single issue or a single draft article of the treaty. I participated in numerous informal negotiating sessions which turned on a single word in the draft text, and which could go on endlessly throughout the night. Once we spent several hours discussing a single comma (see the first line of Article 3(4) of the 1992 Convention for the offending item). The outcome of these negotiations usually had very little to do with legal logic, or the force of intellectual argument, and a great deal more to do with stamina and the ability to stay awake through the night, without a decent meal.

Governments are not the only participants, unlike in the old days. The demands of legitimacy and accountability in international law-making mean that the doors have been opened to all and sundry. For the global warming negotiations there were hundreds of observers and participants, representing corporations (the oil and automobile industries in particular) and non-governmental organizations such as Greenpeace and Friends of the Earth, as well as a myriad of developmental groups like Christian Aid and Oxfam. There were a smaller number of NGOs from developing countries, some of which were highly effective. There were also individuals participating on their own account, like Aubrey Meyer from Willesden, north London, who attended all the sessions and has now made an important contribution with his theory of 'contraction and convergence' (which proposes setting a global cap, and then gradually reducing emission entitlements until each person on the planet has the same emission rights).

The negotiating rooms become a market place for ideas and interests, with individuals lobbying to persuade others why they are right or wrong. The process is not orderly, efficient or predictable. Individual personalities assume great importance, even if they do not represent powerful interests, since no one has a monopoly on good ideas. Other extraneous considerations – who you happen to be sitting next to, where the meeting takes place, the Iraqi invasion of Kuwait – can affect sympathies and outcomes. Negotiations have as much to do with personality as with substance. In sum, the processes of making international treaties bear very little relation to what is described in textbooks. And somehow, at the end of a process which can last years, a treaty will emerge.

This is not before great and unexpected hurdles are overcome. Anyone who anticipated that the first session of the climate negotiations would actually deal with global warming would have been disappointed. There are always issues of process to deal with before the substantive matters are reached. In the global warming negotiations there was an early decision to divide the preparation between two working groups. An immediate difficulty was to elect a chairperson for each of the two groups. Four candidates emerged after two weeks of brittle discussions: a Mexican, a Japanese, a Canadian, and the head of the delegation of Vanuatu, a small island state in the Pacific whose Ambassador, Robert van Lierop, was now the chair of AOSIS.

These four candidates had to be whittled down to two, but in the context of a UN negotiation you needed one chair from a developing country and one from a developed country. The Japan/Vanuatu combination was not acceptable because both countries were members of the Asian group (the United Nations has five groups of countries based on regions and requires balanced representation amongst the regions in allocating jobs in international negotiations). The other possibility was a Mexico/Canada grouping, but that was unacceptable for most delegations because both countries were at the time involved in negotiations with the United States to create a North American Free Trade Agreement. With the United States already antagonistic towards the convention most delegations felt that the appointment of these two chairs would give the US excessive leverage over the negotiations. The compromise was to have two co-chairs in each of the two working groups: Japan and Mexico would chair Working Group One, which broadly dealt with substantive issues of targets and timetables, and Canada and Vanuatu would co-chair Working Group Two, which dealt with the institutional and financial issues.[13] The process issues, structure and chairs occupied the entire first two weeks of negotiations, and were not finally resolved until halfway through the second session, which was held in June 1991 in Geneva. Three of the allotted ten weeks of formal negotiations were used up on this process issue, with just seven weeks left over the following year to conclude the substantive negotiations.

By September 1991, when the third round of negotiations opened in Nairobi, the prospects for a meaningful convention looked bleak, at least from my perspective and those of the small island states. Beyond AOSIS and the EU, at one end, and the US and OPEC, at the other, a number of other important groupings had emerged. The Soviet bloc had more or less collapsed by now, and the support of these countries was being canvassed from both sides. Large developing countries such as China and India wanted action from the industrialized world, but did not want their own economic development to be stymied by a new treaty. Brazil and other Amazonian countries wanted to ensure that the main focus of the treaty was emissions of greenhouse gases into the atmosphere, and were resisting arguments that the forests, which act as sinks by sucking carbon dioxide out of the atmosphere, should also be part of the deal. And there was an increasingly vociferous African group, led by an effective delegate from Mauritania, Ambassador Ould El Ghaouth, who were particularly concerned about the implications of climate change for desertification – the encroachment of deserts into agricultural lands and across towns and cities. As the negotiations unfolded it seemed that no human activity was left untouched. American gas-guzzlers, Vietnamese rice-fields, Amazonian forest fires – everything came under the same spotlight on global warming.

Apart from these daunting economic and lifestyle issues, there were also complex political, legal and cultural factors which had to be taken into account. For example, the small island countries wanted the 'precautionary principle' to be included in the convention: a commitment to action even in the face of scientific uncertainty. They managed to persuade the developing countries (known as the Group of 77) plus China (population 1.3 billion) and Nauru (population 12,809) to support them. This principle requires early preventive action to be taken, to avoid irreversible and serious harm. Although it has been included in the Montreal Protocol, Britain and the United States were vehemently opposed to the inclusion in the Convention of anything which was called a 'principle'. 'If we follow you guys and apply precaution we wouldn't be able to get up in the morning and do anything,' I was told by the late lamented J. R. Spradley, one of America's more colourful but less persuasive negotiators, best known for his hats. The objection to principles had nothing to do with a global warming convention. It reflected a broader concern about the nature of international rules, and in particular their open-ended and ambiguous character. The Anglo-American tradition aims for obligations which are clear and precise. We like to tie down our rules very firmly so that they cannot be 'interpreted' into more onerous obligations, or at least into obligations which are radically different from those which the drafters intended.

This concern seems to spring from a fear – within the common law, Anglo-Saxon legal community – of activist judges who might be prone to take a general principle on precaution and turn it into a more specific obligation, leading, for instance, to the closure of a factory. The English lawyer's nightmare is the Indian Supreme Court decision which ordered the closing down of hundreds of polluting tanneries because they violated a vague and general 'right to life' provision entrenched in India's Constitution.[14] 'We want to stop a fair deal on precaution turning into a ban on out-of-town shopping malls and gas guzzlers,' J. R. Spradley would pronounce, loudly and often. The use of the word 'principle' in the Climate Change Convention was unacceptable to the United States, but even with Spradley's charms the US seemed to find few supporters. The more strongly the US put its case the more entrenched became the opposition, especially from the developing world. 'If the Americans don't want it, we must have it,' was a frequent refrain within the Group of 77. A compromise was found during one particularly animated discussion late in the fifth and final round of negotiations in New York. Sue Biniaz (a very able but occasionally ferocious lawyer from the US State Department, who seemed to disagree with every point I put but with whom I have always maintained very cordial relations) proposed an elegant way around the problem. There would be no insertion of the 'precautionary principle' in the Convention. Instead there would be a reference to the precautionary 'approach', incorporated into an article of the treaty which would be entitled 'Principles'. The words 'precaution' and 'principle' were decoupled. And 'for the avoidance of doubt', as Sue put it, a footnote would be added to the beginning of the Convention which would make it clear that 'Titles of articles are included solely to assist the reader'. That solution would have taken forty or more negotiators many hours of intense deliberation. It is not likely that the point will affect the future well-being of the planet, one way or another, but it seemed important at the time.

This is the way in which international instruments are negotiated. It is about painstaking attention to detail, compromise, and the search for consensus. And it is about trust, amongst delegations and individuals. By May 1992 the last round of negotiations had arrived and there was still no consensus. It looked doubtful whether a convention could be ready for signature at the Earth Summit in Rio, just six weeks away, which all the world's leaders would attend. An additional negotiating session had to be scheduled for later in May in New York. By that time it had become clear that one of the central issues was the unwillingness of the United States and the oil-producing countries to allow a convention which would fix specific targets and timetables for reduction or stabilization of greenhouse gas emissions by reference to a fixed date. President Bush wanted to go to Rio, but he would not do so to sign a treaty which would ruin the American economy. Although the European Community wanted a legally binding commitment to stabilize emissions, it was left to Britain to play its usual role in brokering a final deal which could keep the Americans on board.

A key player was Michael Howard, then Britain's Minister of the Environment and now leader of the opposition Conservative Party. He had practised for many years as a barrister, and has a certain way with words, if not a great attachment to substance. In April 1992 he flew to Washington to try to find a language which would be sufficiently ambiguous to accommodate the different interests at stake and allow the United States to sign up. The text which emerged was masterful in dismantling American objections, but hopeless if the aim was a commitment to real measures to address climate change. The trick in the end was to separate the relevant words into two separate paragraphs: one paragraph committed industrialized countries to limit emissions of greenhouse gases by recognizing the need to return to earlier levels of emissions of carbon dioxide 'by the end of the present decade'; the other paragraph referred to the aim of returning emissions of carbon dioxide 'to the 1990 levels'. But there was no cross-reference or link between the two paragraphs, so that each stood alone. President Bush could sign the treaty in the knowledge that he was not entering into a binding legal obligation to stabilize greenhouse gases at 1990 levels by 2000, since the two dates were kept apart.

But even this language caused difficulties. It went too far for OPEC, and not far enough for AOSIS. Article 2 said that the ultimate aim of the Convention was to achieve stabilization of greenhouse gas concentrations in the atmosphere at a level that would prevent dangerous interference with the climate system. OPEC objected to this language, because it would mean that the Convention would set in train a process which would inevitably lead to restrictions on the production and use of oil and other fossil fuels which produce carbon dioxide. The OPEC countries signalled their objection. It has never been clear to me whether the United States might secretly have been hoping they would succeed. On the last day of negotiations, late into the night, the French chairman of the negotiations, the avuncular French diplomat Jean Ripert, met with a representative group of states, the so-called 'friends of the chair'. He appeared the following morning to present to the assembled plenary a compromise text. This was to be taken up or rejected, it was not open to further negotiation or discussion. The clock had stopped. We had an hour to review the draft.

When we returned, Saudi Arabia, Iran, Nigeria and other OPEC countries objected. To adopt the text as it stood would undermine their economic prospects, they insisted. The chairman asked whether there were any formal objections to the adoption of the text. He looked around the large conference room at the United Nations headquarters in New York, packed to the rafters with official delegates and observers from industry and the NGOs. The OPEC countries vigorously waved their nameplates in the air, trying to attract M. Ripert's attention. He did not see them, although everyone else did. Declaring that he could see no objections, the chairman announced the Convention's text to have been adopted, to great applause and relief. This was consensus in international law-making – not the same as unanimity. International law on global warming was up and running.

*

Of course the framework Convention fell far short of the specific actions needed to respond to the global warming threat which the IPCC had by now confirmed in its second report, published in February 1992.[15] But the Convention was significant. It established a process and institutions to develop the rules, and it made it more difficult for sceptics and opponents to challenge the science or the threat of global warming. The Convention attracted broad support and came into force within a couple of years of its adoption. It now has 189 parties, virtually every country in the world plus the EU. The United States was amongst the first to ratify, and its support will determine its success.

In the meantime the scientific arguments for global warming became ever more compelling, and negotiations began almost immediately to adopt more stringent obligations. In 1997, after three years of negotiations, a Protocol to the Convention was adopted at Kyoto in Japan,[16] after 'one of the most complex multilateral negotiations of modern times'.[17] The Kyoto Protocol goes much further than the

1992 Convention. It was never seriously proposed that developing countries should have specific commitments to limit their greenhouse gas emissions, since the principal responsibility for global warming rests with industrialized countries. If you take all the anthropogenic emissions of greenhouse gases since the Industrial Revolution in the 1780s, industrialized countries are responsible for more than 85 per cent of the total.[18] Today the annual emissions of developed and developing countries are about equal, and over time the emissions of the developing will greatly exceed those of developed countries. Now, however, almost every decent person recognizes that it would be most equitable and efficient for those countries which have benefited the most from lax environmental controls over the past 200 years to bear the burden of immediate actions to address global warming.

Ultimately the Convention and Protocol will succeed if they can contribute to a path of economic development for developing countries which enables them to adopt less carbon-intensive and polluting regimes. In the meantime, the Protocol focuses on getting thirty-nine industrialized countries to reduce their emissions of the main greenhouse gases by 2012, taking 1990 as the starting point. In 1994 the United States entered the Kyoto negotiations with a target of stabilizing emissions at 1990 levels; Japan proposed a 2.5 per cent cut; and the EU a 15 per cent reduction. By 1997 Japan, the United States and the EU (including Britain) had accepted cuts of 6 per cent, 7 per cent and 8 per cent respectively. Other countries, such as Russia, New Zealand and Ukraine, agreed to stabilize their emissions. And for a small number of countries, including Australia and Norway, increases were permitted. Taken together the cuts amounted to just 5 per cent of 1990 emission levels. This may seem insignificant, but since emissions in the United States have grown by nearly 12 per cent since 1990 the true impact of the targets is already onerous.[19] The Blair government has strongly supported the Protocol. In February 2003 Tony Blair announced a target of cutting carbon dioxide emissions to 60 per cent of 1990 levels by 2050. This goes well beyond the Kyoto targets, and legislation is now in place (through EU rules) to give effect to the Kyoto obligations. As with the ICC, Britain's willingness and ability to act undermines much of the force of American opposition to Kyoto, even if in recent months Blair's statements have not been accompanied by the hard actions necessary to achieve his aims.

The Protocol is a complex instrument, with recognized economic implications. Largely at the instigation of the United States, it includes three 'flexibility mechanisms', which rely on free market-based approaches to help countries achieve their emission targets more easily. The US argued that without these mechanisms it would not be in a position to join the Protocol, and the rest of the world bought that claim at face value and accommodated American concerns. The industrialized parties can 'jointly implement' their obligations. A system of emissions trading is created which will allow industrialized countries to trade their emissions in greenhouse gases (so that a company in one country which has exceeded its reduction targets will be able to sell the excess to a company in another country). Once again it was the UK which brokered the deal between the US and the EU – this time through Deputy Prime Minister John Prescott – in the quest for acceptable language, and in the face of considerable opposition to the morality of selling 'pollution permits'. Finally, the Kyoto Protocol creates a 'Clean Development Mechanism', to allow industrialized countries to claim credits towards their own emissions targets, where one of their companies invests in emissions-reducing projects in a developing country.

The Protocol also contains complex conditions which have to be met if it is to enter into force. This is to ensure that the main industrial powers assume the Protocol's obligations and are not disadvantaged economically by the non-participation of others. It also reflects a recognition in international law of the idea that states compete with each other in an increasingly globalized market. Two conditions have to be satisfied for Kyoto to become binding: the Protocol must be ratified by at least fifty-five parties to the framework Convention, and the ratifiers must account for at least 55 per cent of all the greenhouse gas emissions of the industrialized countries. In practice this means that at least two of the three largest emitters – the US (36 per cent), the EU (24.2 per cent) and Russia (17.4 per cent) – must join the Protocol before it will become legally binding.

With the adoption of the Protocol it becomes impossible to deny the very real environmental threat posed by global warming, but also the short-term economic consequences of actions to address climate change, in particular for the most carbon-intensive economies, of which the US is the leader. The final text achieved a balance. It will not prevent global warming, but it does mark a real commitment to take action and provide the basis for more far-reaching measures which could also, eventually, bring on board the developing countries. On the morning of 11 December 1997 the Protocol was adopted by acclamation, welcomed by the major industrial blocs and most of the developing world.

Bill Clinton hailed the Protocol as a 'historic agreement . . . to take unprecedented action to address global warming'.[20] It was 'environmentally strong and economically sound', and reflected 'the commitment of the United States to use the tools of the free market to tackle this difficult problem'. But it was plain he would face significant opposition. In a letter to Clinton, the then former Secretary of Defense Dick Cheney and other members of the Committee to Preserve American Security and Sovereignty (COMPASS) wrote that the Protocol would 'hamstring' American military operations (quite how has never been spelt out) and undermine American sovereignty.[21] By this weird logic, efforts to address global warming became a national security issue. Clinton nevertheless signed the Protocol, in November 1998, although he did not submit it to Congress for ratification, where there was strong bipartisan opposition to the instrument, which, it was said, could only have negative consequences for the American economy.

During the 2000 presidential campaign George W. Bush undertook to reduce emissions of carbon dioxide. Shortly after he took office, his administrator at the US Environmental Protection Agency, Christine Todd Whitman, impressed the G8 Environment Ministers meeting in Trieste, Italy, with a commitment to act on climate change by subjecting carbon dioxide emissions from power plants to limits under the US Clean Air Act.

But within two weeks Bush had written the infamous letter to four American senators and snuffed out the immediate prospects for the Kyoto Protocol. His reasons are not persuasive. First and foremost his claim is based on the absence of scientific consensus. It is doubtful that this claim is anything other than a public relations exercise. The hand of Republican pollster Frank Luntz seems to be behind this part of the strategy: 'Should the public come to believe that the scientific issues are settled, their views about global warming will change accordingly,' he is reported to have written.[22] 'The scientific debate is closing but not yet closed.'

'Not yet closed' is generous. I cannot claim any degree of scientific expertise, but the material I have read and the voices I have heard point compellingly towards the need for precautionary actions. There is a broad consensus in the scientific community that man's industrial activities are causing global warming and that this will probably bring severe disruptions and great dangers for large parts of the world. The most recent scientific report of the IPCC in 2001 is clear.[23] The choice between the scientific arguments of George W. Bush or Sir David King, Britain's Chief Scientific Adviser, is not a difficult one to make. Addressing the American Association for the Advancement of Science meeting in Seattle in February 2004, King left little room for ambiguity: '[T]he current state of climate science is that it's now accepted that we have global warming. It's now accepted that this is largely due to anthropogenic effects. That part of it is not up for argument anymore.'[24] He showed his audience a picture of the ice on the peak of Mount Kilimanjaro in the summer of 1912, comparing it with a picture of the same peak at the same time of the year in 1998. He estimated that the ice on Kilimanjaro would be gone within fifteen years. He provided similarly shocking evidence of a collapse in the size of the South Cascade Glacier in Washington State, between 1928 and 2000. And he described the ever more frequent use of the flood barrier across the River Thames in London, which had been completed in 1982. '[I]t was expected that it would be used roughly once every three to five years and in that first period that is how often it was used. Now, if I tell you that in the year 2000 to 2001 the Thames barrier was used twenty-four times, you will see that the effect of flooding on the Thames . . . has increased very substantially . . . the effects of the warming are already very real,' he concluded. The only question up for argument was what precisely the consequences would be: 'the reason it's up for argument is that we have a massively complex system, the earth itself'. Meanwhile, the British press has reported efforts by the British government to silence Sir David,[25] presumably to maintain a united front with the US at a time of tension over Iraq and in the run-up to the Presidential elections in November 2004.

Against that authoritative view the Bush Administration periodically wheels out a small number of reputable but minority scientists, and focuses on such claims of uncertainty as it can find. One favourite is Professor Richard Lindzen of MIT. In his testimony to the Senate Environment and Public Works Committee on 2 May 2001, he offered the following advice to US law-makers:

[C]arry out only those actions which can be justified independently of any putative anthropogenic global warming. Here, I would urge that even such actions not be identified with climate change unless they can be shown to significantly impact the radiative forcing of climate. On neither ground – independent justification or climatic relevance – is Kyoto appropriate.

Another leading sceptic is Bjorn Lomberg, the controversial Danish ecologist. He doubts the doomsday scenarios but accepts that 'there is no doubt that mankind has influenced and is still increasing atmospheric concentration of CO_2 and that this will influence temperature', that global warming will have serious costs and that it will hit the developing countries hardest.[26] His concern is that the Kyoto Protocol will not make much of a difference, and that it will cost a great deal to implement.

Both points miss the target. International law is process-driven and incremental in meeting its aims and objectives. No one claims that the Kyoto Protocol can, as it stands, prevent global warming or be fully effective in that sense. It is a wake-up call, a preliminary step, complex but important. With the exception of the United States and Australia, it has succeeded in bringing every industrialized country in the world on board. Opposition to Kyoto has a diminishing legitimacy. Bush's call that China, India and the other large, industrial developing countries should now accept targets and timetables for emissions reductions is indefensible. 'Developing countries increasingly find themselves put in a position where they are made responsible for global environmental problems they did little to create,' observes Sir Shridath Ramphal, former Secretary General of the Commonwealth.[27]

By making the argument the Bush Administration plays into the hands of those who consider the United States to be self-interested and unwilling to accept its responsibilities for the consequences of its industrial might. If all other industrialized countries are willing to accept their responsibilities, then why not the United States? The two-tier approach – industrialized countries first, the rest of the world later – worked with the Montreal Protocol and ozone-depleting substances, having been proposed by the US. Why should it not work for climate change? President Bush's plaintive cry that the Kyoto Protocol is flawed because it is not based on 'global participation' is even less persuasive when seen against his Administration's decision to opt out of some international agreements altogether and to suspend or ignore others in the so-called 'war against terrorism'.[28]

*

President Bush described the Kyoto Protocol as being 'an unfair and ineffective means of addressing global climate change concerns'. If it is unfair because it requires the US and other industrialized countries to bear the responsibility of taking the first steps to address a global problem, then the President was expressing a view shared by very few. If it is ineffective because it will not of itself solve the problem, then the President has missed the point – that the Protocol is only a first step, albeit an important one.

Increasingly it seems that the Bush Administration and the federal government are out of sync with growing concerns around the United States. An increasing number of American states – twenty-five – plus Puerto Rico have already adopted their own statewide emissions reduction plans.[29] A growing number of American corporations have taken the same approach, and are pushing the Administration to change tack on the Kyoto Protocol.[30] Even in the US Senate there is growing support for actions which are consistent with the Kyoto Protocol. The bipartisan Climate Stewardship Act 2003, put forward by Senators Lieberman and McCain, would have proposed a reduction in carbon dioxide emission levels to those of 2000 by the year 2010, by capping the overall greenhouse gas emissions from the electricity generation, transportation, industrial, and commercial economic sectors, and creating a market for individual companies to trade pollution credits. It was only narrowly defeated by 43 to 55. So where does the opposition come from?

In September 2003 I served as an adviser to a House of Lords Select Committee which was charged with examining the role of science in the making of international agreements. The Kyoto Protocol was a central part of the inquiry, and the Committee heard evidence from a large number of witnesses from varied backgrounds, including representatives from the large multinational oil companies. Companies like Shell and BP have made it clear that they now accept the threat of global warming to be real. They are taking steps to reposition their business plans, including a move towards renewable energy sources. It was apparent that they have shifted their position to support the Kyoto process and Protocol and that their actions are genuine.

By contrast, the attitude of Exxon Mobil, an American company, verges on contempt for these international efforts. Andrew Swiger is the chairman and production director of Exxon Mobil International. He told a somewhat sceptical House of Lords Committee that the science was inconclusive – 'It has not been settled down yet', directly contradicting Sir David King's evidence.[31] When asked to identify what the gaps in the science were, neither he nor his colleague, Mr Nick Thomas, the public affairs manager of Esso UK, could oblige with an answer. When asked whether Exxon Mobil supported the Bush Administration's decision not to ratify Kyoto, he responded that 'The action not to ratify is consistent with the concerns that we have about Kyoto', referring to the non-participation of developing countries. When asked whether Exxon Mobil campaigned against the US implementing what was recommended by Kyoto, Mr Thomas responded that 'We have certainly not campaigned on any particular position.' The last point seems difficult to accept. The House of Lords Committee was presented with a copy of a leaked memorandum sent by fax from A. G. (Randy) Randol III, Ph.D., Senior Environmental Adviser to Exxon Mobil, based in Washington, DC, to John Howard of the US Government's Council on Environmental Quality. It was dated 6 February 2001, just two weeks into the term of the first Bush Administration, addressing future American participation in the IPCC. It was entitled 'Bush Team for IPCC Negotiations', and among the recommendations it makes were these three points.

1. Restructure the US attendance at upcoming IPCC meetings to assure none of the Clinton/Gore proponents are involved in any decisional activities.
2. Appoint Dr Richard Lindzen . . . to review the US comments to be submitted.
3. Explore the possibility of asking Speaker Hastert to make Dr Harlan Watson, Hse Science Committee, available to work with the team.

No doubt these may be sensible recommendations. But they are inconsistent with the claim that Exxon Mobil did not 'campaign' on any particular positions to be adopted. And, as it turns out, the recommendations were broadly followed by the Bush Administration.

*

What of Britain's attempts to influence the American position? The Kyoto Protocol is another international initiative on which the two countries are poles apart, like the International Criminal Court. Has Britain tried to influence the United States, and if so how? The House of Lords Committee asked representatives of the Foreign and Commonwealth Office (FCO) for information about the steps that had been taken to try to persuade the US to change its position. The same question was put to Bill Rammell, the Minister of State at the FCO. Beyond generalities he seemed unable to give a clear answer. At the concluding press conference following President Bush's visit to Britain in November 2003, no mention was made of global warming. It seems the British government is not willing to take steps to return the US to an 'agrarian economy', as Tony Blair put it.

In its final report, the House of Lords Committee recommended that 'further concrete steps be taken at the highest level of government to persuade the US to take steps consistent with the requirements of the Kyoto Protocol'. However, the special relationship has produced no concrete results, and there is no evidence to indicate that Blair has made the kind of forceful representations which should have been made. The issue has apparently prompted the Queen to make a rare intervention in political matters. In October 2004 *The Observer* reported one of Britain's most eminent experts as saying that 'there has been dialogue between Downing Street and Buckingham Palace on all issues relating to climate change, including the US position and the latest science'.[32] Whether that causes Britain's Prime Minister to stiffen his spine remains to be seen.

5

Good Trade, Bad Trade, Cheap Shrimp

'[I]t was rather striking (of course only in the pleasantest sense) that the rules most honoured in the observance were precisely those which chimed with the financial interests of the proprietors of the establishment; whereas, on the other hand, to those less favourable they were inclined to shut an eye.'

Thomas Mann, *The Magic Mountain* (1924)

Global free trade rules look boring and seem innocuous. Most international lawyers try to steer well clear of them. In fact, they have become the most powerful rules of international law and fuel the engine of economic globalization – which is why they cause people to take to the streets in protest. They are the focus for increasingly bitter claims that international laws are being used by groups of rich countries, led by the US and the EU, to impose their values on the rest of the world. I saw first-hand the potential impact of free trade rules in the 'bananas' case that went to the World Trade Organization in the mid-1990s.

The EU was maintaining a market which reserved a proportion of the EU's banana sales to imports from St Lucia and other former British and French colonies. These countries produce the longer, thinner bananas preferred by British and French consumers. They are more expensive than the small, stubby bananas produced in El Salvador and Honduras and other Central American countries, mostly by American multinational corporations, which are preferred by Germans. Caribbean bananas cost more because they are produced by smallholders, who cannot take advantage of the large-scale economies available to their Central American competitors. Without EU trade preferences the Caribbean bananas would not be able to compete. They would lose market share, and small independent farmers would lose their livelihoods. The US and its allies used the WTO rules to attack the EU preferences, to increase the market share of Central American bananas. The challenge to the EU rules was largely successful, with serious economic impacts for smallholders in St Lucia and elsewhere.

On the surface, international trade rules appear as though they are value-neutral. In fact they imply that values and consequences of economic rationality will tend to trump other values, for example the importance of promoting individual, non-corporate enterprise. Dismantling barriers to trade inevitably means that decisions have to be taken on which other social values – such as labour standards, cultural exceptions or environmental protection rules – should be allowed to be maintained. The logic of international trade leads inevitably to new levels of international governance, with decisions taken by international organizations (such as the WTO) or by judges sitting on international courts (such as the WTO Appellate Body). It is this new level of international governance that leaves a great many people feeling disenfranchised and disconnected from decision-making. Whether we are talking about free trade at the level of the European Community, or the North American Free Trade Agreement, or the WTO, the rules inevitably mean that local values can come into conflict with the aims of global economic liberalization. Until recently the vast majority of people were unaware of this potential effect. As a result of some high-profile trade wars – over bananas, tuna, shrimp, pharmaceuticals, genetically modified organisms (GMOs) – that has now changed. There is a great deal more public scrutiny of international rules which were, for the most part, adopted with little debate or attention at the national level, and little democratic accountability. In this way, the riots in Seattle in 1999, and the emergence of a new Group of twenty-one developing countries at Cancun in 2003, can be seen as a threat to the rules, or, as I prefer to believe, the emergence of a more democratic process in international law-making.

*

The United States and Britain have been leading proponents of global free trade rules, ever since Roosevelt and Churchill formulated Principle Four of the Atlantic Charter in August 1941. The free trade rules were seen – and continue to be seen – as promoting desirable political values. From Roosevelt to Bush, trade is seen as the 'pathway to promote prosperity, the rule of law and liberty', as Robert Zoellick, the United States Trade Representative, told an audience at the National Press Club in Washington, DC, in October 2002.[1] Here is one area where American support for international law seems to have been consistent. But how strong is that support? The EU and the US seem to be involved in long-running trade wars, from steel to GMOs. Developing countries are becoming adept at using the WTO rules to unpick American and European trade barriers, and the free trade rules are being challenged by developing countries for promoting only a narrow range of economic interests, and by an increasingly active civil society fearful that trade imperatives will crush other values. Will the United States maintain its support for these international rules, and will Europe follow suit? As the benefits of the rules begin to flow in a different direction, will they be dumped by their creators? These questions become acute in the face of a series of recent WTO trade disputes.

In March 2004, for example, a WTO panel ruled that the United States regulations prohibiting online gambling violated international trade rules. The tiny Caribbean island state of Antigua and Barbuda (population 75,000) objected to efforts by the United States federal government to crack down on American broadcasters and publishers who advertise on behalf of online casinos, on the basis that they are aiding an illegal enterprise. The crackdown was aimed at stopping Americans using betting and casino games offered by Antiguan companies over the internet. Bob Goodlatte, a Republican congressional representative from Virginia, described the WTO panel decision as 'appalling'. 'It cannot be allowed to stand that another nation can impose its values on the US and make it a trade issue.'[2]

Three months later, Brazil obtained a ruling that the United States was illegally subsidizing (to the tune of $12.5 billion) thousands of American cotton farmers, giving them unfair and illegal competitive advantages in the global cotton market. The *Financial Times* reported that the ruling would put pressure on the US and the EU to dismantle other massive agricultural subsidies. Oxfam, the UK-based aid organization, declared that the ruling would put 'bargaining momentum firmly behind developing countries'.[3] Robert Zoellick warned that further litigation would damage future WTO negotiations.

A few weeks later the EU lost a similar case, also brought by Brazil.

A third case concerned the 'safeguard measures' that Bush had ordered in March 2002 to protect the American steel industry from cheaper steel imports. These measures had restricted imports and increased the duties on steel imports from many countries, including close allies such as Britain. They caused major international tensions. In December 2003 Bush explained that he had decided to end the measures – which had severely curtailed foreign imports into the US – because they had achieved their purpose. They could be lifted, he said, because of 'changed economic circumstances'.[4] The President's comments were remarkable for their omissions: the listener would have been blissfully unaware that the European Community had challenged the American measures under WTO rules, and obtained a ruling that they were illegal. The WTO authorized the European Community to impose punitive trade sanctions up to a value of $2.2 billion,[5] and the Community announced imminent sanctions on products from American states that were crucial in the 2004 presidential election, including citrus fruits from Florida. The international rules became a weapon to influence domestic politics.

It would be naive to imagine President Bush acting differently. In the current climate, politics dictates that he must give the impression of being in control. For his Administration there can be no acknowledgement that so important a decision might have been influenced – not to say dictated – by rules of international law. His omission is all the more striking when compared with the announcement of the temporary safeguards in March 2002: they were, he said, 'expressly sanctioned by the rules of the World Trade Organization, which recognizes that sometimes imports can cause such serious harm to domestic industries that temporary restraints are warranted'.[6]

I find it curious that it is no longer permissible in the United States, committed as it purports to be to 'the rule of law', to trumpet compliance with global rules. At a time when the United States was under constant attack for being a unilateralist, serial violator of international law – the President's decision to stop cheap steel imports was taken against the background of the abandonment of Kyoto and the ICC, detentions at Guantánamo and the war in Iraq – along came an opportunity to proclaim a commitment to multilateralism. Here, at least, is an area in which it cannot be said, as is now fashionable, that the US has no interest in international rules. No country has been more vocal in favour of the WTO's quasi-judicial system for enforcing those rules, a system which has given rise to arguably the most powerful court in the world, the WTO Appellate Body.

*

The World Trade Organization is a real curiosity. Its rules are amongst the most complex, technical and impenetrable international laws so far invented. Yet, along with human rights, these international rules attract great public attention. It could be said that the WTO has played a catalytic role in making the public aware of how far international law has developed, reaching ever deeper into day-to-day life and limiting national sovereignty. WTO ministerial meetings, such as the one held in Seattle in 1999, routinely attract media attention and large numbers of protesters. The WTO is rightly seen as the pumping heart of the globalization project. Trade disputes attract public awareness, because they touch on issues of general public concern, and also, perhaps, because of the sheer size of the financial implications of WTO decisions (in the dispute over US tax breaks for the overseas activities of its corporations the award exceeded $4 billion in value). What is surprising is that the rules have emerged under a 'corner of darkness', as one of my friends put it. For fifty years the global trade rules operated discreetly and out of sight. At the global level it was only in the 1990s, with the dispute between Mexico and the United States over the impact of tuna fishing and dolphins, that public interest was ignited.

In 1941 Churchill and Roosevelt believed that peace and prosperity were inextricably linked to multilateral trade arrangements. The two countries agreed on a far-reaching plan to 'further the enjoyment by all states, great or small, victor or vanquished, of access, on equal terms, to the trade and to the raw materials of the world which are needed for their economic prosperity'. The phrasing of the agreement had not been entirely straightforward, however. President Roosevelt wanted to include the extra words 'without discrimination and on equal terms', but Churchill objected to the change to his draft, on the grounds that it would undermine the imperial preference agreements of 1932 between Britain and several Empire and Commonwealth states. Although Churchill was a long-standing 'free-trader', and not especially committed to the Commonwealth preference scheme, Lord

Beaverbrook, his Minister of Supply, persuaded him that they would not get the support of the Dominion governments unless the preferences were maintained. Roosevelt caved in, agreeing to 'due respect for . . . existing obligations' (the issue re-emerged fifty years later, with the fight over the EU banana import rules).

The American and British governments began to elaborate a formal trade regime as early as 1943, while the Second World War was raging. The basic aim was to establish a system of global rules which would apply to all independent states, and create an international organization with teeth, which would enforce the rules.[7] In 1945 fifteen friendly nations were invited to participate. The United Nations then took over the process, and in 1948 the charter of a putative International Trade Organization was agreed. Parallel discussions were underway in Geneva amongst a smaller, core group of countries.[8] This led to agreement, in 1947, on a broad code of conduct in a document known as the General Agreement on Tariffs and Trade (GATT). This would be a capitalist club, a bulwark against the Soviet bloc. The GATT was limited to concessions in trade in goods. By contrast, a more far-reaching International Trade Organization (ITO) would have tied international trade rules with employment, competition and restrictive practices, a quasi-internationalization of Roosevelt's New Deal. It would also have negotiated commodities and foreign investments. But this agenda was too ambitious, at least in the 1940s. The US Congress was not going to ratify such a far-reaching instrument, one with direct political implications for the role of the state at the national level, and the ITO charter withered. The world had to wait another fifty years – until 1994 – for the World Trade Organization.

For its entire life the GATT was applied on a temporary basis. It is ironic that the icon of globalization was never formally adopted as a treaty. It meant, of course, that national parliaments rarely debated it or acted on it, and it was rarely subject to public scrutiny or accountability. GATT meetings in Geneva took place behind closed doors. The GATT remained, almost to the end of its life, a fiefdom for diplomats and governing elites. In Britain it was not treated as a part of the UN system, which meant that the Foreign Office never got its hands on the GATT. In the last few years of their life, the old GATT rules had become a source of great controversy. By stealth, its

rules were beginning to hurt people on the ground, causing governments to justify domestic measures which constrained trade. Trade
unions, environmentalists and human rights activists joined forces.
For many of these organizations, and many developing countries, the
GATT was a neo-imperial instrument, a post-Second World War
construction which allowed some states (developed, large, powerful
ones) to impose their social, environmental and cultural values over
others, undermining domestic industries, jobs and communities. An
opposing view was that the GATT rules reflected the only decent way
to cement peace and friendship between countries in conflict, by
making them so economically integrated that war would become
unthinkable.

Regional free trade rules, or common markets, have applied this
rationale in Europe, Africa, and North and South America, and Asia
is edging towards its own regional free trade system. The most highly
integrated regional system is that between the European Union's
twenty-five members. That organization began with a rudimentary
1950 treaty creating the European Coal and Steel Community, involving the original six members (West Germany, France, Belgium, the
Netherlands, Luxembourg and Italy). The idea was to create a
common market in coal and steel, to make rearmament and war
between Germany and France an impossibility. In 1957 the scheme
was extended with two more treaties: the Treaty of Rome, which created the European Economic Community (EEC), and another treaty
on the peaceful uses of atomic energy (EURATOM). Originally
intended to remove barriers to trade, it soon became clear that creating a common market necessarily meant addressing other standards
which would affect flows of goods and services and the free move-
ment of people. Gradually standards were developed on everything
from labour to the environment, from agriculture to competition
rules. The original six became the nine (with Britain, Ireland and
Denmark joining in 1973), the nine became ten and then twelve, and
then fifteen, and on 1 May 2004 the total membership grew to
twenty-five with the accession of ten Mediterranean and Central
European countries.[9]

Alongside growing membership, the EEC Treaty was amended on
several occasions to extend its competence and powers, and modify the
institutional structures, which included a powerful executive arm (the

European Commission) and a separate European Parliament. The 1986 Single European Act created a 'single market', and the 1992 Maastricht Treaty established a European Union and committed the members to economic and monetary union. Further changes were made with the 1997 Amsterdam Treaty and the 2000 Nice Treaty, and in 2002 the euro was introduced as the national currency of twelve members. In June 2004 the members agreed on a new Constitution for the European Union, which aims to bring together the numerous treaties and agreements on which the EU is based and define more clearly the respective powers of the EU and the member states, setting out when it can act and when the member states can retain their competence and right of veto. The Constitution will extend the EU's involvement in important areas such as justice, asylum and immigration, and foreign policy. However, it will not come into effect until it has been ratified by all member states, and a significant number have decided that the proposed changes justify putting the decision to ratify to a popular referendum. Given the political consequences of the Constitution that is an entirely appropriate decision.

The EU's experience shows how far the logic of the market and free trade can be taken, if there is political will. The EU is in effect a quasi-federal system created under international law. It is also an important international actor, assuming some of the classical characteristics associated with statehood: early on the European Court of Justice decided that the Community should be able to enter into international agreements in areas over which it exercised internal competence, and the Community has increasingly done so. In areas where it has exclusive competence – such as trade and fisheries – the member states have lost any right to act on their own internationally. Hence Britain no longer acts on its own account on most WTO issues, and its WTO relations with the US are channelled through the EU. In areas where the Community and the member states share competence, for example on the environment, then both are allowed to act internationally. But this gives rise to increasing difficulties in knowing whether it is for the Community or the member state to act, or both, and a growing sense that as the rights of the member states diminish so those of the Community increase. In a current international dispute with Ireland, the British government suggested in June 2003 that the point has now been reached – for certain areas in which the European Community has legislated, such as the protection of the marine environment – where the relationship between Britain and Ireland is no different from that of two Canadian provinces, such as Ontario and Quebec.[10] I was surprised that legal argument was not taken up by the media. While the analogy may be going a tad too far, it does indicate where international trade agreements can lead when they are coupled with extensive legislative, executive and judicial powers (which arrangements such as the GATT, the WTO and the NAFTA do not have). The manifest loss of sovereignty has brought benefits to parts of Europe, including peace and economic prosperity – a success on any count. But that has come at a price, as the disconnection between decision-making in Brussels and the citizens of Europe becomes more marked. This democratic deficit is inherent in all modern international law-making, but is especially pronounced in the field of trade. If it is not addressed, serious consequences will ensue.

*

Overarching regional arrangements such as the EC or NAFTA are the global rules, inspired by the GATT. Fifty-three countries participated in its adoption in 1947, joined in the belief that trade and economic relations were closely connected with higher living standards, full employment and exploitation of the world's resources. The theory was that these social objectives could be achieved by reducing tariffs and other barriers to trade, and eliminating discriminatory treatment in international commerce. The GATT was premised on the principle of economic rationalism, putting into practice the theories of Adam Smith and David Ricardo. Smith saw an analogy between countries and family matters: why make something at home if it would cost more to make than to buy? 'If a foreign country can supply us with a commodity cheaper than we ourselves can make it, better buy it off them with some part of the produce of our own industry, employed in a way in which we have some advantage,' was the way he put it.[11] Ricardo extended this theory in *Principles of Political Economy and Taxation* (1817), which proposed the significance of comparative advantage in producing a product or good in one country, instead of another, and then trading it (a theory which the leading economist Paul Samuelson has rightly described as one of the most difficult for the non-economist to understand). These theories apply a pure economic logic, leaving little room to account for legitimate cultural, social and political differences, which may push governments and citizens towards economically irrational actions. A government may decide, for example, to place restrictions on trade in a product which has been made in violation of fundamental human rights, or minimum environmental standards. Regulating international trade inevitably means taking a view on the legitimacy of such restrictions. It also means banning restrictions if they are not considered, under international law, to be legitimate. So global trade rules necessitate discourse and debate on cultural and social values. The GATT rules come under scrutiny when they are seen to impose – inappropriately – one set of values to the detriment of another. Free trade is not socially or culturally neutral.

The GATT system had to accommodate this tension, and find a balance. The rules appear simple. It is applying them in hard cases which causes sparks to fly. There are four basic principles. First, GATT members – and now WTO members – agree to apply duties and other charges on imported goods equally to all parties, without discrimination. This is known as the 'most favoured nation' principle. It means that all states will be treated no less favourably than the most favoured. So the GATT/WTO is a club of equals. A second principle is that the members agree that they will not increase trade barriers. Third, they agree that any taxes, or charges or regulations, will only be applied in a way that does not discriminate between locally produced goods and the same imported goods. And fourth, the members promise not to impose any form of trade restraint except in the form of customs tariffs and duties. There cannot be quotas, for example. By these means countries agreed in 1947 to establish a multilateral system of rules to increase international trade in goods. These simple rules remain in place today.

The members did recognize, however, that there could be situations in which a GATT member might need to restrict international trade for legitimate reasons. It is at this point – exceptionally – that cultural and social differences, or other legitimate objectives, could justify a restriction of international trade. So in rather vague and general terms the GATT allows members to restrict trade to protect public morals (banning pornography), or to protect human, animal or plant life or health (banning the import of asbestos), or to protect national treasures (banning the export of works of art), or to conserve exhaustible natural resources (banning ozone-depleting substances), or to ensure the availability of products which are in short supply or to protect essential security interests or UN decisions (banning imports of Iraqi oil, after the Gulf War). But these values are not defined in the GATT. In the first instance it is for the GATT members themselves to decide on their application. If another member objects, a group of international judges (who sit on a panel) will decide. What is clear is that the exceptions can only be permitted in rare circumstances, and only if they do discriminate between countries, and they are genuinely intended to achieve their stated purpose. So an exception will not be permitted if it is really a trade restriction which has been illegitimately dressed up as a measure to protect, say, public morals or the environment.

Whether an exception is justified will depend on the facts of any case. As with any legal text there will always be room for interpretation. This means that the dispute settlement mechanism becomes crucially important. The old GATT panels became the arbiters of the legitimacy of public policy, and of social, cultural and environmental matters. In this way, the economic rationale of the rules cannot be divorced from non-economic values. And the rules are not applied in a mechanical fashion, but fall to be interpreted and applied by individual panellists appointed to adjudicate particular disputes.

Over forty years these rules provided the basis for international trade within the GATT club. It was not a truly global system, like the UN, because China, the Soviet bloc and other socialist countries were not included. And the institutions which operated the rules were embryonic, without real teeth. Members could claim that national sovereignty was preserved, that some decisions of GATT panels were not legally binding. From the 1950s to the 1980s the GATT was supplemented by various 'rounds' of negotiations – the Tokyo Round, the Kennedy Round – at which new rules were gradually adopted. In 1986 GATT members launched the 'Uruguay Round' to extend the free trade rules and also create a more formal organizational structure, as well as a new binding system to resolve disputes (the Round is named after a city, country or leader with which it was connected).

The Uruguay Round negotiations were concluded in April 1994. One hundred and twenty-three states met in Marrakesh to sign the Agreement establishing the World Trade Organization. They did not include China, which has since joined, or Russia, which is still negotiating (and whose prospects improve with its recent ratification of the Kyoto Protocol). The WTO is the fully-fledged institutional structure that failed to get off the ground in the 1940s, and is intended to manage the operation of the growing reach of international trading rules. The old GATT rules were incorporated into the new WTO, but nevertheless they remain its core. These rules were extended into important (and sensitive) new areas, so that free trade now encompasses trade in services (the General Agreement on Trade in Services (GATS)) like banking, insurance and financial services, among others. But not all services are included, and those excluded are the ones in which developing countries often have a growing advantage, such as construction and shipbuilding. A second new agreement addressed trade-related aspects of intellectual property rights (TRIPs), and was designed to promote the protection of national and international intellectual property rights (patents, trademarks, etc.) and integrate them fully into the free trade rules. The agreement was intended to end international trade in pharmaceutical products and drugs that do not comply with intellectual property laws, on the basis that a failure to comply with such rules would cause harm to legitimate commercial activities and undermine initiative and creativity. The TRIPs Agreement has already given rise to controversy, when pharmaceutical companies relied on it to try to stop South Africa from providing low-cost, generic treatment against HIV and AIDS. However, following an outcry in April 2001, thirty-nine drug companies dropped a lawsuit to prevent South Africa's 1997 Medicines Act from being enforced, allowing the use of affordable, generic medicines. The impact of the TRIPs Agreement on increasing poorer communities' access to drugs continues to be controversial. This is all the more so after a British government-sponsored Commission on Intellectual Property Rights concluded that IP rights hardly played any role at all in stimulating research and development into tropical diseases in the developing world, which was said to be the rationale for applying intellectual property rules in the first place.[12]

The WTO Agreement established a new institutional framework, including far-reaching provisions on the settlement of international disputes. An all-powerful Appellate Body was created, which is the ultimate authority on WTO law and, as we have seen, the legitimacy of public policy and other exceptions which may be invoked by WTO members. Although the system of trading rules has been extended, there are numerous areas which have not been brought within the WTO system, including many agricultural practices. Efforts to negotiate a new WTO round collapsed in Seattle in 1999, against a background of lack of agreement amongst developed and developing country governments, which helped empower a fragile coalition among NGOs. In November 2001, agreement was reached in Doha, Qatar, to launch a new Round, with the emphasis on economic development and the alleviation of poverty in developing countries. This is referred to as the 'Development Round'. In September 2003, in Cancun, Mexico, the WTO Ministerial Conference, which was intended to take forward the Doha commitments, collapsed without agreement on any agenda items. Divisions were especially bitter on agriculture, which has been excluded from WTO rules at great cost to farmers from developing countries, who are unable to access western markets. A group of twenty-two developing countries, including Brazil, China, India and Nigeria, has now emerged as a well-organized and effective counterweight to the US and the EU. Their main target? The failure of the EU and the US to end the massive farm subsidies which they grant to their agricultural sectors, estimated at billions of euros and dollars. Coupled with Brazil's recent success in litigating an end to American and European cotton subsidies, it begins to look as though these global rules will take a new direction. They do so in the aftermath of the explosion of anti-WTO protest on the streets of Seattle and elsewhere. Naomi Klein has described the events in Seattle as 'the hushed whisper turned into a shout, one heard round the world'.[13] Its full consequences are yet to be felt.

*

The GATT rules had operated more or less out of the public eye for many years. That changed in the early 1990s, when Mexico brought a case challenging an American ban on imports of tuna products caught by Mexican fishing vessels in Mexico's waters and on the high seas. The case turned on the circumstances under which one country could prohibit imports on the grounds that the product had been made in an environmentally harmful way. The United States was applying its domestic environmental standards to fishing activities taking place outside its territory. Mexican tuna was banned because it was not 'dolphin friendly': in taking the tuna the Mexicans were also killing large numbers of dolphins, the US alleged. The American ban appeared to violate two golden rules of international law: 1) that all countries are entitled to fish freely on the high seas; and 2) without agreement to the contrary, one country cannot apply its standards to activities in other countries.

This case posed an additional problem for the US: there were no international rules protecting dolphins, or regulating tuna fisheries off the Mexican coast. The dolphins were not an endangered species under international law. American values – a love of dolphins – were being imposed on Mexico. Mexico challenged the ban under the GATT rules. Two separate GATT panels ruled on the case and found decisively in favour of Mexico. The first decision came in 1991. It ruled that the United States was applying its domestic environmental laws outside its own territory and that this was not allowed by GATT.[14] The GATT panel rejected the American argument that it could restrict trade in tuna to protect dolphins as 'animal life' or conserve them as 'exhaustible natural resources': these exceptions could only be relied upon, said the panel, to protect dolphins *within* the territory of the United States. Since the imported tins of Mexican tuna would not harm the American environment or consumers, the US lost.

The case became a *cause célèbre* among environmental NGOs.[15] Full-page advertisements were taken up in various American newspapers criticizing the free trade rules. NGOs claimed that the GATT rules were undermining American environmental laws, that trade was being given primacy over the environment, that sovereign decision-making was being destroyed. The arguments also caught the public imagination, and the issue became one of the most contentious topics at the Earth Summit in Rio in June 1992. It very nearly prevented agreement from being reached on Agenda 21 and the Rio Declaration, the instruments which global leaders had gathered to sign.[16] The tuna/dolphin case raised a fundamental question: can one country restrict imports to protect the environment outside its own territory? If the answer to that question is yes, then what is to stop that country from banning imports because products are made in violation of health and safety laws, or labour rules, or human rights standards?

But the case could be looked at in another way. From Mexico's perspective (a developing country) it was asked: why should the trade rules allow one country to impose its environmental or cultural values on another, in particular where the international community has not recognized the legitimacy of actions to promote those values, or the need to protect that particular environmental resource? Many felt that the US affection for dolphins was based on little more than sentimental attachment on the part of a generation brought up on the lovable TV dolphin, 'Flipper'.

Free trade cannot be a charter for bullies. The GATT system was conceived as a way of avoiding a situation in which economically large and powerful countries could impose their will (and their values) on smaller or less powerful countries. Yet here was the US doing exactly that. Developing countries were united in their support of Mexico, and felt vindicated when Mexico won the case. I have no doubt that the result was the right one, and the NGO critique of the result was misguided. The real problem was with the reasoning in the decision. It went too far in promoting free trade values, and not far enough in recognizing the importance of environmental and other values (this is not surprising since panels were, in those days at least, usually composed of trade diplomats, with a limited vision). The panel's language seemed to exclude the possibility that there might be *any* circumstances in which one country could ban imports to protect the environment of the producing state, or of the international community as a whole. There will be cases in which unilateral measures applied to activities abroad will be justifiable, especially if the way in which the product is made violates global rules. But this was not such a case, in my view.

Nevertheless, the tuna/dolphin case became symbolic of much that was wrong with the GATT, free trade and globalization. The creation of the WTO, in 1994, provided added impetus for public scrutiny, leading to the 1999 Seattle protests. Church groups, trade unions, environmentalists, development activists, and even a British Conservative, who was a former Member of the European Parliament, dressed as a turtle (in honour of a famous WTO case) came together in the largest anti-globalization demonstration ever held. The WTO rules of international law were the no. 1 target. Public scrutiny of global rule-making is entirely a good thing. The rules are there to

serve the interests of people, not governments or states. Public attention can trigger change: I saw that clearly in some of the earliest
decisions of the Appellate Body, the new, all-powerful judicial arm of
the WTO. Its very first decision (in 1996) concerned a case brought
by Venezuela and Brazil against American standards on gasoline
products. The Appellate Body ruled that the WTO rules are not to be
interpreted in 'clinical isolation' from other rules of general public
international law.[17] Unlike the earlier GATT panels, the Appellate
Body members are not trade diplomats, but are schooled in general
international law. They take a more universal approach, and see
GATT and WTO rules in their broader social context and within the
framework of international law generally. Innocuous as the Appellate
Body's words may have seemed, they marked a very radical departure
from the earlier GATT case law. The tuna/dolphin case seemed to
have slammed the door shut on any possibility that GATT rules
should be interpreted in the light of other global rules, such as those
concerning the environment. For old-style GATT aficionados the
Appellate Body's decision was revolutionary. It signalled a seismic
shift, which was not universally welcomed elsewhere. Developing
countries in particular feared that the WTO would become a battleground for non-trade issues, including human rights and labour
standards. Their concerns were not entirely misplaced. I happened to
be with the GATT's former legal adviser, Frieder Roessler, the day
after the Appellate Body's decision in the Venezuela/Brazil case was
handed down. Walking around the gardens of Harold Acton's renais-
sance estate at La Pietra in Florence, Roessler was appalled by the
ruling. The GATT had previously been treated as a self-contained
regime, one which existed in hermetic isolation from the other rules
of international law. On that view, the purity of the trade rules would
now be tainted by these other international laws on human rights,
environment and labour.

The members of the Appellate Body have certainly not shirked
the bringing of WTO rules into the mainstream of international
law. A further major ruling came in 1998, concerning the huge
global trade in shrimps, when the Appellate Body in effect overturned the GATT panel's tuna/dolphin decisions. Shrimp farming is
a highly profitable activity in more than fifty countries around the
world, with a multimillion-dollar international market. The farmers

are dependent on access to valuable European and American markets. But shrimp farming has major environmental costs. It can be particularly damaging to migratory sea turtles, which drown in shrimp nets. These wonderful creatures migrate across thousands of miles of ocean, and are recognized under international law as being internationally endangered. The 1973 Convention on International Trade in Endangered Species prohibited trade in these turtles. A relatively low-cost device known as a turtle excluder device (TED) had been invented which allows turtles to escape shrimp nets. The United States and other countries required TEDs to be fitted under their domestic laws.

In 1989 the US essentially banned imports of shrimp from certain countries which did not require the use of TEDs, or provide equivalent protection for sea turtles. The ban followed domestic litigation in American federal courts brought by a coalition of NGOs (including the Sierra Club, the Turtle Island Restoration Network, the American Society for the Prevention of Cruelty to Animals, the US Humane Society, and the Earth Island Institute). They argued that US federal law obliged the US government to protect sea turtles around the world, by banning shrimp imports wherever production harmed sea turtles. The claim was upheld by the federal courts, and the US government subsequently banned imports from India, Malaysia, Thailand and the Philippines.

Once again the US was accused of applying its own domestic environmental laws to production occurring outside its own territory. But there were two differences from the earlier tuna/dolphin cases. First, the GATT system had been replaced. The new WTO rules endorsed the concept of 'sustainable development', requiring environmental considerations to be integrated into economic development. And second, unlike dolphins, sea turtles were recognized internationally to be endangered. The four Asian countries challenged the US ban at the WTO. A first instance WTO panel ruled that the American restrictions violated WTO law. The US appealed the case to the Appellate Body, which overturned the panel. The Appellate Body interpreted the GATT exceptions as allowing, under certain conditions, one WTO member to restrict imports on environmental grounds where the aim was to protect shared natural resources, even those located outside the territory of the importing state.[18] The critical issue, said the Appellate Body, is that the resource in question must have some connection with the state taking the conservation measures.

In this case the Appellate Body had little difficulty in concluding that there was a nexus between the United States and the sea turtles which were being harmed in Asian waters. The turtles migrated around the globe and may have moved in and out of American waters. This meant that the United States could in principle take measures to protect the turtles. But the Appellate Body ruled that the ban was discriminatory, since shrimps from other, friendly neighbouring countries, which also did not protect turtles, had not been banned. Under WTO law, said the Appellate Body, all states were entitled to be treated equally.

The Appellate Body also found that the US had acted prematurely. It had not exhausted environmental diplomacy with the four Asian countries before imposing the ban. It should have engaged in across-the-board negotiations with these countries to persuade them to protect turtles, and to try to achieve a negotiated settlement before unilaterally imposing its own rules. Having failed to exhaust diplomacy, the US could not unilaterally impose its own solution. This part of the Appellate Body's decision had significant implications, and not just for environmental bans and trade restrictions. It said, in effect, that a state cannot act on its own until it has engaged, in good faith, in efforts to achieve a negotiated and consensual solution. Coming two years before the Bush presidency, the decision was a shot across the bows of the coming neo-conservative agenda.

The decision in the shrimp/turtles case has been strongly criticized by NGOs and some developing countries. Public Citizen, the US-based advocacy group, argued volubly that this was yet another example of the way in which the WTO rules undermined the right of states to set their own environmental standards.[19] Developing countries, on the other hand, claimed that the decision would open the door to unilateral environmental measures. I do not agree with either critique. The Appellate Body went out of its way to ensure that the values being promoted by the US could only be given effect if they were shared internationally, as reflected in other international agreements. (Interestingly, in support of the US case, the Appellate Body relied on a number of international conventions which the US had neither signed nor ratified, suggesting that such treaties can still have important consequences on non-parties, reflecting the 'will of the international community'.) Before one country can impose its values on another country it must have engaged in proper discussions. So the Appellate Body is balancing competing interests: between free trade and access to markets, on the one hand, and the ability of states to take appropriate and proportionate measures to protect legitimate environmental objectives, on the other. The US has complied with the judgment of the WTO Appellate Body. It negotiated with the four Asian countries on the protection of turtles, reaching agreement with three of them. Malaysia, however, held out, unwilling to adopt the measures to the satisfaction of the US. When Malaysia brought another case to challenge the continued ban on imports of Malaysian shrimp, the Appellate Body ruled that the US had done all that was required. It could ban imports to protect the turtles.[20]

The shrimp/turtle decision has become emblematic of change in the global trade rules. It pointed to the WTO system adopting a more holistic approach, placing trade interests in a broader social context. Ironically, in the age of 'fair trade', by winning the case the US took the trade rules into the very areas of international law in which its support was less deep and less firm. I cannot help feeling that the people who designed the legal strategy for the shrimp/turtle cases took their eye off the broader picture of American politico-legal interests. By winning the arguments in this case the US opened the door to its own future discontent with free trade rules. So although it remains committed, for now at least, to the WTO rules, three factors suggest that over time a different stance may emerge, with the result that as in other areas – human rights, environment – support for multilateralism may wither. First, the developing countries take the WTO into areas, such as agricultural subsidies, which cause economic pain locally. Second, the US continues to lose politically and economically significant cases, in the spheres of steel, cotton and online gambling. Third, the Appellate Body allows other social values to temper the 'purity' of similar trade rules.

*

And what of the 'special relationship' between Britain and the United States, in this discrete area of international law? Ever since the Atlantic Charter these two countries have been among the greatest proponents of multilateral, global trade rules. With the advent of the

EU, Britain has been subsumed into that larger grouping of states. This does not mean that the two countries did not themselves come into conflict, as the differences on colonial-era trade preferences showed. WTO disputes have caused great tension, even before George W. Bush took office. In the bananas case the Appellate Body agreed with the US and its banana-exporting allies that the EU's rules were discriminatory and contrary to WTO law. The WTO authorized the US to impose financial sanctions on the EU and its member states and in September 2000 the Clinton Administration announced that it would apply targeted sanctions on specific EU industries. The products included cashmere made in Scotland. That product was chosen because it was being made in parliamentary constituencies in Scotland in which Labour held only a marginal lead. The targeting of sanctions maximized pressure on the British government to exert influence on the European Community to comply with the WTO ruling, just before the May 2001 parliamentary elections. Scottish cashmere firms breathed a sigh of relief when the threat of sanctions was lifted.[21] The chairman of the Scottish Borders Knitters' Forum described the WTO sanctions as a threat 'hanging over us like the sword of Damocles'. The WTO and its global rules had become domestic political issues.

Three years later, the same trade pressures were applied to domestic electoral politics, but in reverse. After its win at the WTO in the US steel tariffs case, the EU took the American line and targeted products made in electorally marginal American states for rises in import duties and tariffs. One target was citrus fruit from Florida. 'Anyone want to wage a bet whether goods from Florida will take a hit if the EU carries out its threat?' screamed Fort Lauderdale's *Sun Sentinel* newspaper.[22] The pressure forced President Bush to back down. As I have already said, however, he could not mention that he was giving effect to a WTO ruling. Here was international law in action, but no reference was made to that fact. Here also was international law raising issues of sovereignty, democracy and accountability: global rules trumping domestic decision-making.

*

So long as the rules serve its interests, the United States has been a strong supporter of global trade rules, effective institutions and enforceable sanctions, reflecting the clear distinction between its economic interests and its non-economic interests. In 1985 the US had abruptly terminated its acceptance of the jurisdiction of the International Court of Justice to hear disputes brought by or against America. The catalyst was a case filed by Nicaragua, attacking American support for the Contras (the Court went on to rule against the US).[23] By contrast, within the WTO it was the US which led the charge for binding resolution of international trade disputes, prompted by the concern that without such a system countries that violated their trade obligations could not be held to account and would gain unfair economic advantages. Ironic indeed is the call by Robert Zoellick, within a decade, for developing countries to negotiate their differences with the US, and not to litigate. This is one area in which neo-conservatives seem less uncomfortable with multilateralism or a rules-based approach to international relations. This attitude contrasts starkly with the policy on the ICC and the Kyoto Protocol, as we have seen, and with its position in relation to the United Nations and humanitarian law.

How can the difference be explained? Is it that the values have changed, or is something else in play? It may simply be that the US Administration, like other governments, is bending to a corporate agenda, as Noreena Hertz has argued in her book *The Silent Takeover*.[24] In this thesis, where governmental interests are closely aligned to corporate interests, then the rules favouring the latter – opening up new markets, imposing economic liberalization, constraining governmental intervention at the national level – are seen to merit support. It is, after all, far more efficient and less costly to resolve trade disputes by adjudication than by gunboat diplomacy.

Robert Zoellick, the US Trade Representative, has made the economic argument: 'Expanded trade – imports as well as exports – improves our well-being. Exports accounted for 25 per cent of US economic growth over the course of the past decade and support an estimated 12 million jobs.'[25] But the political arguments are intimately connected, premised on the belief that trade and the promotion of political values are linked, along with the rule of law and liberty. 'Erecting new political barriers and closing old borders will not advance the plight of child labourers. It will not liberate the persecuted Christians in China,' Zoellick told an audience at the Heritage Foundation, a right-wing think tank.[26]

At the very least, neo-conservative support for multilateral trade rules confirms that there is no *a priori* objection to multilateralism, or to rules of international law as such. The American position on free trade rules, or on the NAFTA, is flatly inconsistent with the claim that is frequently made that there are constitutional constraints on international commitments.[27] Support for these trade rules is predicated on a belief that public policy objections are met by promoting private economic and commercial interests where they are aligned. To put it another way, when the global rules have a centre of gravity which is economic, then there is a presumption of public benefit which makes them worth supporting. There is a certain irony in this. At the instigation of the US itself, the WTO Appellate Body has now decided clearly that economic rules cannot be taken in hermetic isolation from other rules of international law. The Appellate Body has relied on international treaties which the United States has not joined, such as the Convention on Biological Diversity and the UN Convention on the Law of the Sea. It is the very cases in which the US has sought to defend itself by raising non-economic interests – environment, prohibition of online gambling, etc. – that have come to permeate the trade rules, forming part of the economic system created by the United States.

Here comes the rub. The logic of the Appellate Body's approach in the shrimp/turtle case means that it is the very failure of the United States to participate in multilateral environmental agreements, such as the Kyoto Protocol, which may well open the door to trade sanctions. The day cannot be far off when the EU or some group of countries decides to ban imports of products coming from the US because they are made in a way which harms the climate, because they use energy inefficiently and contribute to excessive greenhouse gas emissions and global warming. Like sea turtles, the climate system is a shared resource. America's arguments and success in the shrimp/turtles case pave the way for future WTO cases against the US for its wilful failure to follow the rest of the international community in taking steps to protect the global environment. As and when that happens, it is less clear that the US would continue to support the WTO system of multilateral trade rules. Like human rights rules, it may be that the constraints, which global trade rules could soon impose, will lead the US to rethink the benefits of a multilateral approach to rule-based trade.

6

A Safer World, for Investors

'Money doesn't talk, it swears.'
Bob Dylan, 'It's Alright Ma (I'm Only Bleeding)' (1965)

In March 1996 I received an unexpected phone call from Stephen Hodgson, one of my former students. He was working in Tirana, the capital of Albania, advising the Albanian government on the reform of its land and agricultural laws. The laws dated back half a century, and had not been changed since the time of the co-operative farms of Enver Hoxha. Hoxha ruled Albania from 1944 until his death in 1985 as a closed, one-party state. For much of that time its great ally was the People's Republic of China. Stephen was working in a dilapidated building on Skendenberg Square, built in the time of King Zog. It was now the Ministry of Agriculture. He was based in the legal adviser's office, and until shortly before our phone conversation had been denied access to a locked wooden cupboard. Inside he eventually discovered a bundle of discarded and mostly unopened Federal Express packages sent from the Secretary General of the World Bank's International Centre for Settlement of Investment Disputes (ICSID) in Washington. They announced that an international arbitration case had been started against the Albanian state by a Greek company, Tradex Hellas. The Greeks were claiming that Albania had expropriated their investment in a melon and cotton farming agricultural joint venture, that this violated international law, and that the investors were entitled to more than $3 million in compensation. For a poor country like Albania this was a significant sum. Stephen explained that ICSID's initial letters had received no response from Albania, perhaps because they were being treated as bills. The three-man arbitration tribunal had therefore been constituted without the benefit of Albanian input (as the ICSID rules allowed). The first hearing was to be held in Frankfurt in two weeks' time. Stephen wanted to know if I could attend on behalf of Albania.

This turned out to be Albania's first real contact with ICSID. In the heady days after the demise of Hoxha's regime, Albania had been persuaded to join ICSID and take steps to protect the tide of valuable foreign investments that were promised to be heading Albania's way. To encourage foreign investment, Albania was told it would be necessary to promulgate various national laws and investment protection treaties. Investors would not come to Albania if they had to go to the local courts, and they should have the right to arbitrate any disputes outside Albania and under the ICSID rules. In this way, so the theory ran, foreign investment would contribute to Albania's economic development. For a country which had had virtually no contact with the outside world for two generations, this was a rude change. Until the 1990s Albania had no treaties to protect the investments of foreigners. It signed its first one, with neighbouring Greece, in August 1991. Twenty-one more were signed within four years.

Under cover of the new Albanian laws and the treaty with Greece, Tradex Hellas became one of the first foreign companies to invest in Albania since the 1930s. However, the investment soon failed and Tradex sued under the ICSID rules. The Albanian President was surprised – to say the least – that his country could be brought before an international tribunal. We had to explain that it was not he personally who was being sued. Plainly, no one had taken the trouble to explain to Albania exactly what it was signing up to, after nearly fifty years of isolation. Ironically, Albania was the first country to be sued at the International Court of Justice in The Hague after the Second World War, for failing to give Britain adequate warnings about mines that had been laid in the Corfu Channel, off the Albanian coast. The mines had damaged two British warships.[1] Albania lost, and the Corfu Channel case has remained engraved on the memories of Albanians as a great injustice, their last brush with international litigation until the Tradex case came along.

The ICSID case was rather more mundane: Tradex alleged that local villagers had revolted and taken over the agricultural joint venture, and that the Albanian government had turned a blind eye, in

violation of its international obligations to protect Tradex's investment. None of the three arbitrators – including Fred Fielding, who
was appointed by Tradex and had previously been a legal adviser to
Ronald Reagan – bought the argument. They all agreed that the
evidence showed that the joint venture had failed because of the
investor's hopeless lack of experience in Albanian farming conditions.
The Albanian witnesses who came to London were decisive. There
was especially animated evidence on what would have been the right
time of the year to plant melons, and the inadequacies of the investment (wrong tractors and too few of them). The expropriation claim
was successfully resisted and Albania's reputation enhanced. The previously obscure ICSID rules made front-page news in Tirana. Our
involvement in Albania's defence and the ability of the international
legal order to do justice brought a ministerial invitation to a celebra-
tion in Tirana, in June 1999, right in the middle of the Kosovo war.
The visit to an appalling refugee camp for thousands of Kosovar
Albanians remains seared in my memory.

*

Like trade, foreign investment protection is an area of international law
which has been strongly and consistently supported by successive US
governments, whether Republican or Democrat, together with Britain
and other capital-exporting countries. The reasons are not hard to find.
These two countries are the world's largest overseas investors and have
been for many years. Their companies and citizens make foreign investments which in 2001 exceeded $300 billion. In 1990 annual flows of
American overseas investment were just $73 billion; by 2001 the figure
exceeded $230 billion. For the United States and Britain, overseas
investments in minerals, manufacturing, services, banking and many
other sectors represent a huge contribution to their national wealth, on
which the future prosperity of both countries depends. Foreign investments need legal stability and certainty. Without protection from
improper interference or expropriation by the host governments, the
corporations will not put their money or efforts into the country. So far
as investments in developing countries are concerned, this usually
means that clear, enforceable international rules are required to provide the protection. Most investors believe that international tribunals,
not national courts, must enforce these rules.

For centuries, countries have been concluding treaties to protect their nationals' legal rights. Since the 1940s, the push for distinct rules of international law to protect foreign investments from expropriation and other forms of interference has accelerated. This protection forms part of the 'collaboration . . . in the economic field' envisaged by Roosevelt and Churchill. Sixty years later George W. Bush welcomed Coalition Provisional Authority Order Number 39, on Foreign Investment. Since it opened much of Iraq's economy to foreign ownership, it was controversial and stretched the limits of what an occupying power was entitled to do under long-established rules of international law. 'Iraq's Governing Council approved a new law that opens the country to foreign investment for the first time in decades,'[2] Bush proclaimed, without a hint of irony.

Foreign investment rules fall into two categories. One category may be found in the various human rights rules which protect property rights. The Universal Declaration of Human Rights, adopted by the UN General Assembly in 1948, prohibits anyone from being 'arbitrarily deprived of his property' (Article 17(2)). The rule has been incorporated into other regional and global human rights instruments, such as the European Convention on Human Rights (ECHR), as well as the more recent African Charter on Human and Peoples' Rights.[3] These instruments provide basic protection for all property. They do not distinguish between local and foreign ownership. But foreign investors and their governments considered that they did not go far enough in protecting overseas investments. In the late 1950s and early 1960s a great number of colonies emerged as independent and sovereign states. They wanted control over their national patrimony, including natural resources. The investor companies and their governments were concerned about their investments being nationalized, particularly valuable Middle Eastern oil concessions. They worried about the enforceability and ambiguity of the human rights obligations. More was needed to encourage foreign investment, and to protect existing investments. So a second category of international agreements emerged. Ironically, these were driven by the consequences of decolonization and the application of the principles of self-determination which Roosevelt had fought for in the Atlantic Charter, and achieved with the United Nations Charter. What you give with one hand you bind with the other.

International agreements for the protection of foreign investments have become closely connected to free trade agreements. Free trade rules are aimed at increasing the flow of goods and services by removing barriers to international trade between countries. Foreign investment agreements aim to increase the flow of money by encouraging overseas investments from the private sector. It is no overstatement to say that the trade and investment rules have underwritten economic globalization. Take these international rules away and global commerce comes to a grinding halt. So it is no surprise that while he was flouting other rules of international law in 2003, President Bush was simultaneously announcing new free trade and investment agreements and initiatives to protect the rights of American investors in Central and South America, in Chile and in Singapore. The Singapore agreement, said Bush, reflected 'a belief in the power of free enterprise . . . to improve lives'.[4] This was good international law, not the bad, constraining kind.

Foreign investment agreements are not a new invention, but they are growing apace. What is surprising, however, is that the great body of treaties which were put in place between the 1960s and the 1990s are obscure and have not been the subject of real public scrutiny or debate. According to Joseph Stiglitz, President Clinton's principal economic adviser, when he was in Cabinet the numerous foreign investment protection rules – such as those in the North American Free Trade Agreement – were agreed more or less without discussion. It seems pretty clear that the British Cabinet, too, has never much deliberated the desirability of foreign investment rules. I doubt that Parliament has ever looked at them. So the dozens of investment protection treaties which Britain has entered into over the last three decades have never been scrutinized by an elected, democratic body. This unfortunate situation may now be changing, following a series of well-publicized recent arbitration awards under the investment rules which Canada, Mexico and the United States adopted in 1994 in the NAFTA. Some of these decisions on investors' rights have been highly controversial. More significantly, after years of a one-way traffic in litigation against developing countries, the developed, capital-exporting countries are being sued. In 1997 the United States was sued for the first time under an investment treaty, by an aggrieved foreign investor. Claims have since been brought, challenging some of the most important institutions of American society, such as trial by jury and political contributions to gubernatorial candidates. Just as American investors could decide not to go to court in Zaire or Argentina, Canadian investors are preferring to challenge the US before international tribunals rather than in the US courts. For a country that prides itself on its legal system, this has come as a rude shock.

These cases have focused public attention on the extent to which the protection of foreign investors' private property rights may prevent a country from adopting or enforcing health and labour standards, environmental rules and human rights norms. How could this be? Because there is a relationship between investors' rights and local laws. The balance in that relationship depends on the extent of the investors' rights: the greater their protection against interference, the more constrained is the ability of countries to adopt domestic laws, and vice-versa. The connection exists because the adoption of social and environmental laws can diminish profitability, for example, if environmental or other rules are costly to implement or where, as occasionally happens, they halt some commercial activities altogether.

A recent case illustrates this. In 1996 Canada adopted new environmental rules to restrict the use of MMT as an additive in gasoline. This is a manganese-based compound which enhances the octane value of unleaded gasoline, but which is thought to be harmful to human health. The Canadian regulations were attacked by an American company as an illegal interference with its investment in a Canadian factory which produced the MMT additive. Ethyl Corporation claimed that the regulations were 'tantamount to an expropriation', but that it had not been compensated for its loss. Ethyl claimed damages of $251 million from Canada. The case was settled, with the Canadian government paying a significantly smaller amount to Ethyl to end the case. But the fact that it had settled supported the view that claims of this kind were available. It opened the door to further cases challenging environmental laws.[5]

Against this background, support for foreign investment agreements which expand investors' rights has come to be regarded by some NGOs as a means of constraining a country's ability to adopt environmental and social norms of their own choosing. The *New York Times* raised eyebrows with an article in spring 2001 about this kind of litigation under ICSID and other rules:

Their meetings are secret. Their members are generally unknown. The decisions they reach need not be fully disclosed. Yet the way a small group of international tribunals handles disputes between investors and foreign governments has led to national laws being revoked, justice systems questioned and environmental regulations challenged.[6]

*

The basic rules of international law that protect the overseas investments of capital-exporting countries date back to the eighteenth and nineteenth centuries and the principles which limit a state from interfering with foreigners or their property. These historical guarantees encompassed both people and corporations, and set minimum international standards of treatment. International rules set a floor below which a state could not fall, but only in relation to foreigners. One early case was the Delagoa Bay arbitration, which followed the Portuguese government's seizure of a concession for a railway line granted to American and British citizens. The matter was considered so important that President McKinley reported the successful conclusion of the arbitration in his State of the Union message in 1900.

Thirty years later, in 1930, another international arbitration tribunal awarded an English company, Lena Goldfields, a huge monetary award (£13 million plus interest, which would be about £400 million today) against the government of the Soviet Union, which had taken a concession back into public ownership, in accordance with socialist principles. The concession to mine gold and other precious metals in the Urals and Siberia was terminated prematurely. The Soviet government abandoned the arbitration, refused to recognize the award, and subsequently repudiated a partial settlement. For more than sixty years the case was a festering sore in relations between Britain and the USSR. It was finally resolved in 1992 when Britain paid out compensation. A 'baleful monument to the absolute power of a State', the venerable English arbitration lawyer V. V. Veeder has called the case.[7]

The process of recovery could be a slow one, sometimes lasting decades. If one state fell below the minimum standards, then the state whose citizen was harmed could complain, and eventually bring a diplomatic claim against the offending state. This could be in the form of a diplomatic note of protest, or maybe something stronger, like sending in the navy to blockade a port and seize customs revenues until the offending state agreed to pay compensation or refer the dispute to arbitration. Respecting the traditional idea that only states had international rights meant that the individual or corporation whose rights had been violated could not bring a claim directly against the offending state. He had to request his own state to take up the claim. If the state declined to do so – for political or other reasons – then he would have no other remedy beyond the courts of the state that had injured his investment.

Over time the system evolved. In some cases states agreed to set up international claims commissions to receive claims from individuals directly. The claims commissions could decide whether the state had violated that individual's rights under international law. In some respects these international claims commissions were forerunners of modern international human rights commissions and courts, although their mandate was narrower. And, of course, they could only receive claims from foreigners. This meant that foreigners were often better protected than nationals. Indeed, even as these rules emerged, the basic principle remained that under international law a state was free to treat its own nationals as it wished. This remained the case until the emergence of international human rights law after the Second World War. Only then could it be said that international law placed constraints on a state's treatment of its own nationals.

By the beginning of the twentieth century a number of claims commissions had been created. One example was the United States–Mexico Mixed Claims Commission, established in the early days of the twentieth century following a period of civil strife in Mexico. It addressed hundreds of cases alleging that Mexico had failed to protect the rights of American nationals in Mexico, and some claims that the United States had likewise failed to protect the rights of Mexican nationals. The cases ranged from allegations that Mexico had turned a blind eye to murder, to the destruction of property. In the case of Thomas Yomans, for example, the US/Mexico Claims Commission found that Mexico was responsible for the acts of Mexican soldiers who had participated in the killing of several Americans. The soldiers had been ordered to quell a riot and end an attack on some Americans, following a dispute over wages with a Mexican worker. On their arrival, instead of dispersing the rioters, the soldiers had opened fire on the house in which the three Americans had taken refuge. One was killed. The other two were killed by the troops and the rioters as they tried to escape.[8]

In the 1950s, the emergence of international human rights law allowed individuals to bring international claims against their own states, at least in some circumstances. In the mid-1960s a number of capital-exporting states – led by the US and Britain – acted to create an institutional system to protect the rights of foreign investors. This would allow states to be sued directly (in the same way that the Albanian President initially found objectionable) by foreign investors, rather than requiring the investors to convince their governments to bring claims on their behalf. The idea was simple. It was premised on the notion that developing countries wanting to attract foreign investment would have to provide certain guarantees not to interfere with those investments. They would undertake not to expropriate or nationalize foreign investments, nor to treat them in a discriminatory or arbitrary manner, nor to take other measures which might be unfair or unjust. These obligations would be coupled with new procedures, allowing aggrieved investors to sue the state directly before an international tribunal.

The timing of the effort to protect foreign investments was significant. In the early 1960s many African, Asian, Caribbean and South American countries gained independence from their former colonial powers. Between 1945 and 1975 the membership of the UN jumped from 51 to 144 states. With independence came sovereignty and, in theory at least, control over natural resources located within their territory, such as oil and gas and other valuable minerals. But full sovereignty was tempered by the reality that under colonial rule long-term resource concessions and contracts had been granted to foreign companies, which would continue to bind the newly independent state. These concessions often allowed western companies to exploit oil, gas and other resources under privileged conditions, such as the payment of low taxes or royalties. There was a tension between the newly independent states who wanted to control these valuable resources, which often represented the most visible form of national wealth, and the former colonial powers whose companies had been granted long-term rights over the same resources and whose efforts and capital, it was argued, had created the infrastructure to exploit them. In the Middle East, in particular, a number of oil-rich Gulf states tried to bring to an early end long-term concessions to oil and gas. The 1960s and the 1970s saw cases of expropriation in Iran, Libya, Kuwait and elsewhere. The abrupt termination of generous, long-term concessions which had been granted to foreign investors pre-independence caused serious political tensions domestically and internationally.

These tensions gave rise to a sustained political debate in the United Nations beginning in the early 1960s. The General Assembly adopted a series of resolutions which were intended to balance the newly independent states' rights of 'permanent sovereignty over natural resources' with the property rights of western companies which had invested in them. By the mid-1970s the developing countries were a significant majority of the United Nations. In 1974, with the support of the Soviet Union, and over the vehement opposition of the major western capital-exporting states, they proclaimed a New International Economic Order. This pronounced the right of developing countries to take full control over their resources without having to pay large amounts of compensation to foreign companies. The New International Economic Order was also reflected in other international laws adopted in the post-colonial period. The UN Convention on the Law of the Sea was adopted in 1982, with rules proclaiming that natural resources beyond national jurisdiction were the 'common heritage of mankind' and should be exploited so that the benefits would be shared equitably.

But the New International Economic Order and its associated rules of equitable redistribution were unacceptable to many western powers, not least the United States, Britain and Germany. In 1979 and 1980 Margaret Thatcher and Ronald Reagan had respectively come to power, pledging to 'roll back the frontiers of the state' and give full rein to economist Milton Friedman's principles of market liberalization. Deregulation and privatization of many state-owned assets, such as water and electricity, were now emerging as part of an incipient neo-liberal political agenda. These two leaders pushed international law and global rules in a new direction. Both Thatcher and Reagan were strongly opposed to the New International Economic Order. They refused to join the 1982 Law of the Sea Convention, at least until its provisions had been amended to provide greater incentives for exploration and exploitation by the private sector (this eventually came in 1994). Ronald Reagan objected to the Convention's principle of 'common heritage of mankind', which required that the mineral resources of the deep seabed should be shared amongst mankind.[9] President Clinton signed the Convention in 1994, and President George W. Bush called on the Senate to ratify it, but doubts remain. BushCountry.org, an outfit dedicated to 'Promoting the Ideals of Conservatism', reflects the tenor of the continuing objections, citing the Convention's close connections to the Climate Change Convention and other international law. 'These treaties are dangerous on their face and malevolent to our Republic,' they wailed, part of 'the insidious wiles of foreign influence'.[10]

Alongside these political moves, the US and Britain also committed themselves to cutting funds from governmental sources of overseas development assistance and replacing them with money from private foreign direct investment. 'Trade not Aid' became the new mantra. Domestic deregulation was accompanied by a new political commitment to promote the private sector overseas: increasing levels of foreign direct investment (FDI) would be the key to wealth creation in the developing world. That meant creating an international legal regime to protect foreign investments.

*

In the 1960s – with considerable prescience – the American and British governments joined others in proposing new international arrangements for the protection of foreign investments, within the framework of the World Bank. The World Bank had been established in 1945 as part of an agreement famously negotiated in just three weeks at Bretton Woods in upstate New York. The Bank was part of British economist John Maynard Keynes's vision of creating an international institutional framework which would provide currency and liquidity stability so as to avoid a repeat of the economic crises of the late 1920s and early 1930s. The World Bank family included the International Bank for Reconstruction and Development (IBRD) to assist in the reconstruction and development of territories by facilitating the investment of capital, including the promoting of foreign investment and the provision of finance to the public sector. Alongside, the International Finance Corporation (IFC) would provide direct financial support to the private sector.

In 1963 President Lyndon Johnson supported the idea that a new institution be created within the World Bank family to promote overseas foreign investment in the developing world. In October 1966, after twenty countries ratified the International Centre for Settlement of Investment Disputes Convention, it entered into force. ICSID did not actually set out the rules which would govern the treatment of foreign investments; instead it aimed to provide a neutral forum within which disputes could be resolved by arbitration. The ICSID system recognized that many foreign investors would not want investment disputes to go to the local courts of the state concerned, and the host state would not want such disputes to go to the national courts of the investor. So ICSID allowed disputes to be resolved by international arbitration, usually before a panel of three independent arbitrators who would be appointed by the parties to the investment dispute. The panel would apply both the law of the host state and international law; the arbitral award would be legally binding and enforceable in the courts of any state that was a party to the ICSID Convention. The ICSID Convention also established an international civil service which serves as the secretariat to the arbitral tribunal. In short, the ICSID system is an internationalized dispute settlement mechanism established under international law that allows an aggrieved investor to bring a dispute against a state without having to involve his own state.

What ICSID does not do, however, is determine precisely which disputes can come before it, or which rules of international law are to be applied. That is left to other rules, usually found in investment treaties or free trade agreements. These treaties are usually bilateral (between two states), but they can also be multilateral (i.e. between three or more states). Since the late 1960s more than 2,000 bilateral investment treaties have been adopted between developed and developing countries (investment treaties between developed countries are a more recent phenomenon; they are being concluded between states such as Singapore and New Zealand, and the US and Australia). A small number of multilateral treaties have also been adopted in some parts of the world, or to govern particular types of investments (for example, in the energy sector in Europe). The United Kingdom has adopted nearly ninety investment treaties since 1975, and the United States more than forty-five. The absence of a bilateral investment treaty tends to discourage investment. Britain has no such treaty with

Mexico, for example, which has tended to limit British investments in that country.

A typical investment treaty does two things. It sets out the substantive obligations to which the parties agree for the treatment of foreign investments. And it provides written consent to ICSID or other forms of dispute settlement. A good example of an investment treaty is the NAFTA, which was adopted by Canada, Mexico and the United States in 1992, and came into force on 1 January 1994. The NAFTA protects foreign investors in three ways: it requires that foreign investors not be discriminated against; that minimum standards of international law be applied; and that there will be no expropriation or other similar acts without payment of compensation. A typical treaty also provides for a range of dispute settlement mechanisms, including recourse to ICSID. Reaction to these NAFTA rules was mixed, and the rules were not universally welcomed. The US business community and some governmental circles tended to see the rules as a great achievement, resolving a fundamental and long-standing disagreement between the US and Mexico. But in Mexico the legal adviser to the Ministry of Foreign Affairs resigned. He considered that the new NAFTA rules would allow US companies to dominate Mexico. NGOs and unions asserted that the investment protection rules were skewed in favour of foreign investors. They would undermine the ability of states to adopt new environmental and labour rules which would provide important social benefits.

*

ICSID got off to a slow start. In the first twenty-five years after the Convention came into force, between 1966 and 1991, just twenty-six disputes were registered by the ICSID secretariat in Washington, DC, about one a year. In the next five years a further twelve disputes were registered. In the period 1998–2003 the number of disputes registered with the ICSID secretariat exceeded ninety. And in the past year alone thirty-one new cases were registered, a massive increase which places a huge burden on an already overstretched international organization. Investors (and their lawyers) have become aware of new international remedies that are available, allowing them to bypass local courts and take control of their own international proceedings. ICSID privatizes the dispute settlement process and takes large bites out of the traditional state-held monopoly in international dispute settlement. But now it is not just developing countries and the former socialist countries of Central and Eastern Europe that have been at the receiving end of lawsuits. Although most cases are against poor or struggling countries, increasingly cases are being brought against developed countries such as the United States, Canada and Spain.

Since the mid-1990s there has been a huge increase in the number of arbitral proceedings and awards. Not that the public will find it easy to get much information about the cases, or what is argued. Despite their great political significance, and the increasing public interest in the cases, the ICSID rules operate on the principle that proceedings take place behind closed doors and beyond public scrutiny unless the parties agree otherwise (which they usually don't). Also, there is no obligation for ICSID awards to be made public, although often they do now make their way into the public domain, either formally or, where the parties have not agreed to publication, as samizdat. To its credit, the United States (and its NAFTA partners, Canada and Mexico) has turned a blind eye to the confidentiality rule. They routinely make their written arguments available on government websites, applying the principle that the public interest entitles the citizens of a state to know what arguments the government is presenting. Almost every other government would rather its citizens did not know what was being claimed, or what it was arguing in its defence.

*

In a great many investment cases the arbitrators have ruled that countries have violated their international obligations to foreign investors. In some cases the behaviour of the state has been outrageous, a good old-fashioned expropriation. But other cases often focus in a more nuanced way on the balance between the rights of foreign investors and host states. Two cases in which I had some involvement illustrate the broader political importance of some investment cases, and the growing tension between the competing goals of protecting private property rights and allowing governments to take reasonable steps to enhance other social objectives.

The first case concerned Costa Rica, and decisions taken in the early 1970s to protect a dry rainforest from encroaching commercial activity. Costa Rica is a country which is widely admired for its

commitment to environmental protection, and in particular the conservation of its unique flora and fauna. Anyone who has visited will
know the extraordinary richness of Costa Rica's Pacific coast and the
extensive virgin and dry rainforest which covers much of its eastern
province. By the mid-1970s only a small portion of this rainforest
remained outside the protected national park of Santa Elena, an area
of some 37,000 hectares (370 square kilometres). In 1974 the government of Costa Rica adopted a decree nationalizing the Santa Elena
reserve. They brought the area into public ownership as a protected
environmental reserve and prohibited commercial activity. But there
was a problem. The area in question had been bought three years
earlier, in 1972, by a group of American investors. They wanted to
build a tourist resort, with numerous hotels and other facilities. They
did not object to the government taking the area, and recognized that
it was genuinely intended to achieve environmental protection benefits. But understandably they wanted compensation for their property.

For more than twenty years the two sides argued about the value
of the property, but they could not reach agreement. In 1996 Costa
Rica was faced with the serious prospect of the loss of American foreign development assistance: in the US there was a move to limit the
flows of development assistance to any country which expropriated
the property of an American national without paying appropriate
compensation, unless the dispute was referred to international arbitration. Against this background Costa Rica agreed to take the Santa
Elena case to ICSID.[11] The issue facing the ICSID arbitral tribunal
was a narrow one: how much compensation were the investors entitled to be paid? Costa Rica had offered $1.9 million, but the invest-
ors wanted $6.4 million plus interest. They claimed this was the 'fair
market value' of their lost investment.

Before the Arbitral Tribunal Costa Rica argued that the amount of
compensation should take into account the public purpose of the
taking, and the broad environmental benefits that the conservation of
the forest would bring to Costa Rica and the region as a whole. The
tribunal was reminded of recent international agreements which committed Costa Rica to take steps to protect its biodiversity, including
the Convention on Biological Diversity, which more than 150 countries had signed at the Earth Summit in Rio in 1992. Costa Rica also
drew the tribunal's attention to the more obscure 1940 conservation

agreement (the Western Hemisphere Convention), arguing that if the Arbitral Tribunal imposed too onerous an obligation on Costa Rica then it would be impossible for developing countries to protect their environmental patrimony. The 1940 Convention committed countries of the Americas to take steps to establish a system of national parks within which all commercial activity would be prohibited. It was the brainchild of President Roosevelt, an innovative effort to extend the American system of national parks more broadly across the continent.

The tribunal was totally unsympathetic to the argument. It rejected any suggestion that environmental objectives could colour the nature and amount of the obligation which Costa Rica owed to foreigners who invested within her borders. It was right that Costa Rica should be ordered to pay compensation for an expropriation which had occurred and for which compensation had not been paid. But the tribunal went further. It decided that the amount of compensation could not be affected in any way by environmental considerations: while an expropriation for environmental purposes could be 'legitimate', the fact that the property was taken for this reason did not affect the nature or the measure of the compensation to be paid for the taking. For good measure the tribunal added: 'The international source of the obligation to protect the environment makes no difference.'[12] In other words, the international rules for the protection of foreign investment and property rights would take precedence over any rules of environmental protection, whether national or international.

This posed a serious problem. Could it be right that one set of international rules should necessarily prevail over another? Does international law recognize an *a priori* hierarchy of values, in which individual property rights (of foreign investors only, not locals) should have primacy over collective environmental (or other social) interests? The answer to that question determines the balance that is to be struck between competing social values. If the decision in the Costa Rica case was correct, then the practical consequence may be to prevent states, in particular developing states, from taking measures to give effect to their international obligations to protect their environmental patrimony. Faced with the payment of 'market value', which could include long-term profits, they may decide that they just cannot afford to adopt the protective measure. Against that, it is of course important to guard against abuse of the right to protect the environment at the cost of foreign (or indeed domestic) property rights. This ICSID decision has been criticized for not striking the right balance. It resembles, in this sense, the old GATT decision on Mexican tuna rather than the new WTO decision on Malaysian shrimp.

A second case was the decision of a NAFTA arbitration tribunal in *Metalclad Corporation v. Mexico*, dating back to August 2000. This was the most controversial (and widely publicized) decision of any NAFTA or ICSID arbitration tribunal, generating more hits on google.com than most other international decisions.[13] The very broad approach to the definition of 'expropriation' which it adopted has only been followed in one other case of which I am aware. Nevertheless the case merits attention, because it shows the potential effect that international arbitral tribunals can have on domestic decision-making, as well as the local impact of obscure international treaties, the provisions of which have never been fully debated by national parliaments. The case raised issues not only about the role of international law in balancing competing social objectives (property rights versus environmental protection), but also constitutional issues of fundamental importance within Mexico on the allocation of decision-making powers between different levels of government (municipality/state/federal) in a federal system.[14] This is termed federalism in the US, subsidiarity in the EU.

A Mexican company owned a green-field (i.e. undeveloped) site in the valley of La Pedrera, near the township of Guadalcazar, in the Mexican state of San Luis Potosí, about 425 kilometres north-east of Mexico City. Guadalcazar is a small town of several hundred inhabitants. Most live in considerable poverty. In 1990 the Mexican company began to operate a hazardous waste transfer station at the site, under an authorization granted by Mexico's federal government. The following year, under local pressure, the federal government ordered the closure of the waste transfer station. This followed the discovery that more than 20,000 tons of waste had been dumped illegally on the site. The Mexican company nevertheless decided that it wanted to build a hazardous waste landfill at the site. The federal government granted two permits for the construction and operation of a landfill, and the state of San Luis Potosí granted a land use permit. In the meantime, however, the local municipality had refused an application to build the hazardous landfill. In fact it did so twice, in 1991 and again in 1992. The municipal council resolved never to allow the proposed landfill to open. The case raised issues that we are all familiar with: central government takes one view on the desirability of a controversial application to dispose of hazardous waste, but the local community and its residents who have to co-exist with the site take a very different view.

In the middle of this dispute, in 1993, along came the Metalclad Corporation from California, which bought the Mexican company and the site. The investment was made in the full knowledge that the local municipality objected to a landfill. Indeed, Metalclad had explicitly made three-quarters of the purchase price contingent upon the resolution of the permit dispute with the municipality. Construction of the landfill then began without the municipal permit having been granted. The municipality ordered a halt to construction. A further application was made for the local construction permit, but again the municipality refused. Nevertheless construction continued. By March 1995 construction of the landfill had been completed, but without the necessary municipal permit. The Mexican federal government then granted authorization to operate the landfill for an initial period of five years. It later increased the annual capacity of the facility to 300,000 tons of waste, from 36,000 tons. The municipality remained steadfast in its opposition. In April 1996 once again it rejected the application for a local construction permit. Metalclad challenged the municipality's refusal in the Mexican federal court, but the court dismissed the application on the grounds that local administrative remedies were available and had not been exhausted. The company appealed to the Mexican Supreme Court. That case was abandoned when the company realized that other remedies might be available, including recourse to the NAFTA's investor protection rules.

By October 1996 the situation was as follows: the facility had been constructed, the necessary federal and state authorizations had been granted, but the remaining permit (which was needed from the local municipality) had not been obtained. To add to Metalclad's difficulties, in September 1997 the governor of the state of San Luis Potosí took a further step which would limit the landfill's prospects: he issued an ecological decree which declared an area of 188,758 hectares within the local municipality, including the landfill site, to be an ecological preserve for the protection of cacti.

It was at this point that the NAFTA rules on the protection of investors came into play. Metalclad started ICSID arbitration proceedings against Mexico, alleging that Mexico had violated its obligations under Articles 1105 and 1110 of NAFTA.[15] Article 1105 of NAFTA requires Mexico to treat Canadian and US investments 'in accordance with international law, including fair and equitable treatment'. The Arbitral Tribunal summarily ruled that Mexico had not treated Metalclad fairly and equitably because it had not provided a transparent and predictable regulatory framework for Metalclad's investment. It held that the municipality's refusal to grant the construction permit was inconsistent with its rights and with Mexican federal laws, which overrode local laws on the relevant environmental issues.

Metalclad also sued under Article 1110 of NAFTA. This provision prohibits Mexico from nationalizing or expropriating an investment of an American or Canadian investor or taking a measure which is 'tantamount to nationalization or expropriation', unless certain conditions have been satisfied, including the payment of compensation. Remarkably, the Arbitral Tribunal ruled that Mexico had indirectly expropriated Metalclad's investment. The reasoning is somewhat tortuous: by tolerating the municipality's refusal to grant the local construction permit, Mexico had, in effect, acquiesced in the denial to Metalclad of its right to operate the landfill as approved and endorsed by the federal government. The decision has the effect of extinguishing local decision-making authority. It is as though the tribunal had decided that the international rules against expropriation allow – even require – central government to override the wishes of a local community, even where that community's actions have not been found to be illegal under local law and the investment was made in full knowledge of local opposition. The tribunal awarded Metalclad nearly $17 million in damages.

To be able to come to such a far-reaching conclusion the tribunal had to adopt a rather broad definition of 'expropriation'. It ruled that:

expropriation under NAFTA includes not only open, deliberate and acknowledged takings of property, such as outright seizure or formal or obligatory transfer of title in favour of the host State, but also covert or incidental interference with the use of property which has the effect of depriving the owner, in whole or in significant part, of the use or reasonably-to-be-expected economic benefit of property even if not necessarily to the obvious benefit of the host State.[16]

On the basis of this definition the tribunal also ruled that the Ecological Decree issued by the governor of San Luis Potosí in September 1997 'had the effect of barring forever the operation of the landfill' and its implementation would, in and of itself, constitute 'an act tantamount to expropriation'.

I have not been able to find a precedent for the definition of expropriation which was adopted by the Arbitral Tribunal in the Metalclad case. The one case that was cited in the decision was totally different. The implications of the award – if followed – are remarkably far-reaching. It could render expropriatory in character many environmental laws, labour standards, and human rights obligations, significantly limiting countries' ability to legislate. In relation to climate change, for example, new anti-pollution laws restricting the use of coal could easily be argued to have the effect of depriving the owner of a coal-fired power plant of a 'significant part of the . . . reasonably-to-be-expected economic benefit of property'. Environmental taxes which discourage the use of SUV cars could be argued to be 'tantamount to expropriation' if it could be shown that the motor company manufacturing SUVs lost a 'reasonably-to-be-expected' economic benefit. Will a country which has adopted such a law be deemed to have expropriated the property of a foreign investor? In relation to the protection of health, for example, could it not be said that restrictions on advertising or the requirement to place health warnings on harmful products could constitute an indirect expropriation of the property owner's packaging?

The controversial Metalclad decision took the rules of international law on the protection of foreign investors' property rights into a new area. This goes well beyond the classical rules of international law, or what NAFTA's negotiators had envisaged. The ruling is based on the unstated assumption that property rights trump all other rights.

It contains no language which would leave much room for legitimate governmental measures to promote other social values, such as health and environmental protection, or human rights. Unlike the decision in the shrimp/turtle case, where the Appellate Body of the WTO was careful to balance different social objectives, the Metalclad decision is one-sided. No doubt the Mexican government can be criticized for certain aspects of its behaviour towards Metalclad, including undertakings which its employees may have been given about the prospects for future environmental authorizations. But those wrongs could be addressed in other ways, and the ruling goes beyond what is necessary to protect the legitimate interests of investors or to encourage investments to be made. It opens the door to the inappropriate use of foreign investment rules to attack governmental actions and laws even when they are reasonable and pursue legitimate objectives.

Needless to say, the ruling has been attacked. 'A vivid illustration of what critics mean when they allege that free-trade deals amount to a "bill of rights for multinational corporations"', is the way Naomi Klein put it.[17] 'We underestimated the potential power grab and damage potential to the fundamentals of governance,' said Lori Wallach, the director of Public Citizen's Global Trade Watch, the Washington-based advocacy group, even before the Arbitral Tribunal gave its award.[18] Wrong, countered the President of Metalclad: 'Neither Canada nor Mexico has internal protections for private property, and there is a tremendous justification for a treaty to override federal, state or local law to provide protections for foreign investment.'[19]

In fact, the system of international law has its own self-correcting mechanisms, so some of the ruling's excesses have been overturned. An obscure and previously unused legal procedure allowed the Mexican government to appeal the decision to the Canadian courts, solely on the basis that the arbitration had been held in the Canadian province of British Columbia. The Supreme Court of British Columbia set aside those parts of the award relating to Article 1105 of NAFTA, on the grounds that the Arbitral Tribunal had gone beyond what it was permitted to do. The Supreme Court also found that the tribunal's analysis of Article 1105 had tainted its interpretation of Article 1110 (on expropriation), so it set aside that part of the arbitrators' award which concerned the Mexican government's failure to override the local municipality's refusal to grant a construction permit. But given the restrictions on its power to review the award under Canadian law, the Supreme Court left intact the tribunal's decision on the effects of the 1997 Ecological Decree: it agreed that the tribunal had given 'an extremely broad definition of expropriation for the purposes of Article 1110', but declared that the definition of expropriation was a legal issue it could not interfere with. So that part of the arbitral award was upheld, even if the Supreme Court was plainly troubled by its implications.

NGOs and the Canadian courts were not the only ones to show their disapproval. The three NAFTA signatories – Canada, Mexico and the US – intervened to show their distaste for the award. In July 2001 they adopted an interpretative statement on Article 1105 of NAFTA, overturning the Arbitral Tribunal's ruling.[20] They also repeatedly criticized the award when claimants subsequently based their claims on its very broad reasoning.

Nevertheless, the Metalclad ruling continues to be relied on in other cases. In Bolivia, a consortium including the Bechtel Group is reportedly relying on the case to attack that government's decision to reverse the privatization of the water supply in Bolivia's third largest city, Cochabamba. The decision followed local unrest as a result of sharp price increases in the cost of water, a story described in the *New Yorker* magazine. And it is not just against 'developing countries' that expropriation claims are being brought. NAFTA cases are pending against the United States, attacking amongst various targets environmental laws in California and the rights of indigenous Indian communities to stop a gold-mining project. The Metalclad decision has generated a backlash and a rethink about the shape and direction of foreign investment agreements. It has also given rise to a new public scrutiny of those international agreements.

*

One immediate effect of public attention is that it has made it much more difficult to supplement the myriad number of bilateral investment agreements with a global investment protection agreement. In 1995 negotiations began at the Organization for Economic Cooperation and Development (OECD) in Paris for a Multilateral Agreement on Investment (MAI) to establish global rules on foreign investment protection. Curiously, the OECD is not a global organization. Its thirty or so members represent only the leading industrial economies, and it is hard to understand why the rest of the world would sign up to a treaty which they were not allowed to negotiate. So the negotiations got off on the wrong footing, and the OECD members could not even get close to agreement on basic issues. The negotiations collapsed in 1998 in the face of opposition from a number of governments, including France, and major NGOs such as Christian Aid, Oxfam, Greenpeace and Friends of the Earth. Insurmountable differences had emerged over the balance to be struck between the obligation not to expropriate (or otherwise interfere with) an investment, and the maintenance, adoption or enforcement of local rules, including rules on culture and language, pollution and health standards, and employment conditions. Three years later there was a renewed effort for a global agreement. Meeting in Doha, the capital of Qatar, in 2001, WTO ministers agreed on the principle of adopting global investment protection rules within the framework of the WTO. They recognized 'the case for a multilateral framework to secure transparent, stable and predictable conditions for long-term cross-border investment, particularly foreign direct investment, that will contribute to the expansion of trade'. They aimed at concluding the negotiations by 1 January 2005. That date has come and gone without agreement. Vivid and sharp differences divide the negotiators on the implications of any future agreement on issues of culture, employment, pollution and health. It is plain that the attention of civil society – NGOs and industry – will make agreement even more difficult. But if that is the price to be paid for rules which have a greater degree of democratic legitimacy, and which have been adopted under transparent and accountable conditions, then it is a price worth paying. Against that, the lack of progress on multilateral rules has led to renewed interest in bilateral agreements, in the negotiation of which the weaker partner invariably has less political leverage.

More significantly, in bilateral negotiations the issues raised by the Metalclad ruling (as well as other cases) are transforming government thinking. So long as restrictions on expropriation and related government actions were seen as a way of constraining developing countries, Washington was happy to support an expansive approach. But as the new and broad definitions of 'expropriation' and similar terms have emerged it has become clear that the actions of American municipalities, states and even the federal government are ripe for attack by aggrieved investors. International rules promoting opportunities for American companies abroad are now being used to challenge American pollution and health standards. A system which was designed to address governmental 'excesses' in the developing world is increasingly being used against those who designed the system.

Ten NAFTA cases have now been filed against the US. In some cases the arbitration process is seen as preferable to an appeal in the national courts. After the United States Supreme Court refused to hear an appeal from the highest court in Massachusetts, in a case brought by a Canadian real estate company challenging a Massachusetts law, the Chief Justice of the Massachusetts court assumed the case was over. 'I was at a dinner party,' Chief Justice Margaret Marshall is reported to have said, when she heard that her court's decision was being challenged to international arbitration. 'To say I was surprised to hear that a judgment of this court was being subjected to further review would be an understatement.'[21] It remains to be seen whether, as foreign investment law increasingly imposes constraints on the US, its support for these rules of international law will continue to grow. The first signs of change are there. Although the Bush Administration has maintained strong support for bilateral investment agreements, the latest drafts to emerge from the bowels of government propose significant changes. Last year the Administration published a new model investment agreement, cutting back the definition of expropriation to a more traditional and restricted meaning. The proposal has met with great opposition from large sections of the American business community, but the US Justice Department and the State Department have weighed in to support more limited investment protections. The changes are not only substantive. Two recent US bilateral agreements – with Chile and Singapore – not only include more restrictive language, but they also envisage mechanisms to permit appeals against decisions of Arbitral Tribunals which stray off course. And the most recent free trade agreement (with Australia) does not include investor-state arbitration at all.

*

The international rules on the protection of foreign investments catalyse international flows of capital. They are an engine of economic globalization. But they can also constrain the application of legitimate health, environmental and employment standards. The Metalclad case put the spotlight on a growing challenge to the legitimacy of these international rules, illuminating their impact on local autonomy and decision-making. The way in which these agreements are made needs to be revisited. As far as I am aware, in Britain there has never been a parliamentary debate on bilateral investment agreements. I recall watching the BBC television programme *Question Time* in the late 1990s, in which a live studio audience puts questions to a panel of leading public figures. In response to a question about the OECD's proposed Multilateral Agreement on Investment, the then Home Secretary, Jack Straw, made it clear that he had never heard about the MAI, that it had not been discussed in Cabinet. The situation in the US was much the same, as Joseph Stiglitz attests. Abner Mikva, a former US Congressman, federal appeals judge and White House general counsel for Bill Clinton, was more biting: 'If Congress had known that there was anything like this in NAFTA they would never have voted for it.'[22]

The Santa Elena and Metalclad cases reflect a tendency to interpret and apply bilateral investment treaties as though they existed in isolation from other international laws. But there should be no *a priori* hierarchy between the private property rights of foreigners and other values, which are also reflected in global rules. The US is belatedly recognizing that foreign investment is a two-way street, and that the US too is vulnerable to challenge. This is forcing a rethink as to the real purpose of the international rules on expropriation.[23] They can be treated as a cost internalization scheme, so that states take into account and meet the full economic consequences of their acts. Or they can be seen as an insurance scheme, in which the state becomes the insurer of last resort against an investment which fails because of the acts of some foreign government. Or they can promote fairness in relations between a foreign investor and the state. They can create conditions in which foreign investment is made attractive and secure – but not at any price. Why should the property of foreign investors be given greater protection than that of nationals, which are subject to general human rights standards? Why should foreign investors be entitled to avoid going to national courts if effective remedies are available? Why should international law allow any particular category of persons to be treated preferentially, and be allowed to internationalize a dispute without first having made at least some minimum effort to engage in available and effective municipal remedies? Why should decisions affecting vital social issues – labour, environment, human rights – be left to arbitrators who serve on a temporary basis and are privately appointed with no longer term institutional or social duties other than to the parties who appointed them?

These are the important questions that demand greater public attention and scrutiny. In the meantime, the ICSID system gives rise to its own curious beneficiaries, and its own consequences for enhancing capital flows to impecunious Central European countries. When I visited Tirana in June 1999 to celebrate Albania's success in the Tradex case, I noticed that Albania's star witness, the expert on melons and cotton, was absent. 'Where is X?' I asked. 'Oh, didn't you hear?' came the response. 'After the hearing we spent a day in London. When we met at the airport he didn't turn up. He stayed in London. He is selling balloons in Trafalgar Square. He sends home the money to his wife and children; they are very happy.'

7

Guantánamo:
the Legal Black Hole

'[A]s critical as the Government's interest may be in detaining those who actually pose an immediate threat to the national security of the United States during ongoing international conflict, history and common sense teach us that an unchecked system of detention carries the potential to become a means for oppression and abuse of others who do not present that sort of threat.'

Sandra Day O'Connor, US Supreme Court, *Hamdi v. Rumsfeld*, 29 June 2004

In January 2002 extremely disturbing images made their way on to television screens and the front pages of newspapers around the globe. They showed groups of bound and shackled men, dressed in orange jumpsuits, on their knees, heads bowed, under armed guard, in narrow enclosures behind barbed wire. Others showed men, also in orange jumpsuits, in the hold of an aircraft, bound and hooded, or wearing blacked-out goggles. These were the first photographs of captives taken in America's 'war on terrorism', a war that followed the 9/11 attacks and the military response of America and its NATO allies in Afghanistan.

These detainees were being held at the American military base at Guantánamo on the island of Cuba, or they were being transported to that base from Afghanistan or other unspecified parts of the world. Within months there were more than 650 detainees, from over forty countries. They were said to be officials and supporters of Afghanistan's Taliban regime, or of the al-Qaeda terrorist organization which was responsible for 9/11. Within a few days Vice President Dick Cheney was explaining on American television that these men were 'the worst of a very bad lot', devoted to 'killing millions of Americans'. They would continue to be held because they 'probably have information that we need to prosecute the war on terrorism'.[1] Later, with Tony Blair alongside, President Bush responded to journalists' questions. He had clearly made up his mind as to their guilt: 'The only thing we know for certain is that these are bad people.'[2] It soon became clear that the 'bad people' would be held at the will of the American President, until he had decided what to do with them. They were being held at Guantánamo because it was outside the sovereign territory of the United States and the Administration believed that this geographic fact would remove all legal protections – both of American constitutional law and international law.

The 'bad people' were put in a legal black hole. They would have no possibility of legal representation. They could have no right of access to any court or tribunal. They could be held until the end of the 'war on terrorism' without charge, indefinitely and for ever if necessary. They would be interrogated. They might face the possibility of truncated military proceedings before tribunals which could apply the death penalty. And they would have no rights under any of the rules of international law which Roosevelt and Churchill had championed in the 1940s. In particular, they would have no rights under the Geneva Conventions of 1949, intended to protect combatants and civilians from the excesses of war and armed conflict.

Amongst the Guantánamo detainees were nine British nationals. As rumours emerged that the conditions of their detention did not meet international standards, the British government faced an acute political problem. Indefinite detention without charge, or access to lawyer or court, violates the most fundamental principle of the English common law and all civilized legal systems. The right to *habeas corpus* is the cornerstone of the rule of law; it is a fundamental norm of international law which was codified at the instigation of the Americans and British in response to the horrors of the 1930s and the Second World War,[3] and means that no government can deprive a man of his liberty unless authorized by a court of law.[4] It is a principle which applies to every citizen and in every state, at all times.

*

The rules of international law which are applicable to the Guantánamo detainees are set out in two separate but related groups of treaties. Both have near universal support, and the US played a central role in promulgating them. They include 'intransgressible norms' of international law, rules which cannot be abrogated under any circumstances. The first set of rules is contained in international agreements which place limits on the conduct of warfare; in particular, they regulate the treatment of combatant prisoners of war and civilians. These rules are known as the *jus in bello*, or international humanitarian law. In their modern form they date back to the middle of the nineteenth century, although their historical antecedents go back much further. The second set of rules – which is more recent – embodies fundamental human rights and was first negotiated in the 1940s, after the Second World War. Notwithstanding these two sets of rules, the Bush Administration claimed the right to treat the Guantánamo detainees without regard to international law, relying on three arguments.

The first is that the Guantánamo detainees have no rights under international humanitarian law because the American President has decided that all of the detainees were 'unlawful combatants'. Al-Qaeda detainees are, it is said, part of a foreign terrorist organization which is not a state and cannot be a party to the Geneva Conventions; hence its personnel are not entitled to proper POW status. As to the Taliban detainees, they do not qualify for POW status because they do not meet the requirements for lawful combatant status, in particular, the need to display a 'fixed distinctive sign recognizable at a distance'.[5] By this logic, neither category is entitled as of right to any of the protections under the third Geneva Convention of 1949, which protects POWs, or indeed any other treaties.

The second argument is that none of the detainees have enforceable rights under human rights norms because they are being held outside the territory of the United States, on land leased from Cuba. The US Solicitor General could not have put it more bluntly in his argument to the US Supreme Court: the International Covenant on Civil and Political Rights 'is inapplicable to conduct by the United States outside its sovereign territory'.[6]

The third argument is that none of the treaties in question, such as the 1984 Convention against Torture, can impose any additional legal obligations beyond those already found in American law. So if it is consistent with American law, then it must be consistent with international law. And, so the argument goes, since the treatment of the detainees – and in particular the conduct of interrogations – is fully consistent with American law, there can be no question of any violation of international law. This has since become a major issue for the treatment of prisoners at Abu Ghraib, in Iraq, and elsewhere.

With these three arguments the lawyers for the Bush Administration have, in effect, constructed a scheme which takes the United States beyond the constraints of international law. Either the global rules do not apply or, if they do, they create no enforceable rights for any of the detainees. It follows that the US is free to treat them entirely as it wishes. This is a startling proposition. It threatens dire consequences for the protection of human rights around the world. It is deeply disturbing that lawyers in the service of a government committed to the rule of law could so advise, and that the advice could then be acted upon. In fact, each limb of the legal analysis is wrong. To appreciate the full extent to which the arguments undermine established principles of international law it is necessary to look a little more closely at the rules.

*

International humanitarian law aims to protect any person who is caught up in war or armed conflicts, whether civilian or combatant. It places constraints on sovereign freedoms, prohibits certain types of weaponry, regulates the conditions under which an occupied territory and its population are to be treated, and creates minimum standards of protection in the treatment of prisoners of war. These rules are regularly invoked by the United States when its soldiers are taken prisoner and have been applied by the US consistently, from Vietnam to Somalia, and no military lawyers are more conscious of the protections afforded by humanitarian law than those of the United States. The rules are overseen by the Red Cross and are well established, even if many non-lawyers will find it curious, or even offensive, that international rules should constrain the conduct of warfare, and in so doing, justify killing. It is frequently argued that the effect of these rules is to make offensive and inappropriate behaviour legitimate. But the rationale is that wars happen, whether just or unjust, lawful or unlawful, and there must be constraints on the actions of soldiers. This is part of law's function as a 'gentle civilizer of nations', as the Finnish academic Martti Koskenniemi has aptly put it.

In their modern form the rules date back to 1868. Meeting in St Petersburg, representatives of sixteen countries adopted a Declaration to renounce the use of small explosive projectiles in times of war. The Declaration was intended to strike a balance between the 'necessities of war' and the 'requirements of humanity'. It aimed to alleviate 'as much as possible the calamities of war' by prohibiting certain weapons which caused unnecessary suffering.[7] The St Petersburg Declaration marked a first attempt at international codification. But it was not the first time that methods and means of warfare had been regulated. Ancient examples include the Hindu prohibition against using poisoned arrows, and similar requirements exist in the Islamic legal tradition and in Roman and Greek laws.[8] Shakespeare's *Henry V* is frequently quoted as dramatizing the barbarity resulting from the unconstrained treatment of prisoners in the name of military necessity.[9]

At the initiative of Russia's Tsar Nicholas II, an international Peace Conference was convened at The Hague in 1899. It was the first of its kind, and produced international rules on the treatment of prisoners of war,[10] as well as codifying the obligations to distinguish between combatants and non-combatants. The 1899 rules applied to combatants, whether as armies, militia or volunteer corps, provided that they met certain conditions: they had to have a fixed distinctive emblem recognizable at a distance, they had to carry arms openly, and they were obliged to conduct their operations in accordance with the laws and customs of warfare.[11] These were rules applied to formal warfare and do not encompass guerrilla warfare, or the activities of al-Qaeda and other terrorist organizations. The acts of such groups – like the provisional IRA – have often been treated as a matter for the ordinary criminal law.[12]

The 1899 Hague Convention required that combatants and certain other individuals who were prisoners of war had to be treated humanely. The idea was to get them off the battlefield. They could then be interned, and even required to work. The governments which held them were obliged to feed, clothe and house them under the same conditions as the troops of the government which had captured them. And – famously – limits were put on the interrogation of prisoners of war:

Every prisoner of war, if questioned, is bound to declare his true name and rank, and if he disregards this rule, he is liable to a curtailment of the advantages accorded to the prisoners of war of his class.[13]

Implicit in this early international rule is a strict limit on the right of the detaining power to interrogate combatants. The Convention assumes that neither the conflict nor detention will be indefinite: the prisoners of war must be repatriated 'as speedily as possible' after the conclusion of peace.

In 1947 the Nuremberg Military Tribunal confirmed that captivity during war is 'neither revenge, nor punishment, but solely protective custody, the only purpose of which is to prevent the prisoners of war from further participation in the war'.[14] The rules were revisited and overhauled after the brutal experiences of the Second World War. The International Committee for the Red Cross had formulated new proposals, as the international guardian of humanitarian law. In 1949 a diplomatic conference in Geneva adopted four new conventions, including Geneva Convention III, on the Treatment of Prisoners of War. This greatly expanded the scope of the protections, and the details. Article 3 of the Convention (which is known as 'Common Arrticle 3' because it is common to all four of the 1949 Conventions) establishes minimum standards for anyone who is taking no active part in hostilities, including a prohibition on 'the passing of sentences and the carrying out of executions without previous judgment pronounced by a regularly constituted court affording all the judicial guarantees which are recognized as indispensable by civilized peoples'. Prisoners of war were to be treated humanely, and protected against 'acts of violence or intimidation and against insults, and public curiosity' (Article 13). This provision is designed to prevent the parading of POWs, or the publication of their photographs. Therefore the broadcasting of images of Saddam Hussein after he was caught in December 2003 is hardly consistent with this rule. Article 4 of the Convention identifies the categories of persons who are entitled to prisoner of war status. Article 5 sets out a procedure which must be followed where status is uncertain:

Should any doubt arise as to whether persons, having committed a belligerent act and having fallen into the hands of the enemy, belong to any of the categories enumerated in Article 4, such persons shall enjoy the protection of the present Convention until such time as their status has been determined by a competent tribunal.

This obligation lies at the heart of the debate concerning the treatment of the Guantánamo detainees – their right of access to a court or tribunal. The Bush Administration has claimed that since there is no doubt that the detainees are not entitled to prisoner of war status there can be no question of giving them access to a 'competent tribunal' to clarify their status. The claim is directly contradicted by the US's own *Field Manual 27–10* (on the law of land warfare), which makes it abundantly clear that a doubt arises whenever a captive who has participated in hostilities asserts a right to be a POW.[15] On its own past practice, it is not for the US to make the determination, and this breach has infuriated many lawyers in the US military and in the Department of State, who are rightly concerned that the precedent will be relied upon against the US. Furthermore, by so acting, by unilaterally deciding that there is no doubt, the Administration circumvents the guarantees of Geneva Convention III. On this approach, the rules which limit how an interrogation may be conducted, or which set the conditions for detention, are made inapplicable. The Red Cross has publicly stated its disagreement with the US,[16] but the US has not budged. The British government, the US's closest ally, took no public stance to contradict the US's position.

The substantive provisions of the 1949 Convention were revisited again in 1977, in the aftermath of the Vietnam War. One Protocol to the 1949 Geneva Conventions was adopted on the protection of victims of international armed conflict and another on internal armed conflict. Geneva Protocol I, as it is known, recognized that there would be some conflicts where the armed combatant would not distinguish himself from the civilian population, as the rules required. Did that person cease to have any legal protections? No. Protocol I makes it clear that certain combatants who do not meet the conditions entitling them to prisoner of war status are nevertheless entitled to protections which are equivalent to those accorded to POWs by the 1949 Geneva Conventions, where such persons are tried and punished for offences which they have committed.[17] This is based on a simple premise: no person can ever fall outside the scope of minimum legal protections. There can be no legal black holes. The point is underscored by Article 75 of the 1977 Protocol I. This is a sort of 'catch-all' for anyone not entitled to the full benefits of Additional Protocol I or the earlier Conventions. Article 75 is unambiguous: any person who is captured by a party to a conflict must be treated humanely and is entitled to enjoy the minimum protections, without discrimination. The particular circumstances of any individual are irrelevant. It provides guarantees for members of the Taliban and al-Qaeda, for 'terrorist' and for 'unlawful combatant'. Nationality is irrelevant. It prohibits violence, including torture of all kinds and threats of torture, and outrages on personal dignity, including humiliating and degrading treatment and any form of indecent assault. A detained person has the right to be informed promptly of the reasons for his detention, and a right to be released 'with the minimum delay possible', except for criminal offences. If there are criminal proceedings, then detainees are entitled to the benefits of 'generally recognized principles of regular judicial procedure'. The presumption of innocence, the right against self-incrimination, and the right to examine witnesses are amongst those basic guarantees.

These rules of international humanitarian law are well established. They were not especially controversial before 2001, even if they were not always respected. The United States is a party to both the 1907 Hague Convention IV and the 1949 Geneva Convention III. It has also signed the Geneva Protocol I but has not yet ratified that treaty. However, it is broadly recognized that Article 75 reflects a rule of customary international law. It is therefore applicable to all states and to all persons. The US Army's *Operational Law Handbook* recognizes the applicability of Article 75 guarantees to the US.[18] When US Attorney General John Ashcroft publicly describes the detainees – collectively – as uniquely dangerous individuals, or when President Bush refers to the British detainees as 'killers' or 'terrorists', they violate these rules of international law. They make it impossible for these and other men to get a fair hearing in the United States, and they make it less likely that the US will be able to obtain respect for these standards when its nationals are captured, a point which has not been lost on the very many US government lawyers who have objected strongly to these decisions.

*

The rules of international humanitarian law deal with armed conflicts. They do not address the international requirements for the treatment by a state of its own nationals, or foreigners, in other situations, when there is no armed conflict, or when a state does not wish to characterize a particular situation as one of armed conflict. International terrorism raises a strategic issue: do you proceed on the basis that an armed conflict exists, in which case humanitarian law applies? If you do not, the rules of criminal law apply, subject to human rights constraints. Britain consistently refused to treat IRA prisoners as POWs on the grounds that it considered there to be no armed conflict. Therefore the IRA was subject to the criminal law, in accordance with international human rights law, a more recent arrival on to the international arena.

Until 1945 there were no general rules of international law which limited a state's treatment of its own citizens and others within its jurisdiction. There were a small number of treaties protecting the rights of some minorities against some discriminatory acts; for example in relation to jobs and languages. And there were some workplace treaties governing working conditions for children and pregnant women. But torture and discrimination, arbitrary detention, mass murder, even genocide, were not outlawed by treaty or prohibited by other clear rules of international law before 1945.

The Second World War changed all that. Led by the United States and Britain, the Allies took radical steps to replace the legal vacuum with a rules-based system of minimum human rights which were to apply universally. With the Atlantic Charter, Roosevelt and Churchill committed the Allies to the principle that 'men in all lands may live out their lives in freedom from fear and want'. The United Nations Charter of June 1945 transformed that principle into an affirmation of 'faith in fundamental human rights'. The Charter identified one of the United Nations' basic purposes as the promotion of 'respect for human rights and for fundamental freedoms for all without distinction as to race, sex, language or religion'. With these simple words the door was opened to a new global legal order, one which would eventually lead to the Pinochet judgment in the House of Lords. For the first time states accepted that they had no unfettered right to act, that they were constrained in the treatment of all people within their territories or within their control. The UN Charter catalysed a hugely ambitious project. Over the next five decades minimum international standards would be put in place which were applicable to all persons, rather than states, across the entire globe.

Within a year of the UN Charter being adopted, the members created a Commission on Human Rights. Two years later, in December 1948, the fifty-eight members of the United Nations General Assembly unanimously adopted a Universal Declaration of Human Rights. It set out a 'common standard for all peoples and all nations' of rights and freedoms of universal application.[19] The Declaration took up the language of the French and American constitutions, but drew on many religious and political traditions. It affirmed everyone's right to life, liberty and security (Article 3). It prohibited arbitrary detention or arrest (Article 9). And it confirmed that everyone was entitled to 'a fair and public hearing by an independent and impartial tribunal, in the determination of his rights and obligations and of any criminal charge against him' (Article 10). This language follows the Fifth Amendment to the US Constitution (the due process clause), which provides that no person shall be 'deprived of life, liberty or property without due process of law'. The Declaration also affirmed the right to guarantees that were necessary for the conduct of a defence in criminal proceedings (Article 11). It codified basic and fundamental rights, at the international level. These were inherent rights to be enjoyed by all human beings of the global village – men, women and children, as well as by any group of society, disadvantaged or not – and were not 'gifts' to be withdrawn, withheld or granted at anyone's whim or will.[20] The Declaration was endorsed by the UN General Assembly the day after the adoption of the Genocide Convention on 10 December 1948. Eleanor Roosevelt had led the US delegation negotiating the Universal Declaration. In her speech to the Assembly that day, she described mankind as being on the threshold of a great event:

This Declaration may well become the international Magna Carta of all men everywhere. We hope its proclamation by the General Assembly will be an event comparable to the proclamation of the Declaration of the Rights of Man by the French people in 1789, the adoption of the Bill of Rights by the people of the United States, and the adoption of comparable declarations at different times in other countries.[21]

It took another twenty years for a legally binding global treaty to be agreed: the International Covenant on Civil and Political Rights was finalized in December 1966, and entered into force in March 1976. The US became a party in 1992, under the presidency of George Bush Senior. On issues concerning detainees, the Covenant generally follows the approach taken by the Universal Declaration, although greater detail is provided. Article 2(1) commits each party 'to respect and to ensure to all individuals within its territory and subject to its jurisdiction the rights recognized in the present Covenant, without distinction of any kind', including national origin. The Human Rights Committee of the United Nations has confirmed that the Covenant applies not just to acts taking place on a state's territory.[22] This makes it crystal clear that the position adopted by the Bush Administration in the Guantánamo case before the US Supreme Court is wrong in the eyes of the main body charged with interpreting the Covenant. The Covenant's obligations apply to Guantánamo Bay in Cuba because it is under the exclusive control and 'jurisdiction' of the United States.

*

A few days after 9/11 President George W. Bush declared a 'war on terror'.[23] The choice of words was significant, although it is now clear that not all the implications were fully thought through and there was no consultation with allies. The formulation took the response to 9/11 outside the ordinary criminal law into the laws of war and armed conflict. Unlike the British government in respect of the IRA, the Bush Administration seemed to be characterizing the struggle as an international armed conflict, although without a state on the other side. In so doing, the Administration placed itself within the constraints of international humanitarian law. This created a dilemma: should 'enemy' individuals be treated as combatants, and if so subject to the laws of war? Or does it mean that they are to be treated as criminals, with all that implies, and subject to the criminal laws of the United States and other countries which may wish to prosecute them?

We now know that the Administration took a conscious decision to use the 'war on terrorism' as a further means to propel its assault on global rules. The US Deputy Assistant Attorney General, John Yoo, could not have been clearer when, in May 2002, he said of the treatment of Guantánamo detainees: 'What the Administration is trying to do is create a new legal regime.'[24] And, he might have added, without bothering to engage our allies and treaty partners. What we did not know then, but do know now because of a series of leaked internal legal opinions which were first published by *Newsweek* magazine and others, is that shortly after 9/11 a small number of government lawyers started focusing on what a new legal regime should look like. The Administration's political masters asked their lawyers to devise ways to minimize the constraints on the Administration in fighting its 'war'. The lawyers assigned to the task were mostly political appointees, not career civil servants, many of whom have objected in strong terms to the advice that was given. One object was to allow as much information as possible to be obtained from detainees. To do that it was necessary to limit, or even suspend, the application of international rules which would constrain techniques of interrogation, including possibly the use of means which could be considered as torture or at least cruel, inhuman or degrading. In December 2001 and January 2002 there was a furious exchange of legal opinions between the Department of State, which plainly wanted to respect the international rules as far as possible, and the Departments of Justice (under John Ashcroft) and Defense (under Donald Rumsfeld), which wanted to limit them. The Ashcroft and Rumsfeld line prevailed. US Secretary of State Colin Powell's argument that al-Qaeda and Taliban fighters should be given access to an Article 5 military tribunal was rejected. In his memorandum of 25 January 2002, White House General Counsel, Alberto Gonzales, made clear the benefits of a determination by the President that, in the circumstances of this war on terrorism, Geneva Convention III did not apply to al-Qaeda or the Taliban:

this new paradigm renders obsolete Geneva's strict limitations on questioning of enemy prisoners and renders quaint some of its provisions [. . .]

Powell's response the following day rejected the argument. He pointed out numerous factual inaccuracies and omissions in Gonzales's reasoning. Powell added that the argument 'is likely to be rejected by foreign governments and will not be respected in foreign courts or international tribunals which may assert jurisdiction'.[25] An equally robust memorandum from William Taft IV, legal adviser to the State Department, made the point that a decision to apply the Geneva Conventions would demonstrate that the 'US based its conduct not just on its policy preferences but on its international legal obligations'.

But he was not sufficiently persuasive. On 7 February 2002, President Bush accepted the conclusions of the Justice Department. He determined that neither Taliban nor al-Qaeda detainees qualified as prisoners of war, but that the American armed forces should treat the detainees humanely and 'in a manner consistent with the principles of Geneva'. However, this was only to be 'to the extent appropriate and consistent with military necessity'. If it was not appropriate, or military necessity required otherwise, then they need not be treated humanely. America was unbound.

Taking the US outside the global legal order was not the path initially chosen after 9/11. On 12 September 2001 the United States had gone to the UN Security Council and obtained a unanimous resolution which condemned the attacks and called on the international community to redouble its efforts to 'prevent and suppress terrorist attacks'. By characterizing the attacks as 'terrorist' the intent seemed to have been to subject the perpetrators to criminal law and process, as the relevant international conventions on terrorism require.[26] But Security Council Resolution 1368 went further. It recognized also the 'inherent right of individual or collective self-defence'. This was not an authorization to use force, but rather a recognition that the circumstances allowed the US to use force in accordance with international law. The resolution's bifurcation was not accidental: it opened the door to military action in Afghanistan. This began with air strikes on 7 October 2001 and by mid-November the Taliban's hold on the country had collapsed. Kandahar was the last city to surrender to anti-Taliban tribes.

An immediate consequence of the Afghan war was the detention of a large number of non-Americans. Many were suspected of being associated with the Taliban government or al-Qaeda. The detainees were held in various parts of Afghanistan, including Kandahar and the now notorious air base at Bhagram. Other detainees were brought to Afghanistan after they had been arrested (and in some cases kidnapped) in other countries, including Pakistan, Malawi and Bosnia.[27] Afghanistan provided a new base from which to fight the 'war on terrorism'. But what to do with the detainees? Were they combatants to be treated as prisoners of war, or were they regular criminals to be subjected to the American courts? Or did they have some other status? The answers to those questions were set out in President Bush's order of 7 February 2002, but also in an earlier Executive Order of 13 November 2001. This established military commissions to try non-Americans who were suspected of 'violating the rules governing the conduct of warfare'.[28] It took nearly three years for the first preliminary hearings to be held, in August 2004. In November 2004, the first trial before a military commission – of Salim Hamdan, reputed to be a driver of Osama bin Laden – was halted by a federal judge in Washington, DC, who ruled that the proceedings lacked the basic elements of a fair trial and violated the Geneva Conventions.

The November 2001 Executive Order applied only to non-Americans whom the President believed to be associated with acts of international terrorism which could harm the US. The Order authorized the detention of persons 'outside or within' the US, and established the ground rules for the conduct of military proceedings. Under these rules the US President has a central role: the prosecutor and adjudicating panels are to be military officers answerable only to him, and it is the President alone who is responsible for the final review of any verdict. However, within two months of the Order's adoption, and well before any proceedings had been initiated against the detainees, the Administration had already decided that the Guantánamo detainees were terrorists and killers.[29]

The military commissions are conducted in secret and the prosecution may rely on secret evidence and witnesses. There is no appeal to any civilian court. The jurisdiction of the military commissions includes acts, such as terrorism, which are generally regarded as criminal and not ordinarily part of humanitarian law and the laws of war. Defendants are to have no right of access to the courts of any other country or to any international tribunals, including human rights courts, and will not be able to choose their own counsel. Communication between defendants and their advisers is restricted. Lord Steyn, the British law lord, has described these tribunals as 'kangaroo courts'.[30] He is right.

After the President's Order was adopted it received global criticism. It has since been amended, but only marginally. Kenneth Roth, Executive Director of Human Rights Watch, has summarized the shortcomings: 'a defendant could be sentenced to death without a public trial, the presumption of innocence, a right to appeal, or even proof of guilt beyond reasonable doubt'.[31] Amnesty International described the President's Order as 'inconsistent with the principles of law and rules of evidence applied to people charged with criminal offences in the US courts'.[32] The US National Association of Criminal Defense Lawyers told its members that it would be unethical for them to represent an accused person before any proceedings, as the rules precluded adequate or ethical representation.[33] Mary Robinson, the United Nations High Commissioner for Human Rights at the time, castigated the US for failing to ensure that detainees were entitled to the protection of international human rights law and humanitarian law, in particular the relevant provisions of the 1966 Covenant and the 1949 Geneva Conventions. The US subsequently blocked her reappointment. And for more than two years the British government made no public criticism, beyond mouthing generalities about some unspecified 'reservations' it might have.

The building blocks were now in place. Steps were being taken to suspend the application of the Geneva Conventions, and proceedings were to be directed towards inadequate military commissions. All that was needed was a place to hold the detainees, where the risk of legal challenges would be removed. The search was on for an 'appropriate' detention camp to round up the terrorists, meaning a secure location outside the United States. The Administration's lawyers dug up a useful decision of the US Supreme Court from 1950. In *Johnson v. Eisentrager* the Supreme Court had ruled that twenty-one Germans, captured in China, imprisoned at an American base in Germany, and subsequently convicted by a US Military Commission, had no right to appeal to the American courts. This was because non-Americans captured and detained outside the territory of the US lacked the 'capacity and standing to invoke the process of [US] federal courts'.[34] The judgment seemed to provide the key: holding the detainees outside the US would avoid the risk of US legal proceedings. This would allow a more 'flexible' approach to interrogations.

The naval base at Guantánamo Bay was the oldest American military base outside US territory. It was in the south-eastern corner of

Cuba, only about 400 miles from Miami, Florida. The American base dates back to December 1903, when the US concluded a treaty with Cuba to lease forty-five square miles at Guantánamo Bay for use as a coaling station. The treaty was reaffirmed in 1934, and extended indefinitely in time. The US pays an annual rent of just $2,000, in gold coins. After being used as a detention camp for Haitian refugees in the 1990s its utility was declining. The 'war on terrorism' provided a new lease of life. The centennial issue of the *Guantánamo Bay Gazette*, published by the US government, proudly describes the camp as being 'at the forefront of the war against global terrorism'.[35] In a radio interview in December 2001, Michael O'Hanlon, Senior Fellow at the Brookings Institution, a well-known think tank in Washington, DC, gave an idea of the Administration's thinking in choosing Guantánamo:

[W]e can sort of do what we want to there. It's on foreign soil and yet the foreign government doesn't have much say in how we use the place. We've used it to detain people in the past [. . .] It's an important base, but it's not the most important operationally for training in the U.S. military, so you can use it for other reasons without disrupting other kinds of military priorities too much. And it's close enough to the United States, you can imagine flying in various intelligence experts to interview these detainees and try to get information from them. So, for a number of reasons, it seems the best choice and I think Rumsfeld is right here to have selected it.[36]

It is ironic that an old treaty with Cuba should be relied on to avoid American obligations under other treaties. But that is one bit of international law which is appreciated by the neo-conservative appointees who advise the Justice and Defense Departments in the Bush Administration.

*

As early as the end of January 2002 the British Foreign Office had confirmed that three of the detainees were British nationals.[37] Two other British nationals, Ferroz Abbassi and Moazzam Begg, were also among the first detainees to arrive at Guantánamo Bay. They had been arrested in Afghanistan. Eighteen months later, in July 2003, they were included in the first group of six Guantánamo detainees to be singled out for proceedings before a military commission. But even then they were not charged, and no information was provided by the

Pentagon as to what they were alleged to have done in Afghanistan, or anywhere else. By December 2004 they still had not been charged and no proceedings had begun.

Media attention has focused on legal concerns, including the conditions under which the detainees were being held. In January 2002, nothing much was known. The detainees had no access to lawyers, and correspondence with families took months, and was censored. The Red Cross visited, but in the initial months maintained a traditional silence. In October 2003, however, more than eighteen months after the camp had been opened, a top Red Cross official broke with tradition and publicly attacked the conditions at the American base. Christopher Girod led a Red Cross team which inspected the detention camp. It was intolerable, he said, that Guantánamo was used as 'an investigation centre, not a detention centre'. He told the *New York Times* that 'the open-endedness of the situation and its impact on the mental health of the population has become a major problem'.[38]

In March 2004, five of the British detainees were released. The 'Tipton Three' – Shafiq Rasul, Ruhal Ahmed and Asif Iqbal – claimed that their interrogations had begun immediately upon arrival at Guantánamo, and that the British secret service, MI5, had participated. They disclosed that they had been held in solitary confinement for three months after they were wrongly identified as being pictured meeting with Osama bin Laden and the leader of the 9/11 hijackers, Mohammed Atta. Under interrogation they gave confessions which were only proved to be false when MI5 provided documentary evidence to show that they had been in the UK on that date. They described interrogation sessions lasting many hours. Ruhal Ahmed described an interrogation session which took place in Afghanistan before he was transferred to Guantánamo: 'All the time I was kneeling with [an MI5] guy standing on the backs of my legs and another holding a gun to my head.'[39]

In May 2004, another released British detainee, Tarek Dergoul, aged twenty-six, described his experience. He had been transferred to Guantánamo after initial detentions at Bhagram and Kandahar, in Afghanistan. He claimed the Americans paid $5,000 for him, to troops loyal to the Northern Alliance. He too described being held in an isolation block, and intensive interrogation. He also described the pre-interrogation process:

They had already searched me and my cell twice that day, gone through my stuff, touched my Koran, felt my body and my private parts. And now they wanted to do it again, just to provoke me, but I said no, because if you submit to everything you turn into a zombie.

I heard a guard talking into his radio, 'ERF, ERF, ERF,' and I knew what was coming – the Extreme Reaction Force. The five cowards I called them – five guys running in with riot gear. They pepper-sprayed me in the face and I started vomiting; in all I must have brought up five cupfuls. They pinned me down and attacked me, poking their fingers in my eyes, and forced my head into the toilet pan and flushed. They tied me up like a beast and then they were kneeling on me, kicking and punching. Finally they dragged me out of the cell in chains, into the rec. yard, and shaved my beard, my hair, my eyebrows.[40]

Not all the detainees were youthful. Camp Delta prison at Guantánamo Bay must have had a geriatric wing. In the autumn of 2003, *Channel 4 News*, an English television programme, broadcast an interview with an elderly Afghan shepherd. He had recently been released after sixteen months at Camp Delta, when it had become clear that he had been picked up in error. He was one of the more than seventy detainees who had been released from Camp Delta, without charge, apology or compensation. Others included Mohammed Sadiq, a ninety-year-old Afghan, and Mohammed Hagi Fiz, described in Florida's *St Petersburg Times* as a toothless and frail man with a bushy beard who claimed to be 105 years old and weighed just 123 pounds. Fiz's family had no idea where he was: 'All they know is that I went to a doctor for treatment and disappeared.' He was released after eight months at Guantánamo, without apology.[41]

Well before the British detainees went public with their allegations of mistreatment, the British government went on the defensive and was forced to justify its approach to the legality of Guantánamo and the treatment of detainees. Early on Foreign Secretary Jack Straw hinted that all the detainees had legal rights, even if they were members of the most dangerous terrorist organization in the world: 'Whether or not technically they have rights under the Geneva Convention, they have rights under customary international law.'[42] But on the very same day his colleague, Defence Secretary Geoff Hoon, took a different tack. Responding to complaints that British nationals had been removed from Afghanistan hooded and manacled together and then flown for twenty-four hours in that condition, he responded assertively: 'There is no doubting the legality in the way these combatants have been imprisoned. There is no doubting the legality of the right of the US . . . to remove them for trial.'[43] If I have come to learn anything about the internal workings of the British government it is that words are carefully chosen by ministers and their civil servants. Mr Hoon's statement is unlikely to have been made unless the British government had rather more information than it was letting on. That would be consistent with the later statements of the British detainees that they had been interrogated by MI5 even before they were taken to Guantánamo.

The British Prime Minister was rather more circumspect. He told the House of Commons that the detainees should be treated 'humanely and in accordance with the Geneva Convention and proper international norms'.[44] This seemed to suggest that the Geneva Conventions were applicable, in the eyes of the British government. But by the end of January 2002 American actions had become a major international issue.

It is a well-established principle of many legal systems that you must not prejudice a possible future trial – whether criminal or military – by publicly commenting on the guilt of the defendants. President George W. Bush was not deterred. Within weeks he had already made his personal views clear and broadcast them around the globe. The Guantánamo detainees were 'unlawful combatants', and they had no rights under international law. They were 'terrorists'; they were 'killers'. There appeared to be no effort to consider each detainee's case individually, and the President was not reined in by his Attorney General (unlike Britain's Home Secretary David Blunkett, who was rebuked by Lord Goldsmith when he made inappropriate comments in another terrorism case in Britain). In fact, US Attorney General John Ashcroft had no qualms about the risk of prejudging future trials. Within a month of Camp Delta's having opened for business he was describing the prisoners as uniquely dangerous individuals and terrorists who had been participants in a 'war crime setting', responsible for killing innocent women and children.[45]

From the outset it was clear that the die was cast. For the Bush Administration, the detainees' guilt was not in question. They were being held for one of two reasons: to obtain additional intelligence information, or because it had been determined that they were dangerous.[46]

*

In setting up Camp Delta in Guantánamo Bay in Cuba the Bush Administration was acutely aware of America's obligations under international law: a strategy was devised to work around them. 'New thinking in the law of war' was the way Bush himself put it.[47] In this way he treats international rules as though they are private contractual rules which the US – as the more powerful contracting party – is free to apply or disregard as it sees fit. Rules which were previously seen as encapsulating American values now imposed unnecessary constraints in fighting the 'war on terrorism'. So they were deemed to be inapplicable, because the detainees were foreigners outside US territory, and because they were combatants who either did not respect the laws of war (Taliban) or cannot invoke them because they are not associated with a state (al-Qaeda). No value is given to the benefits which the rules may provide to Americans, a point which Colin Powell made in his 26 January 2001 memo. Suspending Geneva, he wrote, would 'undermine public support'. It is hard to see how you can win hearts and minds with this approach, which may also provoke foreign prosecutions against US nationals. For example, are private contractors used in the war effort in Iraq to be treated as unlawful combatants? And in the face of America's disavowal, what of the British? Again, silence.

Very early on the Red Cross went public, challenging the concept of 'unlawful combatants' as non-existent in international law. 'You can look through the Geneva Conventions and you will not find it.'[48] Holding the detainees outside the US and reclassifying them as 'unlawful combatants' made it possible to bypass their legal rights. It created the possibility of indefinite detention. And it purported to remove the international legal constraints which prevented interrogators from going beyond the requirement of information as to name, rank and serial number.

A number of Guantánamo detainees brought challenges before the American courts. One case was brought by two of the British detainees (Shafiq Rasul and Asif Iqbal) and two Australian detainees (David Hicks and Mamdouh Habib) to challenge the claim by the US government that it could hold the claimants indefinitely without charge or proof of wrongdoing and with no opportunity for the detainees to establish their innocence. Specifically, they argued that the American courts must give them a judicial forum in which to challenge the factual basis for their detention and its legality under the American Constitution and international law.[49] A second case was brought by the relatives of a group of twelve Kuwaiti detainees.[50] Up to the Federal Court of Appeal these cases failed. The American courts declined jurisdiction, relying on the 1950 US Supreme Court decision in *Johnson v. Eisentrager*.[51] Then, in November 2003, the US Supreme Court decided it would hear the cases on appeal, limited to the narrow point of determining whether the Guantánamo detainees should have any right to challenge their detentions before US federal courts. The decision came as a surprise to the Bush Administration.

Even as the US courts and the British government had been silent, the English courts had sprung into action. How could Guantánamo detainees bring an action in Britain? Through the creative lawyering of Louise Christian. Ms Christian is a campaigning public interest lawyer, based in London, who has a string of high-profile legal successes to her name. She took the case on behalf of Ferroz Abbassi and his mother, Zumrati Juma, challenging the failure of Britain's Foreign Office to take adequate steps to protect the basic human rights of a British citizen. She was inviting the courts to step in to fill the void left by the British government's inaction. Her argument was based on two propositions. First, that Ferroz Abbassi's continued detention violated his fundamental rights under international law, and second that the British government had an obligation in English law to take steps to protect those rights. The argument faced serious hurdles. Not least, she had to persuade the English courts to hear a case which touched on sensitive issues of foreign relations. Such issues have always been treated as a matter for the executive branch of government, and not for the courts. Once she was over that hurdle she would then have to persuade English judges that the US – Britain's closest ally – was violating fundamental human rights, the Geneva Conventions and international law.

Abbassi also had to persuade the English courts that he had a right to force the British government to make diplomatic representations to the US. This argument was helped by some obscure Foreign Office rules, issued in 1988. They set out government policy on diplomatic representations for British citizens denied justice abroad.[52] In 1999 this policy was extended to cover situations where it was alleged that the state of detention was violating international law.[53] This was precisely the case of the British detainees at Guantánamo.

The case put the British government on the back foot. In the autumn of 2002, as the case was heard, the British government was laying out its arguments for action against Iraq. A first dossier, setting out the evidence of Saddam Hussein's continued possession of weapons of mass destruction, and the threat he posed, had been published in September 2002. This was not the moment to engage in public criticism of the US. By then British civil servants had made several visits to the British detainees. But the government had still not expressed any public views as to whether the American position on the Geneva Conventions and the treatment of detainees was consistent with international law. A case before the English courts would mean inevitable public attention being given to the UK's stance.[54] The Foreign Office has consistently taken the position that megaphone diplomacy is ineffective. It prefers its views to be communicated in a discreet, confidential manner. There is much to be said for this approach. On some issues, however, the time comes when a clear public statement is required, especially if you want to avoid the charge that your relationship has ceased to be that of a friendly state, and has become that of a servant state. The indefinite detention of your nationals at Guantánamo is such a time.

The British government defended the English court proceedings with its usual vigour and thoroughness. It succeeded in getting the case thrown out by the first instance court, on the grounds that the case would require the court to enter the 'forbidden domain' of foreign relations. But in July 2002 the Court of Appeal gave Abbassi's lawyers permission to challenge the government's inaction. It set a hearing date for September 2002. The case was fast-tracked. That fact, and the presence of Lord Phillips, the Master of the Rolls and the second most senior judge in the country, as presiding judge, reflected its importance. But the hurdles were considerable. It came as no surprise that the Foreign Office should choose to mount a defence based on the argument that America's actions were simply not justiciable before the English courts. It would be wrong, they argued, for the courts of one country to express a view on the behaviour of another. In one of the most forensically superb pieces of advocacy I have ever seen, Nicholas Blake QC destroyed that argument: '[a]n old view', he said, 'which takes no account of modern developments in international law and human rights'.

The Court of Appeal rejected the government's defence, cautiously but robustly. It ruled that it was 'free to express a view in relation to what it conceives to be a clear breach of international law, particularly in the context of human rights'.[55] In reaching that conclusion, one of the cases it relied on was a landmark 1976 judgment of the House of Lords that the English courts should not recognize a Nazi law which constituted a grave infringement of human rights.[56] The parallels are not identical, but the point was not lost on the many readers of the judgment.

On the merits of the case – was Ferroz Abbassi being treated properly in accordance with international legal standards? – the British government decided that it would not disclose to the court what its views were. In response to Abbassi's claim that he was being arbitrarily detained, the government merely put before the Court of Appeal the arguments which were being made by the US: the detainees were enemy combatants who posed a serious threat to the United States, would be treated humanely, and were being held in accordance with the laws and customs of war. The British government also put before the Court of Appeal the US government's rejection of the recommendation adopted by the Inter-American Commission on Human Rights – a human rights body of the Organization of American States of which the US is a member – that the US should 'take the urgent measures necessary to have the legal status of the detainees at Guantánamo Bay determined by a competent Tribunal'.[57] But the British government expressed no view of its own as to the strength of these arguments: its silence was deafening.

The English Court of Appeal, on the other hand, was not silent. It invoked the principle of *habeas corpus* and the fundamental principle of English law that every imprisonment must be treated as unlawful unless it can be justified. The Court relied on the famous dissenting words of Lord Atkins in a House of Lords judgment given during the Second World War:

Amid the clash of arms, the laws are not silent. They may be changed, but they speak the same language in war as in peace.[58]

The Court approached the case on the basis of human rights law, rather than humanitarian law. Relying on the 1966 Covenant, it ruled unanimously that Ferroz Abbassi was being detained arbitrarily in a 'legal black hole'. This was in breach of fundamental human rights, and it contravened basic principles recognized in international law and in English and American law. It was the absence of legal remedy that really irked the Court, prompted by the British government's tendentious argument that it could imagine some circumstances in which the indefinite detention of a person without charge might not be arbitrary. Pressed by Lord Justice Robert Carnworth to give a single example, counsel for the British government was unable to do so. The Court's response?

What appears to us objectionable is that Mr Abbassi should be subject to indefinite detention in territory over which the United States has exclusive control with no opportunity to challenge the legitimacy of his detention before any court or tribunal.[59]

The Court did not order the Foreign Office to make any particular representations to the United States. Since that would have an impact on the conduct of foreign policy at a delicate time, it was a matter for the government to decide what to do, and how. But the judgment made clear that silence was not an option. The Court expressed the hope that its deep concern and anxiety would be drawn to the attention of the American courts.

The judgment added great authority to those who were relying on international law to challenge the conditions of the Guantánamo detainees. Guantánamo's 'legal black hole' has become a recurring phrase. The judgment also added to pressure from the public at large and from Members of Parliament. By the time President Bush arrived on a state visit to London in November 2003, the international legal issues were the subject of considerable media attention and coincided with the US Supreme Court's preliminary decision to accept a challenge from some of the Guantánamo detainees. By then Lord Goldsmith, the British Attorney General, had assumed the role of principal negotiator with the United States. Yet even then, eighteen months into the detentions, the British government had not set out its view on the minimum standards to which the British and other detainees were entitled under international law. There was no unambiguous condemnation of the treatment, unlike that from the Court of Appeal. Could the detainees be interrogated? Under what conditions? Could the results of any interrogations be used in any criminal or military trials? Should the detainees have access to a tribunal to determine their status? Under what conditions could any trials of criminal activity be conducted? On all these questions the British government was silent. Even more telling was the government's decision not to present any arguments in the Guantánamo proceedings before the US Supreme Court. That was left to the detainees, NGOs, groups such as the Commonwealth Law Association, and to a cross-party group of more than 150 Parliamentarians from the Palace of Westminster.

That is not to say that the British government – and in particular the Attorney General – did not engage actively with the Americans regarding the Guantánamo detainees. I do not know what was said behind closed doors. But with what influence, and to what effect? As early as January 2002 Foreign Secretary Jack Straw expressed a preference for the British detainees to be returned to Britain to face justice.[60] But that view was not universally supported. The Prime Minister identified two options: either there would be sufficient undertakings from the United States about the form of any trial the detainees would face before an American military commission, or the detainees would be returned to the United Kingdom.[61] The Americans appeared willing to allow the detainees to return, but only if they were charged and tried. This presented a serious obstacle in the form of the independent Crown Prosecution Service, the body which would have to decide whether to initiate criminal proceedings against any of the detainees. Lord Brennan QC, a former Chairman of the English Bar, wrote that it would be 'next to impossible' to produce a case against the detainees.[62] Even if there was a case on the basis of any material that had emerged from the interrogations – including 'confessions' extracted under interrogations of the kind described by Tarek Dergoul and the Tipton Three – such material would not be admissible as evidence in any criminal proceedings since it would have been obtained in violation of internationally recognized due process rights. They had had no access to lawyers. If the detainees were to be returned, they would almost certainly have to be released. Having held these 'bad people' without charge or trial for two or more years, that option seemed unacceptable to the US.

The British government therefore shifted the focus on to the conduct of any proceedings against the detainees. By its account it has sought to persuade the US that any trial of British citizens must be conducted 'in accordance with proper international law'. But Chris Mullin, a junior Foreign Office minister, adopted a rather deferential posture: 'the road chosen by the US is clearly set down, and we have to negotiate around that position'.[63] The decision to charge two of the British detainees, in July 2003, caused the British government to revisit its approach. (The approach may be compared to that taken by Paraguay, Germany and Mexico: when the US failed to respect its obligations to provide consular access under the 1963 Convention on Consular Relations, those three countries went off to the World Court in The Hague.) In July, after the detainees had been held for eighteen months without charge or trial, the Prime Minister told the House of Commons that now was 'the right time to make active representations', since the rules for the military commissions had not yet been drawn up.[64] This statement elicited a robust reaction from Professor Ruth Wedgewood, an American legal academic who had advised the US Department of Defense on the military tribunal rules. The rules had long been debated and in the public domain since November 2001, she wrote in the *Financial Times*. The US had been consulting with the British government for months on the question of how to make the trials work well. 'From the chatter of certain British ministers,' she added, 'one might think that the rules and the decisions to prosecute came as a great surprise.'[65]

What exactly had the British government been doing since the detentions became public? For a start, it had been defending its own anti-terrorist practices before the English courts, including the indefinite detention of a number of non-nationals, alleged to have links with al-Qaeda, who could not be removed from the country.[66] Could it be that Britain's public silence on the rights of the Guantánamo detainees had been influenced by its domestic stance? And might it be that interrogations of the Guantánamo detainees – in which MI5 had reportedly been involved – were providing useful evidence for the UK cases? The British government has confirmed that evidence obtained through torture at Guantánamo (or elsewhere) would be admissible in proceedings before the Special Immigration Appeals Commission (SIAC), which would assess the legality of the detention of non-UK nationals.[67] We know very little about the representations which have been made to the US. We do know that public criticism was muted: the government did not make plain – publicly and unambiguously – its condemnation of 'the utter lawlessness at Guantánamo Bay', as Lord Steyn put it.[68]

A series of meetings was held between British and American officials, led by Lord Goldsmith and William Haynes, the General Counsel of the US Department of Defense. By October 2003 there had been four rounds of talks. The US agreed to suspend military commission proceedings against British nationals, pending the outcome of the talks.[69] Lord Goldsmith summarized the British position: 'my objective in these discussions is to ensure that the British detainees . . . are assured of fair trials that meet international legal standards, wherever those trials take place.' The British government was opposed to the death penalty 'in all circumstances', he added, noting that the detainees should also have the benefit of legal advice.[70] Beyond that no details were provided. According to news reports, Washington gave assurances that it would not seek the death penalty against the British detainees,[71] but the Pentagon did not officially confirm this to be the case. In addition, but subject to unspecified conditions, undertakings were reported to have been given that British civilian lawyers would be able to act as consultants on the legal defence teams, that it might be possible for the sentences to be served in Britain ('to the extent feasible in accordance with US and UK law'), that trials would be open to the media ('subject to any necessary security restrictions'), and that conversations between defence lawyers and detainees would 'exceptionally' not be recorded by the authorities.

Matters dragged on. Reports circulated that the Red Cross was becoming increasingly concerned about the mental condition of the detainees. In August 2003 the US Department of Defense suggested that the US was considering whether further assurances could be given.[72] This followed media reports that Abbassi and another British detainee, Moazzam Begg, were expected to confess to war crimes and provide assistance to investigators on other cases. In September 2003 Lord Goldsmith reiterated his support for the rule of law and the right to a fair trial: '[T]hose suspected of being terrorists are not outside the law, nor do they forfeit their fundamental rights by virtue of that fact.'[73] But again the criticism was muted and limited to future trials, rather than being concerned with the continued detention of the present detainees without access to the courts or legal advice. Reports began to circulate about 'good old-fashioned torture' at Guantánamo. One report described detainees being tied to a spot and having rubber bullets fired at them, and being made to kneel cruciform in the sun until they collapsed.[74] The following month President Bush made a state visit to the UK. 'The deepest beliefs of our nations set the direction of our foreign policy,' he told an invited audience in Whitehall, with Blair sitting with him. 'We value our own civil rights, so we stand for the human rights of others.'[75] 'Unless they are at Guantánamo,' one of my Sri Lankan students added, during a class that week.

A few months later, on 9 March 2004, the 'Tipton Three', together with Tarek Dergoul and Jamal al-Harith, returned to Britain. The five men, described by Donald Rumsfeld as 'the hardest of the hard-core lethal terrorists',[76] were released without charge. After hundreds of hours of interrogation sessions it became clear that the men were not terrorists or a threat to society. But there has been no apology for their detention, and no compensation.

In April 2004, the US Supreme Court heard oral arguments in the Guantánamo cases. The *New York Times* reported that the opening remarks of the US Solicitor General (whose wife had been on one of the 9/11 hijacked planes) – 'The United States is at war' – rankled with the Justices. The British government did not intervene in the case (although it did intervene – and lose – in another US Supreme Court case to argue that US courts should not exercise extensive jurisdiction over human rights violations occurring outside the US). A few days before the judgment – no doubt coincidentally – Lord Goldsmith once again set out his concerns about the proposed military proceedings announced for two of the British detainees. The tone was more forthright, and was reported as such. 'We must be flexible and be prepared to countenance some limitation of fundamental rights if properly justified and proportionate,' he told a meeting of the International Criminal Bar Association. But, he added, 'there are certain principles on which there can be no compromise. Fair trial is one of these –

which is the reason we in the UK have been unable to accept that the US military tribunals proposed for those detained at Guantánamo Bay offer sufficient guarantees of a fair trial in accordance with international standards.'[77] 'What took you so long?' asked an editorial in *The Independent* newspaper. Shortly afterwards it emerged that Britain had abandoned efforts to change the rules for the military tribunals. We 'have to be realistic', Defence Secretary Geoff Hoon told the BBC. And in the face of a second case brought by Ferroz Abbassi it became apparent that Tony Blair had now formally asked for the return of the four remaining British detainees.[78]

*

On 28 June 2004 the US Supreme Court handed down its landmark ruling in *Rasul et al. v. Bush*. By six votes to three, the Court decided that US federal courts did have jurisdiction to determine the legality of the executive's potentially indefinite detention of individuals held at Guantánamo who claimed to be wholly innocent of wrongdoing. The majority applied the historical principles of *habeas corpus* from English law, and found that the facts of the case were different from the 1950 decision in *Eisentrager*. The Guantánamo detainees were not nationals of countries at war with the US, and they denied wrongdoing. They had not been charged, and had had no access to a tribunal. And, most significantly, they had been imprisoned in territory over which the US exercised 'exclusive jurisdiction and control'. Since the Bush Administration had conceded to the Court that an American citizen held at the base could challenge his detention in the federal courts, there was nothing in the relevant statutes which suggested that non-Americans should be treated differently.

'What matters', wrote Justice Kennedy in a concurring judgment, 'is the unchallenged and indefinite control that the United States has long exercised over Guantánamo Bay.' He was not persuaded by the arguments of military necessity:

Perhaps, where detainees are taken from a zone of hostilities, detention without proceedings or trial would be justified by military necessity for a matter of weeks; but as the period stretches from months to years, the case for continued detention to meet military exigencies becomes weaker.

The judgment was a crushing blow for the Bush Administration's entire legal strategy. As Justice Scalia put it in his scathing dissent, in which he was joined by Chief Justice Rehnquist and Justice Clarence Thomas, Guantánamo Bay was now subject to the oversight of the federal courts. It was, he said, 'a foolish place to have housed alien wartime detainees'.[79]

*

The judgment followed the same principles that had been applied by the English Court of Appeal. Although the Supreme Court did not refer to any international obligations, its approach is consistent with the values which Eleanor Roosevelt pushed for in the Universal Declaration of Human Rights. It marked a further step in making good 'a monstrous failure of justice', as Lord Steyn had described it, although the end may yet be a long time in coming. The treatment of the Guantánamo detainees is totally inconsistent with the Geneva Conventions and its Protocol I, and with human rights law. For short-term gain the US sought – on a unilateral basis – to accord to itself the right to declare a war and extend the application of military rules without giving its victims the minimum rights which international law provided. The Supreme Court saw straight through that. The legal logic which led to the decision to locate the detainees at the offshore camp at Guantánamo also underpins the Administration's arguments that the Geneva Conventions and other rules of international law are inapplicable. Moreover this is the work of the same legal team which provided the arguments sustaining the torture and other cruel and inhuman acts which occurred at Guantánamo, Abu Ghraib and elsewhere. It is all part and parcel of John Yoo's 'new legal regime', now in a state of collapse.

Within a few days of the Supreme Court judgment it became clear that Guantánamo might not survive, at least in its present form. The Pentagon confirmed that all options were open, even relocating the detainees to the US mainland. 'There is no reason to keep them overseas anymore,' it was said. Within days it announced the release of another group of detainees. The threat of legal review had an immediate effect as the Administration redoubled efforts to reach agreement with foreign governments willing to take custody of detainees.[80] In January 2005 the British and American governments announced that the four remaining British detainees at Guantánamo would be released.

Guantánamo has had terrible consequences for the lives of many of the individual detainees as well as their families. To hold people on an indefinite basis without due process over extended periods of time runs contrary to elementary principles of justice. It is an approach which threatens the very heart of human rights law. But the rules of international law, it turns out, have not been fatally undermined. Indeed, they have been shown to be robust in providing an independent standard to judge the propriety and legitimacy of state behaviour. It may be that over time the early certainties will be replaced with second thoughts. There was a glimmer of hope a couple of years after the first Executive Order on military tribunals was adopted. In April 2003 Donald Rumsfeld protested about the treatment of American prisoners of war, who had been filmed in the streets of Baghdad after their capture by Iraqi forces. He complained that Iraq was not complying with its obligations under Geneva Convention III, to protect prisoners from 'public curiosity'. The media response was predictable. A memorable cartoon in *The Independent* newspaper in London showed Rumsfeld clutching a shredded copy of the Geneva Conventions, which had been stuck together again with sticky tape. And in November 2004 a federal judge in Washington, DC, halted the first trial before a military commission of a Guantánamo detainee, Salim Hamdan. Why? Because, ruled the judge, Geneva Convention III stipulated minimum protection even for an alleged al-Qaeda operative; because there was doubt as to Hamdan's status as a prisoner of war and he was therefore entitled to access to a competent tribunal to determine his status under Article 5 of Geneva Convention III; and because Common Article 3 of the Geneva Conventions was applicable.[81] It seems that obligations put in place by the US and others after the Second World War are proving harder to dislodge than at first envisaged. The words of a former American President of the World Court, writing about another international agreement – also ignored by the US – come to mind: 'Citizens of no state have a higher interest in the observance of those obligations than the peripatetic citizens of the United States.'[82]

8

Kicking Ass in Iraq

'This isn't 'Nam, it's bowling. There are rules.'
The Big Lebowski (1998)

The war in Iraq in 2003 brought the rules on the use of force into mainstream political debate. In many parts of the world the legality of the war was a major issue: the subject of debates in legislatures, front-page news in many papers and even an item worthy of vitriolic editorials in others. The prospect of an illegal war without Security Council backing added to the numbers who marched and demonstrated in February and March 2003. But this was not the case in the United States. Once the US Congress had given President Bush authority to use force, the legality of the war under international law became almost a non-issue. The view from inside the Bush Administration was reflected in the attitude of John Bolton, Under Secretary of State, who dismissed any suggestion that international law could constrain the actions of the US or that domestic constitutional requirements alone were not sufficient to confer legitimacy on the use of force. Any other approach, he wrote, 'will result, over time, in the atrophying of our ability to act independently'.[1] Bush's own view was even blunter. The day after 9/11, Donald Rumsfeld outlined the limits which international law placed on a military response. 'I don't care what the international lawyer says,' Bush retorted, 'we are going to kick some ass.'[2]

Disbelief having been suspended in the US after 9/11, this attitude set the country's mood and went more or less unchallenged. As the troops prepared to cross into Iraq, sensible people like Anne-Marie Slaughter, Dean of the Woodrow Wilson School at Princeton and

President of the American Society of International Law, could write in the *New York Times* that a war would be 'illegal but legitimate'[3] (a claim which, to her credit, she rescinded a year later, concluding that the 'invasion was both illegal and illegitimate').[4] It was sufficient for the President to declare that Saddam Hussein had to be removed because he was a bad man with weapons of mass destruction (WMD). (After the war, in an interview in December 2003, Bush said that it made no difference whether Saddam Hussein had WMD or the intention of acquiring them.)

That attitude contrasted sharply with the position in Britain. The issue of legality was a constant constraining influence on the Prime Minister's public statements on Iraq, and he repeatedly stated that Britain would only act within the limits of international law. So great was the pressure on the British government that a late public statement had to be made in the name of the Attorney General three days before the war, justifying its legality without a further Security Council resolution explicitly authorizing force. The statement to the House of Lords was unprecedented but necessary. Establishing the legality of the war was vital to keep three key constituencies on board: Cabinet ministers on the verge of resignation; backbench Labour MPs who might vote against the war when the matter was brought before the House of Commons; and Admiral Sir Michael Boyce, the UK Chief of Defence Staff, who wanted a clear and unequivocal opinion before committing troops.[5] While the Attorney General's statement may have had the short-term effect desired by the Prime Minister – pulling the trigger on British military action – over the longer term doubts festered about the circumstances in which it had been given. The government's refusal to publish the Attorney General's full advice raised more questions. Its report into intelligence failings in Iraq, the Butler Inquiry, which was published in July 2004, provided troubling insights into the timetable and manner in which the Attorney General had advised. In September 2004 the normally circumspect UN Secretary General, Kofi Annan, took the unusual step of publicly stating that the Iraq War was illegal. And in November 2004 Sir Stephen Wall, a senior foreign policy adviser at 10 Downing Street during the war, broke ranks with his former boss, acknowledging that 'we allowed our judgement of the dire consequences of inaction to override our judgement of the even more dire consequences of parting from the rule of law'.[6]

Before turning to these issues – the legality of the war and the circumstances in which the British government advised itself force was lawful – it is necessary to set out some background on the rules governing the use of force and their application in the period after the Second World War, including in Iraq in 1991.

*

Until the twentieth century there were no international rules prohibiting the use of force by one state against another. The Covenant of the League of Nations was adopted in 1919 but it fell far short of outlawing war. Members of the League simply agreed to exhaust other avenues before resorting to war, and to go to the League's Council and – somewhat optimistically – arbitral or judicial procedures.[7] If the Council failed to resolve the dispute the Members could use force: 'the right to take such action as they shall consider necessary for the maintenance of rights and justice'.[8] The test was subjective; there were no formal criteria to meet.

In 1928 renunciation of war as 'an instrument of national policy' was taken a step further. A number of states signed the Kellogg–Briand Pact, named after the foreign ministers of the United States and France. The Pact condemned war as a method for solving 'international controversies'. It committed the signatories to renounce war between themselves but it left open various exceptions. For example, it did not apply in relations with states which had not joined the Pact; it was not a global code. The League of Nations and the Kellogg–Briand Pact did not prevent the Japanese invasion of Manchuria in 1931, or Italy's conquest of Abyssinia in 1936, or Germany's incursions across large parts of Europe, or Russia's attacks on Finland in 1939. It could not prevent the Second World War, although that terrible conflict reignited the idealistic spirit of US and British governments.

In August 1941 Franklin Roosevelt and Winston Churchill had expressed their belief 'that all of the nations of the world, for realistic as well as spiritual reasons, must come to the abandonment of the use of force'. The Atlantic Charter argued for the disarmament of nations threatening aggression beyond their frontiers, pending the establishment of 'a wider and permanent system of general security'. In the midst of war this was a visionary document, standing in sharp contrast to the attitude adopted by the US and British governments after 9/11. On 7 December 1941 came the attacks on Pearl Harbor. The project was postponed but not cancelled. The aspiration of limiting the use of force became a central part of the Charter of the United Nations, which was adopted in San Francisco in June 1945. After much deliberation, Britain and the US joined with forty-five other countries to outlaw the use of force, except under the most limited of conditions. Article 2(4) of the UN Charter declares that 'All Members shall refrain in their international relations from the threat or use of force against the territorial integrity or political independence of any state, or in any other manner inconsistent with the Purposes of the United Nations.'

There are two exceptions. The first is self-defence: Article 51 of the UN Charter states that nothing in the Charter 'shall impair the inherent right of individual or collective self-defence if an armed attack occurs against a member of the United Nations'. However, the right is not open-ended; it exists only until the UN Security Council 'has taken measures necessary to maintain international peace and security'. The compromise language of Article 51 is not free from ambiguity, as more than sixty years of practice and volumes of academic commentary make clear. Article 51 has raised many questions. Can self-defence be invoked before an armed attack has taken place? If there is a right of 'anticipatory self-defence', as it is called, can it be invoked where another state acquires – or is in the process of acquiring – weapons of mass destruction?[9] Article 51 of the UN Charter has been described as myopic, for its failure to anticipate, let alone address, the rise in surrogate warfare prompted by rogue states and international terrorists.[10] The issue of anticipatory defence is a pressing one, because President Bush's post-9/11 National Security Strategy committed the US to act pre-emptively to forestall or prevent hostile acts.[11] In March 2004 the British Prime Minister gave a speech in which he affirmed the existence of a 'duty and a right to prevent the threat materializing' of the proliferation or illegal acquisition of WMD.[12] This has been taken by some as endorsing the US's declaration of the right to strike pre-emptively, going beyond anticipatory self-defence. These assertions are based on the erroneous view that the events of 9/11 and of the Iraq War demonstrate the inadequacy of the global rules. I disagree. The Bush doctrine itself – and Blair's low-level support for it – poses a fundamental threat to the international legal order without adequately addressing the threats posed by organizations like al-Qaeda and by failed states.

The UN Charter allows for a second exception, where force has been authorized by the UN Security Council, acting under Chapter VII of the UN Charter. Apart from economic sanctions and other non-military measures available under Article 41 of the Charter, Article 42 allows the Security Council to 'take such action by air, sea or land forces as may be necessary to maintain or restore international peace and security'. For nearly fifty years, until 1990, Cold War rivalries prevented the Security Council from exercising its military powers: the US and Soviets said they would veto any Security Council resolution which threatened their interests, as they were entitled to do under the UN rules. With the collapse of the Soviet bloc in 1989 a reinvigorated Security Council emerged.

The first time the Council acted to authorize the use of force against another state under Chapter VII was on 29 November 1990, when Iraq unlawfully invaded Kuwait.[13] Resolution 678 authorized member states 'to use all necessary means' to uphold and implement previous Security Council resolutions and to restore peace and security in the area.[14] Since then Chapter VII powers have been relied upon regularly to authorize different measures, for example in Somalia, the Balkans, Liberia, Sierra Leone, Haiti and East Timor.

There is a third situation in which it is claimed that force may be used, apart from that of self-defence or where the Security Council has authorized it. This is the 'humanitarian intervention' exception, where massive violations of fundamental human rights are taking place. This exception has long been contentious. Smaller and developing countries in particular are fearful that 'humanitarian intervention' will be used to justify the use of force when the established rules do not permit it. They are right to be concerned, until clear criteria have emerged and are accepted by the international community as a whole. In 1988, following Saddam Hussein's use of chemical weapons in Halabja, there were some calls for international intervention, but these were not acted upon. There was a shift in international practice in the 1990s, to protect the rights of the Kurdish minority in northern Iraq, who were persecuted by Saddam Hussein after the Gulf War in 1991. Calls for international intervention were stepped up after the gross failures to intervene to prevent genocide and other atrocities following the break-up of the former Socialist Federal Republic of Yugoslavia (in 1991), and the genocide in Rwanda (in 1994). The law evolves with changing values, and as human rights' considerations become entrenched they will influence the law in this area.

When tensions flared up in Kosovo in 1998, the Security Council condemned the excessive use of force by the Serbian police and demanded that both sides take steps to avert 'an impending humanitarian catastrophe'. Although the Security Council threatened to 'consider further action and additional measures to maintain or restore peace and stability in the region', it was clear that enforcement action would be vetoed by Russia or China. In March 1999 NATO acted unilaterally, without authorization by the Security Council. A majority of the Council's members supported the arguments put forward by the Dutch Ambassador: states could not 'sit back and simply let the humanitarian catastrophe occur' just because one or two permanent members of the Security Council were following a rigid and limited interpretation of the UN Charter.[15] (The same principle is applicable now to the unfolding catastrophe in the Darfur region of Sudan.) But that view was not universal and Russia, for one, condemned it. It was, Russia maintained, 'in no way based on the Charter or other generally recognized rules of international law'.[16] The Security Council declined to act and was thus relegated to a peripheral role. After the conflict, however, the Council took steps to deploy an international civil and security presence in Kosovo.[17] Some saw this as ratifying retroactively the NATO mission (China abstained from the resolution, precisely on the grounds that it might be seen as legitimating NATO's use of force).

Humanitarian intervention in Kosovo prompted Tony Blair to make one of his earliest forays into the reform of international law. In the summer of 1999, after Kosovo, he proposed a doctrine of 'international community', which could permit intervention to protect human rights. But he fell well short of intimating a right of preemptive strike. That was for later.

*

There will always be doubt about the extent to which international law can really limit the use of force by states. There have been countless examples of force being used in the sixty years since the UN Charter was adopted, but it is noteworthy that when states do use force they invariably try to justify their actions in law. If nothing else, there is acceptance that force is subject to legal constraints: since the

UN Charter was adopted it can no longer be argued that the use of force is beyond the rules of international law.

Nevertheless many people, including some newspaper editors, continue to believe that the idea of applying global rules to military force is absurd. As doubts grew about the Attorney General's advice on Iraq, a leader in the *Sunday Telegraph* newspaper in London made the point with brutal simplicity:

The 'legality' or otherwise of the war is a non-subject, for the simple reason that there is no binding body of international law which compels obedience, either in morality or in fact, from the sovereign nations of the globe. [. . .] The invasion of Iraq may or may not have been 'illegal' under international law. The point, however, is that the whole issue of 'international legality' is a gigantic irrelevance.[18]

It is extraordinary that a leading British newspaper could express such an ignorant and dangerous view in the twenty-first century, pandering to the 'little Englanders' among its readers and oblivious to Churchill's role in bringing about the 'gigantic irrelevance'. No doubt the opinion is shared by some readers of the *Sunday Telegraph*. But altogether more worrying is that the opinion seems to reflect the views of many who are close to the US government, and even the US President himself.[19]

Despite the views expressed in the *Sunday Telegraph*, it is a striking feature of modern British political debate that the legality of the Iraq War should be such a central issue. I am not quite sure why this is the case. Britain is no more legalistic a country than the United States – although it is a less powerful one. This makes it more dependent on respect for the rules. Robert Cooper, a former foreign policy adviser to Tony Blair, describes a popular perception that 'the United States is unilateralist because it has the strength to act on its own; Europe's attachment to treaties, the rule of law and multilateralism comes from weakness and wishful thinking.'[20] There may be a grain of truth in that, but it is over-simplistic. The Prime Minister was trained and has practised as a barrister; he is sensitized to legal arguments and surrounded by lawyers. He also recognizes that the law adds legitimacy to difficult actions. In the run-up to the Iraq War he and various members of his Cabinet missed no opportunity to stress that any decision to go to war would have to be justified under the United Nations

Charter. The British government's public position marked it out from that of the United States. The Bush Administration paid lip-service to 'legalisms', as President Bush put it. But there was never any sustained public debate about the legality of going to war. The American press was not interested. Most academics in the US kept their heads below the parapet, and those who tried to raise legal arguments often found that they could not get their letters published. In Britain the reaction was very different. In early 2003 the details of various UN Security Council resolutions were being picked over, line by line, in the newspapers, on radio, on television. To understand the legal issues in March 2003 it is necessary to go back to August 1990, and the first Gulf War.

*

The Security Council had acted decisively after Iraq had invaded Kuwait on 2 August 1990. That very day the Council condemned the invasion. Resolution 660 called on Iraq to withdraw immediately from Kuwait. Four days later, the Council froze Iraqi assets and imposed wide-ranging sanctions. Iraq still did not withdraw. On 29 November 1990 the Council adopted resolution 678. This authorized member states 'to use all necessary means to uphold and implement resolution 660 (1990) and all subsequent relevant resolutions and to restore international peace and security in the area', if Iraq did not withdraw by 15 January 1991. 'All necessary means' is the well-understood formulation authorizing force. There was no withdrawal.

The first Gulf War thus began on 17 January 1991, duly authorized by the Security Council. It ended on 28 February 1991, when Iraq capitulated. On 3 April 1991 the Security Council adopted a ceasefire in resolution 687. That resolution also imposed new obligations on Iraq to disarm and to destroy all chemical and biological weapons of mass destruction, and not to acquire or develop nuclear weapons. It established a system of far-reaching UN inspections to ensure Iraqi compliance. These continued until 1998. Then the UN inspectors were pulled out of Iraq. By the time President George W. Bush came into office in January 2001 the UN inspectors had been out of Iraq for nearly three years.

With hindsight it seems obvious that George W. Bush was committed to the removal of Saddam Hussein from the outset of his presidency. It remains unclear why. There was no hard evidence that he threatened the region, or that he was associated with al-Qaeda, although he must have been a constant reminder of the impotence of the first Bush presidency and the limits of American power. In the mid-1990s several people who were to become leading advisers and members of his government – including Dick Cheney, Donald Rumsfeld and Paul Wolfowitz – had called for his removal. 'From the very beginning, there was a conviction that Saddam Hussein was a bad person and he needed to go,' former Treasury Secretary Paul O'Neill told CBS viewers.[21] The events of 9/11 and resurgent Islamic terrorism provided a perfect pretext, even if there was no firm evidence of collusion between Iraq and al-Qaeda or any hard evidence of the existence of WMD in Iraq. Within two days of the attacks on the twin towers, Rumsfeld was asking the National Security Council: 'Why shouldn't we go against Iraq, not just al-Qaeda?'[22] After all, Saddam had manufactured and used chemical weapons in the late 1980s, against his own people. His Ba'ath regime had perpetrated appalling violations of human rights since 1968. And he had invaded Kuwait in 1990. It was plain, so the argument went, that he posed a threat to the region and to American interests, all the more so if he was in alliance with al-Qaeda and Islamic terrorists.

On 5 April 2002 Bush declared in a television interview that 'Saddam needs to go'.[23] The US seemed willing to proceed on its own, but needed some sort of coalition, to limit charges of unilateralism and shore up domestic support. By then the British Prime Minister was on board, having concluded that nothing would stand in the way of Bush. Tony Blair had privately signalled his commitment to regime change: on 18 March 2002 Sir David Manning, Blair's foreign policy adviser, had written to the Prime Minister confirming that he had told Condoleezza Rice that 'you would not budge in your support for regime change'.[24] But unlike Bush, Blair knew this could not be stated publicly, as the use of force to effect a change of regime was plainly contrary to international law. Michael Foster, MP, an assistant to the British Attorney General, confirmed that Lord Goldsmith was later 'asked the question – would regime change be lawful *per se*, and he said no, it wouldn't'.[25] As Manning recognized, regime change would not get past 'a press, a parliament and a public opinion that was very different from anything in the States'. The justification would have to be dressed up as something else. According to John Kampfner, a British political commentator:

The question was not if there would be a war, but on what terms it would be fought. [Blair and Manning] told the President that he had the power to do it on his own, that Britain would support him come what may, but in order to maximize his case he should try to build a larger coalition, preferably through the UN.[26]

It has been suggested that Blair had no choice. But there are plenty of instances when the US and Britain did not stand together, from Suez in 1956 to Vietnam in the 1960s. Blair's reaction also stands in sharp contrast to the stance taken by Margaret Thatcher in 1983, when the US invaded Grenada, ostensibly at the invitation of other eastern Caribbean states. Admittedly Grenada was on a different scale to Iraq, but it seems hard to imagine Blair writing to Bush as Thatcher did to Reagan:

This action will be seen as intervention by a western country in the internal affairs of a small independent nation, however unattractive its regime. I ask you to consider this in the context of our wider East–West relations and of the fact that we will be having in the next few days to present to our Parliament and people the siting of Cruise missiles in this country. [. . .] I cannot conceal that I am deeply disturbed by your latest communication.[27]

Why Blair joined in remains a great mystery. The fact that he declared his hand so early and unreservedly seems impetuous. But go along he did. As regime change as such was out of the question, Blair needed an alternative public justification. A key meeting apparently took place in mid-July 2002, at which various ministers, including the Attorney General, were present. They were reminded that the Prime Minister had told President Bush that the UK would support military action to bring about regime change, so long as a coalition had been created, the Israel–Palestine crisis was quiescent, and UN weapons inspectors had been given a further opportunity to eliminate Iraq's WMD. Those present were told that in Washington military action was now seen as inevitable, justified by the linking of terrorism and WMD, although the intelligence and the facts were being fixed around policy. The Foreign Secretary Jack Straw complained that the case with thin, not least because Saddam Hussein was not threatening neighbours and had a lesser WMD capability than Libya, North Korea or Iran. The meeting also considered the legal issues, including a March 2002 paper prepared by Foreign Office legal advisers. Even at this stage the British government was acutely aware of the legal difficulties. The Attorney General confirmed that self-defence and humanitarian intervention were not justified, and that as matters then stood, claiming the authorization of the Security Council would be difficult. The Attorney General was instructed to consider legal advice with the Foreign Office and Ministry of Defence. The chosen route was to build up the intelligence to support the claim that Saddam had weapons of mass destruction, which could provide a potential legal justification. This meant persuading Bush to take the United Nations route, which Blair achieved by working with Colin Powell. Four months later, in November 2002, the Security Council unanimously adopted resolution 1441, which is of central importance to any assessment of the legality of the Iraq War. It merits careful consideration in the context in which it was adopted.

Resolution 1441 stated that Iraq 'has been and remains in material breach of its obligations under relevant resolutions, including resolution 687 (1991)', and that it had failed to co-operate with UN inspectors and the International Atomic Energy Agency (IAEA). It afforded Iraq 'a final opportunity to comply with its disarmament obligations under relevant resolutions of the Council'. It set up an enhanced inspection regime, requiring Iraq to provide (within 30 days) an accurate, full and complete declaration of its programmes to develop chemical, biological and nuclear weapons. And it decided that false statements, or omissions in the declaration, would constitute a further material breach and would be reported to the Security Council. The resolution directed Hans Blix (the head of the UN inspectors) and Mohammed ElBaradei (the head of the IAEA) to report to the Security Council any failure by Iraq to comply. On receipt of a report the Council would then convene 'to consider the situation and the need for full compliance with all of the relevant Council resolutions'. The resolution concluded with a warning that Iraq 'will face serious consequences as a result of its continued violations of its obligations'. But the resolution did not authorize states 'to use all necessary means' to implement its requirements – nor did it imply such authorization. France, Germany, Russia and China objected.

Between November 2002 and March 2003 the UN and the IAEA

resumed inspections in Iraq. Messrs Blix and ElBaradei reported regularly to the Security Council, with highly charged meetings taking place on three occasions. Despite the inspectors' failure to find any WMD, the US and Britain continued to claim that their own intelligence disclosed that Iraq had failed to disarm and was violating its Security Council obligations. American and British troops were moved in around Iraq. Blair pushed strongly for a second Security Council resolution which would give legal cover for the use of force. The purported justification for force was taking shape: mention of regime change was studiously avoided in lieu of Saddam Hussein's failure to disarm, in violation of Security Council resolutions. 'The purpose in our acting is disarmament,' the Prime Minister told the House of Commons.[28] 'The truth is . . . We went to war to enforce compliance with Security Council resolutions,' he said a year later.[29] The signals may have been mixed but, unwittingly perhaps, barrister Blair had boxed himself into a corner of diminishing legal options.

In January and February 2003, the US, Britain and Spain laid the groundwork for a further resolution. Throughout this period Britain's approach – and Blair's public statements – is suggestive of the fact that there was a background of legal opinion that explicit Security Council authorization was needed to use force, and that 1441 did not provide such authorization. By the end of January Blair had been told that the start date for the military campaign was pencilled in for the middle of March, and 10 Downing Street was being advised that a second Security Council resolution should be sought as soon as possible. On 24 February 2003 the three countries tabled a draft Security Council resolution. The draft stated that Iraq's declaration pursuant to resolution 1441 (2002) contained 'false statements and omissions' and concluded that 'Iraq has failed to take the final opportunity afforded to it in Resolution 1441'. But it had little support. The same day, France, Germany and Russia tabled a separate memorandum on inspections, stating that 'the conditions for using force against Iraq are not fulfilled'. By the first week of March it was becoming obvious that the prospects for the second Security Council resolution were grim. The US and Britain were expending considerable efforts to persuade the six key swing votes – Mexico, Chile, Guinea, Cameroon, Angola and Pakistan – to support their draft. The battlelines were drawn. Efforts to persuade the swing votes included high-level

ministerial visits to Africa and prime ministerial diplomacy, in particular with Prime Minister Lagos of Chile and President Fox of Mexico.
Clare Short (then Britain's Minister for International Development)
described the pressure that was brought to bear on these states,
including inducements in the form of development assistance.[30] Some
of these countries later complained that their diplomats in New York
were being bugged, in violation of international law.[31] If true, these
allegations would confirm London's great attachment to a second
Security Council resolution.

The reason for Blair's attachment to a second resolution is not
hard to find. As one observer put it, a second resolution was needed
'to provide political, diplomatic and even legal authority for a military conflict to which [Blair] was already committed'.[32] That is an
understatement. Britain was committed to compliance with international law, and there was mounting opposition in Britain to any
Iraq war without explicit UN backing. But Britain had not argued –
and could not argue – that it was entitled to use force against Iraq in
self-defence (under Article 51 of the UN Charter). Appearing on
MTV on 8 March 2003, the Prime Minister accepted that it was not
plausible to claim that Saddam Hussein's Iraq posed an imminent
threat to Britain.[33] This was despite the claim made in the British
government's dossier of September 2002 that the Iraqi military are
'able to deploy [chemical and biological] weapons within 45 minutes
of a decision to do so'.[34] This claim was later abandoned as the
limited intelligence on which it was based referred only to battlefield
chemical weapons, not long-range missiles. In July 2004 the Butler
Inquiry concluded that the '45-minute' claim should not have been
included in that form.[35]

Regime change and other arguments – pre-emptive strike and
humanitarian intervention – were also not available under international law. As of spring 2003 Britain had not accepted the premise of
the new US National Security Strategy, which argued for a right in
international law to use force pre-emptively.[36] And it could not be
argued that the situation in Iraq was similar to that in Kosovo in April
1999, justifying force to prevent an overwhelming and imminent
humanitarian crisis. Whilst that could conceivably have been argued
in the late 1980s when Saddam was using chemical weapons against
Kurdish villages, and was used in 1991 to justify the creation of

Kurdish safe areas in Iraq from which Iraqi troops would be excluded, in 2002 and 2003 the facts on the ground in Iraq did not allow such a claim to be made. However brutal and appalling Saddam Hussein's behaviour had been in earlier years (during the time when he was an American ally fighting a war against the regime of the ayatollahs in Iran, and receiving Donald Rumsfeld as an esteemed visitor), there was not a humanitarian crisis of that kind in Iraq in 2003.

That left the second Security Council resolution, which was going down the drain. The six swing countries were being remarkably resilient. 'A little too independent', I was told by one seasoned UN observer. An alternative legal basis had to be found. By early March the only argument left, the only plausible justification, would be to run the argument that the Security Council had somehow already authorized the use of force.

It was not difficult to predict that Tony Blair would have to make this argument, which had already circulated in academic circles and had been raised in informal meetings of the Security Council. Fifteen British and other European academics – myself included – foresaw that Britain would claim that resolution 1441 (and possibly also the earlier resolutions 678 and 687 of 1990 and 1991) might somehow be claimed to authorize the use of force. This was even more likely if (as the British government feared) France or Russia were to veto a second resolution. We wrote a letter to the Prime Minister to pre-empt a claim which the overwhelming majority of our academic colleagues around the world considered to be without any merit:

We are teachers of international law. On the basis of the information publicly available, there is no justification under international law for the use of military force against Iraq. [. . .] Neither Security Council resolution 1441 nor any prior resolution authorizes the proposed use of force in the present circumstances. Before military action can lawfully be undertaken against Iraq, the Security Council must have indicated its clearly expressed assent. It has not yet done so. A vetoed resolution could provide no such assent.

We agreed on the law but were divided on whether an express Security Council resolution would make it a just war. To accommodate both views we added a further statement: 'A lawful war is not necessarily a just, prudent or humanitarian war.' We also sent a copy to *The Guardian* newspaper, which published it the following day, on 7 March. (The *New York Times* declined to publish a similar letter from American academics.) It ran as a lead story on the front page and was picked up by the BBC and the wire services. For the next couple of days, radio and TV were full of interviews and news stories about the legality of any war on Iraq. The arguments for and against the legality of an Iraq war even made it on to breakfast television chat shows. The effect was catalytic, as the legality of the war became a significant political issue. During a crucial ten-day period after 7 March, the Attorney General was required to provide a clear and decisive statement on the legality of force in the absence of a further Security Council resolution.

In unprecedented circumstances, on 17 March 2003 the Attorney General was invited to respond to a parliamentary question on the legal basis for the use of force by the United Kingdom against Iraq. The written answer required just 337 words. It set out with remarkable economy the basis for his view that authority to use force against Iraq existed from the 'combined effects' of UN Security Council resolutions 678, 687 and 1441. The argument was beguilingly simple:[37]

1. In Resolution 678, the Security Council authorized force against Iraq, to eject it from Kuwait and to restore peace and security in the area.
2. In Resolution 687, which set out the ceasefire conditions after Operation Desert Storm, the Security Council imposed continuing obligations on Iraq to eliminate its weapons of mass destruction in order to restore international peace and security in the area. Resolution 687 suspended but did not terminate the authority to use force under Resolution 678.
3. A material breach of Resolution 687 revives the authority to use force under Resolution 678.
4. In Resolution 1441, the Security Council determined that Iraq has been and remains in material breach of Resolution 687, because it has not fully complied with its obligations to disarm under that resolution.
5. The Security Council in Resolution 1441 gave Iraq 'a final opportunity to comply with its disarmament obligations' and warned Iraq of the 'serious consequences' if it did not.
6. The Security Council also decided in Resolution 1441 that, if Iraq failed at

any time to comply with and co-operate fully in the implementation of Resolution 1441, that would constitute a further material breach.

7. It is plain that Iraq has failed so to comply and therefore Iraq was at the time of Resolution 1441 and continues to be in material breach.

8. Thus, the authority to use force under Resolution 678 has revived and so continues today.

9. Resolution 1441 would in terms have provided that a further decision of the Security Council to sanction force was required if that had been intended. Thus, all that Resolution 1441 requires is reporting to and discussion by the Security Council of Iraq's failures, but not an express further decision to authorize force.

The argument is well spun and could, at a pinch, win the prize for the most plausible response to the question: what is the best possible argument to justify the use of force in Iraq in March 2003? But it masks a host of complex issues. It is a bad argument, and very few states and virtually no established international lawyers see its merits. On 18 March, the day after the argument was published, the Foreign Office's Deputy Legal Adviser, Elizabeth Wilmshurst, tendered her request for early retirement or resignation. 'I regret that I cannot agree that it is lawful to use force without a second Security Council resolution,' she wrote. After noting the evolution of the legal views, she added: 'I cannot in conscience go along with advice within the Office or to the public or Parliament – which asserts the legitimacy of military action without such a resolution, particularly since an unlawful use of force on such a scale amounts to the crime of aggression; nor can I agree with such action in circumstances which are so detrimental to the international order and the rule of law.'

The Attorney General's reliance on resolution 678 is misconceived. That resolution was only intended to get Iraq out of Kuwait. It required that Iraq comply fully with resolution 660, which demanded that 'Iraq withdraw immediately and unconditionally all its forces to the positions in which they were located on 1 August 1990'. There was nothing in resolution 660, or any other resolution adopted between that one and 678, which mentioned regime change, or the overthrow of Saddam Hussein's government. The British Ambassador to the UN at the time, Sir Crispin Tickell, was one of the main drafters of resolution 678. He clearly understood that the resolution would have no purpose beyond the removal of Saddam Hussein's forces from Kuwait. Similarly, writing in his memoir in 1995, Colin Powell is explicit: 'The UN resolution made clear that the mission was only to free Kuwait. [. . .] The UN had given us our marching orders, and the President intended to stay with them.'[39] His British counterpart, Sir Peter de la Billiere, does not demur: 'We did not have a mandate to invade Iraq or take the country over.'[40] The same point is made by others who were in power at the time. John Major was Prime Minister when resolutions 678 and 687 were adopted. In his view: 'Our mandate from the United Nations was to expel the Iraqis from Kuwait, not bring down the Iraqi regime [. . .] We had gone to war to uphold international law. To go further than our mandate would have been, arguably, to break international law.'[41] No ambiguity there.

If resolutions 660 and 678 did not provide any basis for overthrowing Saddam Hussein in 1991, how could they have done so in 2003? A right to use force which did not exist in 1991 cannot 'revive' in 2003. Similarly, the ceasefire established by resolutions 686 and 687 was premised on the use of force only to remove Iraq from Kuwait. Resolution 687 stated expressly that it was for the Security Council to implement the resolution and secure peace and security in the region. Moreover, there is nothing in 687 which allows one or more members of the Security Council – or the British Prime Minister – to decide what further steps are needed.

Whether right or wrong, it is the very essence of the system of collective security which America and Britain created, and which gave rise to resolutions 678 and 687, that decision-making is collective. It is not individual, or prime ministerial. And this was the view put by the Foreign Office legal advisers in a note which was first circulated in March 2002. They concluded that since the ceasefire had been proclaimed by the Security Council in resolution 687, 'it is for that body to assess whether any such breach of those obligations has occurred. The US have a rather different view: they maintain that the assessment of breach is for individual member states. We are not aware of any other state which supports this view.' Moreover, as Professor Vaughan Lowe, the Chichele Professor of International Law at the University of Oxford, has written: 'there is no known doctrine of the revival of authorizations in Security Council resolutions'.[42]

Even if resolutions 678 and 687 could be construed to authorize a right to use force to overthrow Saddam Hussein – which they do not – on what basis could such a right be said to 'revive'? Did resolution 1441 provide a basis for the revival of the right to use force, as the British Attorney General implies? There are established rules and practices for interpreting Security Council resolutions, like any other international agreements.[38] Resolution 1441 must be interpreted in good faith, in its context, and in the light of its object and purpose. All these elements seem to have been ignored by the Attorney General. If that approach leads to any ambiguity or obscurity then it is appropriate to look at the preparatory work involved in the negotiation of the resolution. The preparatory work would be unhelpful to the argument and it too seems to have been inadequately considered. The operative paragraph 4 of resolution 1441 provides that

false statements or omissions in declarations submitted by Iraq pursuant to this resolution and failure by Iraq at any time to comply with, and cooperate fully in the implementation of, this resolution shall constitute a further material breach of Iraq's obligations and will be reported to the Council for assessment in accordance with paragraphs 11 and 12 below.

Paragraph 11 provided for the inspectors (the United Nations Monitoring, Verification and Inspection Commission (UNMOVIC) and the International Atomic Energy Agency) 'to report immediately to the Council any interference by Iraq with inspection activities, as well as any failure by Iraq to comply with its disarmament obligations'. By paragraph 12 the Council decided 'to convene immediately upon receipt of a report . . . to consider the situation and the need for full compliance with all of the relevant Security Council resolutions'.

Any argument that by resolution 1441 the Council was reviving the authority to use force contained in resolution 678 is defeated by the wording of paragraph 4 of resolution 1441. It is absurd to claim that the requirement in that paragraph for 'assessment' by the Council could be met merely by a report to, and discussion of, Iraq's failures by the Security Council: the clear intention of the drafters is that the Council would take a decision after assessing the situation – whether Iraq had committed a breach of its obligations sufficient to justify force. Resolution 1441 is not a revival of the authorization to use force; it requires that the Council meet again and decide upon the situation in the event of an adverse report from Messrs Blix or ElBaradei. This is plain from the language of the resolution, and is not altered by any statements made at the time of the resolution's adoption. As the Russian Deputy Foreign Minister, Yuri Fedotov, put it on 8 November 2003: Russia, with the support of France, China and other UN Security Council members, took steps to remove the most unacceptable formulations from the draft, including 'provisions which would permit an automatic unilateral use of force'.

In adopting resolution 1441, the understanding of all but a tiny minority of the members of the Security Council was that it would be for the Council to decide what to do if Iraq failed to comply with the requirements of that resolution. When resolution 1441 was being negotiated, the drafters were well aware of the 'revival' argument. During one of the informal sessions, they had put before them a 1998 article setting out the views of a senior legal adviser at the US State Department.[43] This articulated the revival argument which was eventually relied on by America and Britain as well as the claim that the US alone could determine the existence of a material breach of a Security Council resolution. There is no indication that other members of the Security Council accepted that view.

Against that background, it is difficult to understand on what basis the Attorney General could claim, as he did, that resolution 1441 merely required reporting to and discussion by the Security Council of Iraq's failures, but no express further decision to authorize force. 'The Attorney General must have overlooked completely the entire context of the negotiations to reach the conclusion he did in respect of 1441,' I was told by one diplomat who was involved throughout the negotiations of 1441. The US Permanent Representative to the United Nations John Negroponte said in his Explanation of Vote that 'resolution [1441] contains no "hidden triggers" and no "automaticity" with the use of force'.[44] Sir Jeremy Greenstock, the UK Permanent Representative, was even clearer:

We heard loud and clear during the negotiations the concerns about 'auto-maticity' and 'hidden triggers' . . . there is no 'automaticity' in this Resolution. If there is a further Iraqi breach of the disarmament obligations the matter will return to the Council for discussion as required in Operational Paragraph 12. We would expect the Security Council then to meet its responsibilities.[45]

In adopting resolution 1441, the great majority of the members of the Security Council understood that it would be for the Security Council to decide what to do if Iraq failed to comply. The consequences of that were spelt out by Lord Thomas in a House of Lords debate: 'Neither the United Kingdom nor the United States is entitled to enforce the "will" of the Security Council.'[46]

I believe that the Attorney General's argument – that a non-existent authority to use force can 'revive' at the behest of three of the fifteen members of the Security Council – makes a mockery of the UN sys-tem. The claim has rightly been called 'risible'.[47] It undermines Britain's credibility at the UN. 'My Ambassador was very very angry when the British used the "revival" argument in March 2003,' I was told by a senior adviser to one of the Security Council members that had negotiated resolution 1441. It caused Kofi Annan to speak out, describing the actions of the UK and the US diplomatically as lack-ing legitimacy.[48] The Attorney General would have known that his arguments would face considerable difficulties before an English court or the World Court.

*

In what circumstances could the Attorney General have been pre-vailed upon to lend Britain's name to such a weak and dismal argu-ment? Was the 17 March statement an accurate summary of his advice? Was his advice shared by the legal advisers at the Foreign Office? Did his views change over time? Why was the advice so late? In Britain these questions are being asked because the Attorney General's advice raises issues about the integrity of government and the law. The story behind the legal arguments masks a bigger ques-tion: were the legal arguments corrupted to pursue an illegal regime change in Iraq?

The British government first considered the legal options in the spring of 2002. In early March of that year officials circulated interdepartmental advice, stating that regime change of itself had no basis in international law, and that in the absence of evidence of Iraqi complicity with international terrorism self-defence could not be justified.[49] The paper did identify a possible argument that Iraq might be in material breach of its WMD obligations. It concluded, however, that any such claim would only succeed if the five Permanent Members and a majority of the fifteen members of the Security Council could be persuaded that there was 'incontrovertible' proof of 'large-scale activity'.[50] This was a reasonable approach. It acknowledged that 'general legal opinion' did not recognize the right of the US or Britain to make such a finding on their own.

Despite these conclusions, Tony Blair had already expressed his support for regime change, as reflected in Sir David Manning's memorandum of 18 March 2003, which only came to light eighteen months after the war, when it was leaked.[51] This memorandum, and the interdepartmental advice, issued more or less contemporaneously, show the disparity between the Prime Minister's private objectives and the advice his government was receiving on what international law would allow. Much of the next year was spent in efforts to bridge this gap.

The Foreign Office was the government department leading on these issues. It therefore fell, initially, to its lawyers to advise on the conditions, if any, under which force could be lawful. The Foreign Office's legal advisers in London are highly respected, in Britain and around the world. In the period up to November 2002, before resolution 1441 was adopted, they were clear in their view that force could only be used against Iraq if explicitly authorized by a further Security Council resolution or resolutions. The adoption of resolution 1441 did not cause them to change their view. My understanding is that the Foreign Office legal adviser and his colleagues were crystal clear in advising that resolution 1441 did not authorize the use of force, either on its own or taken in conjunction with the earlier Iraq resolutions of 1990 and 1991, and that without a further resolution the United Kingdom could not lawfully use force against Iraq to ensure compliance with Iraq's WMD obligations.

This conclusion was not shared by their minister, Jack Straw. He was willing to adopt a more open and more flexible interpretation of the law. Perhaps the Pinochet case, when he was Home Secretary, had emboldened him to push at the limits of international law. He told the Butler Inquiry that he had concluded that a further resolution was not essential once 1441 had been adopted. It seems then that there was a clear disagreement between Jack Straw and his own legal advisers as to what should happen next. In the circumstances it was for the Attorney General to set out a definitive view, which would be the government's formal legal advice. The Ministerial Code of Conduct requires the Attorney General to 'be consulted in good time before the Government is committed to critical decisions involving legal considerations'.[52]

In January 2003 the Foreign Office legal advisers told the Attorney General of their views and asked for his. There is nothing to indicate that he did not share the unequivocal views of the legal advisers at the Foreign Office in London. However, he did not deliver a final view until mid-March, which left the Foreign Office and the government in limbo and without definitive advice in the crucial period during which a further Security Council resolution was being proposed and negotiated. Whether that delay was due to the indecision of the Attorney General or to other circumstances is unclear. It appears that he was not asked by the Prime Minister to provide formal advice until the last possible moment. Robin Cook, who resigned from the Cabinet shortly before the war in honourable protest, has noted his alarm when Tony Blair told the Cabinet on 11 April 2002 that 'the time to debate the legal basis for our action should be when we take that action'.[53] It seems that 10 Downing Street did not want a formal legal opinion in January or February 2003. But the key point is that the Attorney General did not then advise that no further resolution was needed.

If the British government had received clear advice that a further resolution was not needed it would not have been sensible to make the Herculean efforts it did during January and February 2003 to obtain such a resolution. A diplomat from one Security Council member state, who was closely involved in the negotiations, described to me a widespread recognition that the fact that such negotiations were taking place was wholly inconsistent with any claim that no further resolution was needed: 'The mere fact that the whole debate on having a new resolution happened between November and March showed that they [the Americans and the British] knew that the revival theory – relying on old resolutions – wasn't working and another resolution was needed.'

Efforts to obtain a second resolution dragged on and finally collapsed in the first week of March. By then there had been a significant development. On 11 February 2003 Lord Goldsmith met with John Bellinger III, legal adviser to the White House's National Security Council. The meeting took place in the White House. An official told me later: 'I met with Mr Bellinger and he said: "We had trouble with your Attorney, we got him there eventually."' When I put this to Mr Bellinger, he reflected and then told me: 'I do not recall making such a statement,' adding diplomatically, 'I doubt that an individual of Lord Goldsmith's eminence would adopt a legal argument based on pressure from the US government.' In any event, this seems to have been the moment at which the Attorney General's views shifted. Two weeks later, on 28 February, he informed the Prime Minister's office of his views.

The Attorney General's formal advice to the Prime Minister is set out in a minute dated 7 March 2003. By then the troops had been deployed. It is a thirteen-page document which states the various arguments on the need for a further resolution. It was sent only to the Prime Minister, although it was seen more widely, by the Foreign Secretary and Defence Secretary amongst others. It concludes that no further resolution is needed. It was sufficient for the Prime Minister – not the Security Council – to decide that Iraq had failed to comply with its disarmament obligations and that there was hard evidence of non-compliance and non-cooperation with resolution 1441. But the advice was not exactly clear-cut. It recognized that if the argument were to come before a court of law it might well be unsuccessful, so that the use of force against Iraq could be found to be illegal. It would be safer to have a second resolution. So concerned was the government about the possibility of such a case that it took steps to put together a legal team to prepare for possible international litigation.

Lord Goldsmith's advice of 7 March appears not to have been sufficiently clear for Admiral Sir Michael Boyce, the Chief of Defence Staff, or his legal advisers. On 10 March, against the crescendo of voices arguing that a failure to obtain explicit Security Council authorization would render force illegal, Sir Michael sought a clearer assurance of the war's legality.[54] What he was looking for, he has subsequently said, was a short and unambiguous note from the Attorney General (a further indication that his minute of 7 March was too ambiguous to be relied on). He wanted to be sure that military chiefs and their soldiers would not be 'put through the mill' at the International Criminal Court:

I asked for unequivocal advice that what we were proposing to do was lawful. Keeping it as simple as that did not allow for equivocations, and what I eventually got was what I required . . . something in writing that was very short indeed. Two or three lines saying our proposed actions were lawful under national and international law.[55]

His concerns had been 'transmitted' to the Attorney General through the Prime Minister. Sir Michael did not feel the need to ask himself what he would do if he did not receive the short note he was seeking: 'I was reassured I would get what I asked for and I was prepared to take that at face value.' If the reassurance came from the Prime Minister, then Blair, at least, was confident that the Attorney General would provide the necessary support.

My understanding is that the Attorney General's views became 'clearer' only after his legal advice of 7 March. On 13 March the Attorney General communicated his 'clearer' views – that the better interpretation of 1441 was that it was lawful to use force without another resolution – at a meeting with Baroness Morgan, Director of Political and Government Relations at 10 Downing Street, and Lord Falconer, at the time a Home Office minister. The Attorney General also informed Lord Falconer and Baroness Morgan that the Prime Minister was entitled to certify the existence of a material breach by Iraq. On 14 March, Sir Michael was provided with the short written reassurance he had sought. On 15 March the Prime Minister confirmed in writing 'unequivocally [his] view that Iraq has committed further material breaches' of Security Council resolutions. But on what basis did the Prime Minister make that vital determination? Having wrongly concluded that it was not for the Security Council to make that determination, the Attorney General fell into further error: he provided no clear guidance on the standard which the Prime Minister should apply in making his determination. In any event,

10 Downing Street then proceeded to set out the Attorney General's view in the answer to the parliamentary question which was published on 17 March.

I have already explained why Lord Goldsmith's advice was wrong. It was for the Security Council and not the Prime Minister to make a finding of Iraqi non-compliance, a view that had been put forward by the Foreign Office legal advisers as early as March 2002. But even if the Attorney General's advice was right, it is remarkable that he could have omitted a crucial step, by not requiring the Prime Minister to take full and proper account of the Blix and ElBaradei reports or the current views of the British Joint Intelligence Committee on Iraq's actions under resolution 1441. The crucial line in the Attorney General's statement to the House of Lords on 17 March is paragraph 7: 'It is plain that Iraq has failed so to comply . . .' Plain to whom? Plain according to what standard? What may have been plain to the Prime Minister was not plain to most of the rest of the world.

In March 2003 it could not be said there was 'incontrovertible' proof of large-scale WMD activity in Iraq. The Blix and ElBaradei reports did not find such proof. There was no assessment of Iraqi compliance by the British government's Joint Intelligence Committee beyond an 'Initial Assessment' on 18 December 2002, shortly after Iraq had submitted its weapons declaration as required by 1441. The Butler Report was critical of the fact that there was no re-evaluation of the quality of the intelligence in early 2003, given what it called the 'generally negative' results of the UN inspections.[56] So even on the widely discredited basis put forward for the legality of the war – Iraq's material breaches – it is hard to see how the use of force could be justified. In March 2002 the British government proceeded on the basis that a claim of material breach required incontrovertible proof of large-scale WMD activity; a year later Blair departed from that standard.

*

The Attorney General's public statement of 17 March 2003 was not a summary of the written advice of 7 March or of any other formal legal advice. It did not explain the basis on which the Prime Minister had found a material breach. What happened to cause the Attorney General to revisit his opinion by ditching those parts of his earlier advice that offered a more balanced view? His statement of 17 March made no mention of any doubts or alternative views. It provided no response to the numerous members of the Security Council who had reacted angrily to the 'revival' argument and to the claim that the US and Britain alone could determine the existence of a material breach of 1441. Nor did it refer to his previously expressed view that it was likely that a court would rule that the use of force in these circumstances would be unlawful. Moreover, no legal developments had occurred, in the Security Council or elsewhere, to transform the situation from that which existed in January and February or on 7 March 2003, when earlier advice had been given, to that of 17 March 2003.

There is nothing in the public domain to suggest that new facts had emerged in that period to indicate conclusively that Saddam Hussein was violating resolution 1441. If anything, the contrary was true: on 7 March Hans Blix had given his third presentation to the Security Council. He concluded that although Iraqi co-operation was not complete it was accelerating. No weapons of mass destruction had been found, and thirty-four al-Samoud missiles had been destroyed. Mohammed ElBaradei had comprehensively demonstrated that one of the British government's central claims, that Iraq had sought to obtain supplies of uranium from Niger, was totally unfounded. There is no indication that the Attorney General caused the Prime Minister to consider these points.

Clare Short has suggested that the Attorney General might have been 'leaned on' by the Prime Minister. Without a clear explanation – or publication of the totality of the advice given by the Attorney General in the period prior to resolution 1441 and then during the period between November 2002 and 17 March 2003 – it is difficult to know what took place. It is clear, however, that the statement made in the House of Lords on 17 March 2003 was neither a summary nor a précis of any of the earlier advices which the Attorney General had provided, including the minute of 7 March. The published statement appears to be a recasting of a plausible argument into the succinct and decisive opinion of law which Sir Michael Boyce had requested. The 17 March statement does not seem to have been accompanied by a formal and complete legal opinion or advice in the usual sense, whether written by the Attorney General, or independently by a barrister retained by him. When the issue was addressed in a Cabinet meeting on the morning of 17 March, ministers were provided with just two pieces of A4 paper, the same document that was delivered in the House of Lords later that day. The Ministerial Code of Conduct requires the full text of any advice to be made available in papers to the Cabinet.[57] None was provided. There was no discussion, and no minister raised any question as to the basis upon which the Prime Minister had decided that Iraq was in material breach of resolution 1441.

The statement by Lord Goldsmith produced the desired result, at least in the short term. Sir Michael Boyce and the military were satisfied, as were many Labour MPs, who were wavering in their support of the government in the House of Commons motion supporting the use of force. Clare Short did not resign from the Cabinet, remaining for a few weeks more.[58] The Prime Minister got the legal advice he needed. War was waged. But the issue did not go away, and questions surrounding the Attorney General's final advice continued to fester.

A year after the war, in February 2004, criminal proceedings against Katharine Gun, a junior translator at a British government spying centre, were dropped. In the run-up to the war, Gun had leaked to *The Observer* newspaper a copy of an email from the US National Security Center to British intelligence. The email sought Britain's assistance in bugging Chilean and Mexican diplomats on the UN Security Council whose votes were needed to obtain the resolution which the Attorney General subsequently concluded was not needed. Gun was prosecuted under Britain's Official Secrets Act, but a few months later the case was dropped. Over the following days the British government came under pressure to explain the circumstances in which the case had been dropped. Renewed calls were made to publish all of the Attorney General's legal advice on the war. The government refused, adding to the suspicion that any release could include embarrassing material.

A few months later, in September 2004, Kofi Annan's unambiguous statement that the war was illegal darkened the cloud which hung over the British government, harbouring the suspicion that an artificial and erroneous legal argument had been cobbled together to justify regime change. In November 2004 an article in the *New Statesman* described 'how Blair, together with the Americans, leaned on the UK Attorney General . . . to change his mind about the legality of the war'.[59] Surprisingly, this prompted the Attorney General to respond with a

letter published in the journal the following week: 'I confirm again
. . . that it was my genuine and independent view that action was lawful, under existing Security Council resolutions.'[60] Despite the robust
response I suspect that the cloud will continue to hang over those
most closely associated with the advice until it is published in full.

*

The Iraq War posed fundamental challenges to the established international legal order. It has brought the international community to a
'fork in the road . . . a moment no less decisive than 1945 itself, when
the United Nations was founded', as the UN Secretary General put it
in his speech to the UN General Assembly in September 2003.[61] I
have explained why the legal arguments put forward by the US and
British governments to justify the war are unsustainable. I agree with
Richard Perle that international law did not permit force to overthrow Saddam Hussein.[62] I disagree, however, that it required the
international community to 'leave him alone'. The UN's system of
collective security had contained Saddam Hussein, better than most
would have expected. The inspections which resumed in November
2003 and which were brought about by the threat of force were
working, and it remained open to the Security Council to authorize
force as and when it considered such action necessary.

Contrary to the views of the British government, neither France
nor any other state had said that it would veto any resolution at any
time and irrespective of the circumstances. The suggestion by the
Prime Minister that he was entitled to override an 'unreasonable' veto
is an outrageous one. Britain created the system of Permanent
Members and vetoes, and must live with it. The simple fact is that the
great majority of states who sat on the Security Council in March
2003 did not consider that the circumstances, as they were then
known to be, could justify the use of force. History has shown that
they were right and that the US and Britain were wrong. No WMD
have been found. It could be said that the UN system worked. No
amount of bullying by two Permanent Members could buy the votes
they wanted.

In the meantime the illegality of the war continues to taint the
process of reconstructing Iraq. We cannot know how different things
would have been if the Security Council had duly authorized force.
But they surely could not have been more difficult if the international

community had been less divided and if there had been a proper UN-led process of reconstruction, rather than the Anglo-American effort whose motives are distrusted by almost every Iraqi I have met, including so many of its present government officials.

More broadly, the events of the past three years have shown that the circumstances in which the UN rules on force were established have changed. It is not credible any more to proceed on the basis that the international legal order is founded on a body of sovereign states who are willing to play by the established global rules. Nowadays, there are failed states in which no government controls the territory; there are clandestine groups, such as al-Qaeda and others, who have made it clear that they intend to obtain weapons of mass destruction, and that they will use them if they can. The threats they pose are real. Such threats can only be met fully over the long term if the civilized world acts together in accordance with agreed basic values and principles. That necessarily means a system of rules, under international law. Undermining the rules diminishes the effectiveness of the response. Ignoring the rules de-legitimizes actions and makes smaller states feel vulnerable. Relying on bad legal arguments destroys the credibility of governments. And credibility is important right now. My concern with the Anglo-American war on Iraq is that it will make it more difficult to act when there is a real threat: at a time when unity is needed to address actual challenges, these two countries have broken ranks and acted unilaterally where there was no immediate threat. Their actions have undermined trust in the intelligence services and in governance. The challenge for international law is to ensure that the rules balance the legitimate interests of two groups of states: those that feel vulnerable to international terrorism and weapons of mass destruction, and those that feel vulnerable to the response to that threat, especially unilateral responses.

A year after the Iraq War, in the aftermath of the collapse of the case against Katharine Gun and the call for the Attorney General's legal advice to be published, the British Prime Minister delivered another emotive speech, from his constituency at Sedgefield in the north-east of England. It was an important speech, but confusingly constructed upon a series of false premises. It was woven around an idealized 'doctrine of international community' which the Prime Minister had first invoked in a speech in Chicago in 1999, in the aftermath of Kosovo. The Sedgefield speech moves seamlessly between different issues. It goes from the responsibility to use force to protect human rights (humanitarian intervention) to the entirely different issue of the right to use force pre-emptively to prevent threats from weapons of mass destruction materializing. The Prime Minister argued in favour of both. He recognized concerns that the US and its allies will use these emerging doctrines to do whatever they want, 'unilaterally and without recourse to any rules-based code or doctrine', but he is not persuaded by the concerns, and he raises the spectre of international rules which are totally inadequate to meet modern challenges.

I am not persuaded by his argument. He has aligned himself with a US Administration which behaves as though international law does not matter, that has withdrawn from international agreements with impunity, and that is willing to bully other states which seek to promote initiatives such as the ICC and the Kyoto Protocol. The Prime Minister may believe that global rules matter, but ultimately his actions speak louder than his words. His actions on Iraq have degraded the international rule of law and contributed to a dangerous fiasco. They suggest a rather lesser attachment to the international rule of law than he professes.

9

Terrorists and Torturers

*'International law? I better call my lawyer. [. . .] I don't know
what you're talking about by international law.'*
George W. Bush, 11 December 2003

What do you do, as an international lawyer, when your client asks you to advise on the international rules prohibiting torture? Do you start with the rules, ask yourself how an international court – or your allies – might address the issue, and reach a balanced conclusion? Or do you focus on narrower issues of the relevance, applicability and enforceability of the international rules in the national context, and reach a conclusion that you know – if you ask yourself the question – no international court would accept? Let me put it another way. Do you advise, or do you provide legal cover?

When the now notorious Abu Ghraib photographs and testimonies entered the public domain we did not know that lawyers in the US Department of Justice and elsewhere had provided detailed legal advice to the US government on the international torture rules. But over the weeks that followed a rich source of leaked legal memos and opinions threw light on the logic which provided the context in which Abu Ghraib could happen. The documents argued, in short, that the international rules were inapplicable, irrelevant or unenforceable. They suggested that interrogation practices could be defined without reference to the constraints placed on the United States by its international obligations. So long as the practice was consistent with US law, it would be fine. The advice ignored the plain language of the 1984 Convention against Torture and other treaties and rules which bound the US. The advice ignored the definition of torture in international law, and the prohibition against torture under any circumstances. Even more outrageously, it proposed defences, immunities and impunity. In an effort to limit the damage, the White House declassified and released a great deal of material, although by no means all the advice. But it turned out that the White House material had not been reviewed very carefully. Some of it was even worse than the earlier leaked material. Parts of the advice were then disavowed.

The photographs were monstrous, and so were the legal opinions. How did it come to this, at the beginning of the twenty-first century, after more than fifty years of human rights and humanitarian law? How could the government of a country so strongly committed to the rules set its lawyers on such a task? And how could it be that the lawyers would get it so badly wrong?

*

The 'war on terrorism' has led many lawyers astray. This phoney 'war' has been used to eviscerate well-established and sensible rules of international law, which the US has in the past supported, relied upon and often created. In the minds of the politically appointed legal advisers the argument runs something like this: 1) the US faces an unparalleled threat, presenting a clear and present danger; 2) all necessary means may be used to obtain information from captives, who are to be treated as combatants rather than ordinary criminals; and 3) international law is inapplicable and/or unenforceable and/or irrelevant, and in any case the rules of international law must be interpreted to allow a threatened state to do everything necessary to protect itself. I should make it clear that this is not the kind of legal analysis which would be applied by the vast majority of legal advisers in the US State Department or the US Army's Judge Advocate General's Corps, or by legal advisers to the British government or almost any other government in the world. The advice I would have expected to see would run something like this. There are two sets of international rules governing torture and interrogation practices: a first set prohibits torture; a second set provides that torture cannot be used against terrorists, whether they are combatants or criminals. The governing principle must be: do unto others as you would have them do unto you.

Torture and other cruel and inhuman treatment has been internationally outlawed since the end of the Second World War. The 1948

Universal Declaration of Human Rights stated that 'No one shall be subjected to torture or to cruel, inhuman or degrading treatment or punishment'. It allows for no exceptions. Similar language can be found in the International Covenant on Civil and Political Rights (Article 7) and the American Convention on Human Rights (Article 5(2)). Both are binding on the US. The 1949 Geneva Convention III prohibits physical or mental torture and any other form of coercion against a prisoner of war (Article 17). It designates such acts as 'grave breaches' of the Convention (Article 130). Geneva Convention IV prohibits an occupying power from torturing any protected person (Article 32), as well as all other 'measures of brutality' (Article 283). And the 1977 Geneva Protocol I – the relevant provision of which reflects customary law – prohibits 'torture of all kinds' and any other outrages on personal dignity, against any person under any circumstances. Even the threat of such acts is banned (Article 75(2)). These are the standards to which all detainees are entitled as of right.

The 1984 Convention against Torture takes these general obligations and codifies them into more specific rules. It prohibits torture and 'other acts of cruel, inhuman or degrading treatment or punishment'.[1] It criminalizes torture and seeks to end impunity for any torturer by denying him all possible refuge. The House of Lords ruled that Augusto Pinochet's claim to immunity could not withstand the 1984 Convention. The Convention defines torture broadly: 'any act by which severe pain or suffering, whether physical or mental, is intentionally inflicted on a person'. It encompasses acts which have been authorized – or acquiesced in – by a public official, and it includes acts carried out to obtain from the victim or from a third person information or a confession (Article 1). The Convention is categorical that there will be no circumstances – even a 'war against terrorism' – in which torture is permitted:

No exceptional circumstances whatsoever, whether a state of war or a threat of war, internal political instability or any other public emergency, may be invoked as a justification for torture.[2]

Similarly, the Statute of the International Criminal Court treats torture and other inhumane acts as war crimes and crimes against humanity. These are parts of the Rome Statute that the United States has not objected to, as far as I am aware.

This is one area in which the rules of international law are clear. It does not matter whether a person is a criminal, or a warrior combatant, or a lawful combatant or an unlawful combatant, or an al-Qaeda militant, or a private American contractor. He may not be tortured. He may not be subjected to other cruel, inhuman or degrading treatment. If he is, then the perpetrator of such acts must be punished under the criminal law. And any person who threatens torture, or who is complicit or participates in torture, is also to be treated as a criminal. Complicity can include a commanding officer or a political official. It can include a legal adviser who gives the green light to torture. It can include a prime minister or a president.

This absolute prohibition is related to the second set of rules, addressing the status of the terrorists: are they to be treated as criminals or combatants? The answer will depend on the particular individual. If he was a member of the Taliban's regular armed forces, or of Saddam Hussein's Republican Guard, then he is a combatant, and must be treated as such. Once caught, he is entitled to protection under international humanitarian law, including the Geneva Conventions and Protocols. Even if it is suspected that he has information which may assist in the 'war on terrorism' there are strict constraints on his interrogation. He cannot be tortured or treated inhumanely under any circumstances.

What if he is a suspected member of al-Qaeda who is thought to have planned a suicide attack? Or an insurgent in Iraq after the March 2003 conflict, who is suspected of laying roadside bombs targeting the Coalition Provisional Authority? Is he a combatant or a criminal? International law generally treats such people as criminals, not warriors. Britain adopted that approach in respect of the IRA, whose claims to be treated as combatants were always rejected, largely on the grounds that applying the laws of war would add legitimacy to their efforts. The 1997 International Convention for the Suppression of Terrorist Bombings followed that reasoning, and made it a criminal offence to bomb a public place or a state or government facility with the aim of causing death or destruction. The United States, Britain and more than 120 other states supported that approach. States which are parties to the Convention agreed to subject any person who is thought to have engaged in terrorist activities to criminal process, by prosecuting them or extraditing them to a country that will prosecute them. The US became a party in June 2002, after 9/11.

Nowhere does the 1997 Convention say that these criminals are exempt from the ordinary protections of the law, or that you can torture them or treat them inhumanely. Quite the contrary. The Convention explicitly guarantees 'fair treatment' to any person who is taken into custody under its provisions. That includes the rights and guarantees under 'applicable provisions of international law, including the international law of human rights'.[3]

Taken together, the rules prohibiting torture and criminalizing terrorism allow no exceptions. The rationale is simple: torture is morally wrong and, according to the US Army's *Field Manual*, is a poor technique which leads to unreliable results. In 1999 the Israeli Supreme Court gave a unanimous landmark ruling that prohibited the Israeli Security Services from using physical abuse of suspected terrorists during interrogation. 'This is the destiny of democracy,' wrote Chief Justice Barak, 'as not all means are acceptable to it, and not all practices employed by its enemies are open before it.'[4] His words have a strong resonance today:

Although a democracy must fight with one hand tied behind its back, it nonetheless has the upper hand. Preserving the Rule of Law and recognition of an individual's liberty constitutes an important component in its understanding of security. At the end of the day, they strengthen its spirit and its strength and allow it to overcome its difficulties.

The Court said that it was not deciding whether the so-called 'necessity' defence could be available. This might be invoked in the 'ticking time-bomb argument' (where an arrested suspect is thought to hold information concerning the location of a bomb which has been set and will explode imminently). Such a case would have to be decided on its own merits, as and when it arose. What the state could not do, ruled the Israeli Supreme Court, was to invoke a necessity argument to justify directives and authorizations which would use 'liberty-infringing physical means' during the interrogation of those suspected of terrorist activities. The Court noted the absolute prohibition on torture and cruel, inhuman and degrading treatment in international law: there were no exceptions and 'there is no room for balancing'.

*

The events of 9/11 reopened a door which the Israeli Supreme Court wanted to close. Very shortly after the attacks the Bush Administration set in motion the procedures which led from the interrogation centres at Kandahar, Bhagram and Guantánamo to the torture of detainees at Abu Ghraib and elsewhere. According to media reports, President Bush signed a secret order giving new powers to the CIA and authorizing it to set up a series of detention facilities outside the US, and to question those held in them with 'unprecedented harshness'. Guantánamo was established as a place to gather information beyond the constraints of international law and US law. The US Supreme Court's judgment in *Rasul* in June 2004 initiated the unravelling of that effort. What the Supreme Court has not yet addressed, but which US federal courts may yet have to consider, is whether the interrogation regime at Guantánamo was consistent with American law and America's international obligations. The Guantánamo model of interrogation technique seems to have been applied in Afghanistan, and to have been exported to Iraq, including to Abu Ghraib, where the Geneva Conventions are recognized as being applicable.

We know nothing about the covert CIA regime. As to Guantánamo, the full story is yet to be told, including how far up the hierarchy the decision-making went. But much is known. The first detainees arrived on 11 January 2002. They were subjected to interrogations in accordance with the principles set out in the US Army's *Field Manual 34–52*, which was published in 1987. *FM 34–52*, as it is known, sets out 'the basic principles of interrogation doctrine and establishes procedures and techniques applicable to Army intelligence interrogations'. It makes clear that the principles and techniques of interrogation are to be used within the constraints established by The Hague and Geneva Conventions. *FM 34–52* is unambiguous in its prohibition of the use of force, or threats of force. It says:

The use of force, mental torture, threats, insults, or exposure to unpleasant and inhumane treatment of any kind is prohibited by law and is neither authorized nor condoned by the US Government. Experience indicates that the use of force is not necessary to gain the co-operation of sources for interrogation. Therefore, the use of force is a poor technique, as it yields unreliable results, may damage subsequent collection efforts, and can induce the source to say whatever he thinks the interrogator wants to hear. However, the use of force is not to be confused with psychological ploys, verbal trickery, or other non-violent and non-coercive ruses used by the interrogator in questioning hesitant or uncooperative sources. [. . .] Additionally, the inability to carry out a threat of violence or force renders an interrogator ineffective should the source challenge the threat. Consequently, from both legal and moral viewpoints, the restrictions established by international law, agreements, and customs render threats of force, violence, and deprivation useless as interrogation techniques.[5]

According to the Pentagon, by the summer of 2002 it had become clear that *FM 34–52* was not producing the desired results. The Pentagon wanted to use 'additional interrogation techniques' on Guantánamo detainees who were alleged to have close connections to the al-Qaeda leadership and planning figures, including 'financiers, bodyguards, recruiters and operators'.[6] This included individuals who were 'assessed to possess significant information on al-Qaeda plans' and who demonstrated resistance to the relatively light interrogations set out in *FM 34–52*.

Lieutenant Colonel Diane Beaver, a US Army lawyer, was asked to advise on the legal position. More aggressive interrogation techniques than the ones referred to in *FM 34–52*, she wrote, 'may be required in order to obtain information from detainees that are resisting interrogation efforts and are suspected of having significant information essential to national security'.[7] Her memorandum of 11 October 2002 described the problem: the detainees were developing more sophisticated interrogation resistance strategies, because they could communicate amongst themselves and debrief each other. This problem was compounded by the fact that there was no established policy for interrogation limits and operations at Guantánamo and 'many interrogators have felt in the past that they could not do anything that could be considered "controversial"'. According to her memorandum, America's international obligations are irrelevant and interrogation techniques – including forceful means and restraints on torture – are governed exclusively by US law.

Her analysis provides a useful insight on how to get around international law. President Bush's Executive Order of 7 February 2002 determined that the detainees were not prisoners of war. It followed, therefore, that 'the Geneva Conventions limitations that ordinarily would govern captured enemy personnel interrogations are not binding on US personnel conducting detainee interrogations at [Guantánamo]'. In fact, Lt. Col. Beaver went even further: 'no international body of law directly applies'. She is not saying that there are no international rules; rather, the international rules are either not applicable or not enforceable. To reach this extraordinary conclusion she reviews various international conventions which establish binding norms for the US – including the 1984 Convention against Torture, the International Covenant on Civil and Political Rights, and the American Convention on Human Rights – and then explains why not one of them creates any obligations which could actually be applied so as to constrain interrogators. This was either because the US had entered reservations which gave primacy to US federal law, or because the treaty was not 'self-executing' (meaning that although it might bind the US under international law it did not create rights for individuals which they could enforce in the national courts). It is striking that no mention is made of customary international law, reflected in particular in Article 75 of the 1977 Geneva Protocol I. *FM 34–52*'s reference to the 'restrictions established by international law, agreements, and customs' is simply bypassed. The logic of the argument is grotesque. It means that international law is irrelevant. Can you imagine how the US would react if another country tortured an American and defended it by saying 'Oh, terribly sorry, but the international treaty we signed up to which prohibits torture isn't enforceable in our domestic law so we don't have to apply it'? That is Lt. Col. Beaver's logic.

In the meantime, over at the US Department of Justice, her civilian colleagues had not been idle. On 1 August 2002, a few months before Lt. Col. Beaver produced her advice, Alberto Gonzales, Counsel to President Bush, received two memoranda. Apparently these were not related to Guantánamo, but to interrogations carried out elsewhere, including those conducted by the CIA.

One memorandum was from John Yoo, a Deputy Assistant Attorney General.[8] He had been asked whether interrogation methods used on captured al-Qaeda operatives, which were lawful under a US statute, could nonetheless lead to prosecution at the ICC, or violate the 1984 Convention against Torture. The question seems to have arisen to address the possibility that an interrogation carried out on the territory of a country which had joined the ICC might fall foul of the ICC rules. Yoo is known in academic circles as a sceptic about international law, and his opinion is replete with basic errors of law. Since the US is not a party to the Rome Statute, he wrote, the US 'cannot be bound by the provisions of the ICC treaty nor can US nationals be subject to ICC prosecution'. The first point is right, but the second is wrong. Individuals, not states, are defendants before the Court. If a CIA operative commits torture, rising to the level of a war crime or a crime against humanity, on the territory of a state which is a party to the Statute, then he can be prosecuted at the ICC. The Rome Statute is totally clear on that point. A first-year law student could work that out.

As regards the Convention against Torture, Yoo concluded that American participation was premised on the view that the definition of torture in the Convention was 'in the exact terms' of the relevant US federal statute. This is significant, because the Convention sets a lower threshold for acts to be defined as torture. On Yoo's analysis, then, if an act was not to be defined as torture under US law, then it could not be torture under the Convention. The argument is hopeless. It is one of the most basic rules of international law that in the event of a conflict between an international rule and a domestic rule the international rule will prevail. Once that rule is overridden – as Yoo proposes – there is no international law left. Why bother negotiating a treaty on torture? Each state would be free to substitute its own definitions for those of the Convention. But more seriously, Yoo has misunderstood what the US did in ratifying the Convention. It did not enter a 'reservation' redefining torture and setting the bar at a higher level; it entered an 'understanding'. This is an entirely different thing. Whilst a reservation can change the international legal obligation, an 'understanding' cannot. Yoo writes that Germany commented on the United States' reservations, but 'did not oppose any US reservation outright'. In fact Germany said the understandings 'do not touch upon the obligations of the United States of America as State Party to the Convention'. So it is the definition in the Convention – the international definition – which prevails. No amount of wilful misreading by a senior Justice Department legal adviser can change that.

The second memorandum received by Gonzales was a longer one

from Jay Bybee, an Assistant Attorney General and, presumably, Yoo's boss.[9] It addressed the standards of conduct required by the 1984 Convention against Torture, as implemented by US federal law. Administration officials have confirmed that the Bybee memo 'helped provide an after-the-fact legal basis for harsh procedures used by the CIA on high-level leaders of al-Qaeda'.[10] *Newsweek* magazine has reported that the 1 August 2002 memo was prompted by CIA questions about what to do with those captives alleged to be top-ranking al-Qaeda terrorists, such as Ibn al-Shaykh al-Libi and Abu Zubaydah, who had turned uncooperative. Relying on the same starting point as Beaver and Yoo – we are supreme and our law trumps everything – Bybee dispenses with all established canons of treaty interpretation and concludes that torture covers only the most extreme acts, limited to severe pain which is difficult for the victim to endure. 'Where the pain is physical,' he writes, 'it must be of an intensity akin to that which accompanies serious physical injury such as death or organ failure.' Anything less, he implies, will not be torture and will be permissible. And where the pain is mental, then it 'requires suffering not just at the moment of infliction but it also requires lasting psychological harm, such as seen in mental disorders like posttraumatic stress disorder'.[11] This is the most shocking legal opinion I have ever come across. Such 'legal' analysis, by a man who is now a federal judge, bears no relation to the definition which the US and 120 other countries signed up to in the Convention against Torture.

And it gets worse. According to Bybee, the US Congress can no more interfere with the President's conduct of the interrogation of enemy combatants than it can dictate strategic or tactical decisions on the battlefield. So the President is freed from all legal constraints. Laws that would prevent the President from gaining the intelligence he believes necessary to prevent attacks upon the US would be unconstitutional.[12] The US Assistant Attorney General concludes that under the current circumstances certain criminal law defences of necessity and self-defence could justify interrogation methods needed to prevent a direct and imminent threat to the US and its citizens. This overrides the Convention against Torture's absolute prohibition on torture in all circumstances. But that prohibition is not applicable in US law, advises Bybee, because it has not been included in the relevant federal statute. The US Congress must therefore have intended to permit the 'necessity or wartime defense' for torture.[13] Finally, he concludes that self-defence could allow a government defendant to argue that using torture in an interrogation could be justified 'on the basis of protecting the nation from attack'.[14]

The assessment of international law is plain wrong. I can't comment on the position under American law but I am happy to defer to Harold Koh, Dean of the Yale Law School and an acknowledged expert in US constitutional and international law: the memos are 'blatantly wrong. It's just erroneous legal analysis. The notion that the president has the constitutional power to permit torture is like saying he has the constitutional power to commit genocide.'[15] The analyses of Beaver, Bybee and Yoo are deeply flawed, and scary. Anyone who has even the most rudimentary understanding of international law will see that. Yet these are the memoranda the White House was willing to put in the public domain.

*

The 'global war on terrorism' was therefore used to justify the need for 'additional interrogation techniques' – at Guantánamo, in Afghanistan and in Iraq, and secretly elsewhere under CIA control. Against the backdrop of this legal advice, the US Army's Lt. Col. Jerald Phifer requested approval for a new 'interrogation plan' at Guantánamo.[16] The additional techniques – going beyond *FM 34–52* – were divided into three categories. Category I included two techniques: yelling and deception. Category II required additional permission and included the use of stress positions (such as standing) for up to four hours; the use of falsified documents; isolation for up to thirty days; deprivation of light and auditory stimuli; hooding during questioning and transportation; twenty-eight-hour interrogations; removal of comfort items (including religious items); removal of clothing; forced grooming (shaving of facial hair etc.); and using detainee-specific phobias (such as fear of dogs) to induce stress. Category III was to be used only for 'exceptionally resistant detainees', who would normally number no more than 3 per cent of the total (that would be twenty people at Guantánamo). This category required approval by the Commanding General, with appropriate legal review and information to the Commander of the US Southern Command (USSOUTHCOM). It covered the 'use of scenarios designed to convince the detainee that death or severely painful consequences are imminent for him and/or his family'; exposure to cold weather or water; use of a wet towel and dripping water to induce the misperception of suffocation; and use of mild, non-injurious physical contact such as grabbing, poking in the chest with the finger and light pushing. All of these are plainly inconsistent with international law, as are most of the Category II techniques. Nevertheless, Phifer's memorandum implied that even more might be available: it added that any of the Category III techniques 'that require more than light grabbing, poking or pushing will be administered only by individuals specifically trained in their safe application'.

In another memorandum on the same day – 11 October 2002 – Major General Dunlaver concluded that these techniques did not violate US or international law. He relied on Lt. Col. Beaver's legal analysis which, it will be recalled, had determined that no international laws were actually applicable. Beaver gave the green light to all three techniques, although not without reservation. The use of a wet towel to induce suffocation should be used with caution, she wrote, because 'foreign courts have already advised about the potential mental harm that this method may cause'. Pushing and poking 'technically' constituted an assault. And the US Torture Statute specifically mentioned death threats as an example of 'inflicting mental pain and suffering'. Nevertheless, she concluded that the proposed methods of interrogation should be approved, subject to proper training and prior legal and medical review before their application. Others were cautious about Category III. General James T. Hill wrote to the Chairman of the US Joint Chiefs of Staff, asking that lawyers from the Department of Defense and the Department of Justice review Category III. He was unclear whether all the techniques in Category III were legal under US law, he wrote, and was 'particularly troubled by the use of implied or expressed threats of death of the detainee or his family'.[17] But he wanted as many options as possible at his disposal.

If any legal reviews were carried out they have not been made publicly available. However, it appears that there were no legal objections to techniques that plainly violate the 1984 Convention against Torture and the requirements of the Geneva Conventions, including Protocol I.

It would be interesting to know what the lawyers at the US State Department would have made of all this. Perhaps they never got a chance to have their say. On 2 December 2002 Donald Rumsfeld personally approved Categories I and II. He also approved the grabbing, poking and pushing technique in Category III.[18] As to the other Category III techniques, he concluded that whilst these could be legally available, a blanket approval was not warranted 'at this time'. 'I stand for 8–10 hours a day,' Rumsfeld added in a handwritten comment. 'Why is standing limited to 4 hours?'

The approval remained in force for only six weeks, and was rescinded by Rumsfeld on 15 January 2003. When this fact was made public, in June 2004, it stated that Rumsfeld had 'learned of concern about the implementation of these techniques'. No further explanation was provided. But more was needed, beyond *FM 34–52*. So Rumsfeld directed the Pentagon's General Counsel to establish a Working Group on the interrogation of detainees held by the US armed forces. The Group was headed by Mary Walker, the US Air Force's General Counsel. It included top civilian and uniformed lawyers from each military branch, and consulted with the Justice Department, the Joint Chiefs of Staff, the Defense Intelligence Agency and other intelligence agencies.[19] Again it seems the State Department was excluded.

The Working Group reported on 4 April 2003. It recommended thirty-five interrogation techniques to be used on unlawful combatants outside the United States, subject to certain limitations. The legal analyses put forward by Yoo and Bybee were broadly accepted, with the effect that international law could be taken as imposing no constraints above and beyond US law. A military lawyer who assisted in preparing the report said that political appointees heading the Working Group wanted to assign to the President virtually unlimited authority on matters of torture.[20] Military lawyers were uncomfortable with that approach, and focused on reining in the more extreme interrogation methods, rather than challenging the President's constitutional powers.[21] The report accepted the principle that unlawful acts might not give rise to criminal liability, in view of the necessity and self-defence arguments. And it concluded that the prohibition against torture 'must be construed as inapplicable to interrogations undertaken pursuant to [the President's] Commander-in-Chief

Authority'.[22] This sweeping conclusion brushed aside fifty years of international laws.

On 16 April 2003 Donald Rumsfeld approved the use of only twenty-four of these techniques, for the purpose of interrogating unlawful combatants at Guantánamo. Seven techniques went beyond what *FM 34–52* allowed. Four of the techniques could only be used with Rumsfeld's approval because, it was said, other countries might consider them to be inconsistent with the Geneva Conventions. They were the use of incentives to co-operate; 'pride and ego down' (referring to the exploitation of a prisoner's loyalty, intelligence or perceived weakness); good-cop-bad-cop interrogation; and isolation.

Rumsfeld did not approve eleven of the thirty-five techniques recommended by the Working Group, at least in this document. They included mild physical contact, threats to transfer to a third country, the use of prolonged interrogations, forced grooming, prolonged standing, sleep deprivation, physical training and slapping. They also included one technique which appeared in the Abu Ghraib photographs, namely increasing anxiety by use of aversions ('simple presence of a dog without directly threatening action'), and they included removal of clothing and hooding, two techniques which US Senators found especially troubling when they questioned Rumsfeld's Deputy, Paul Wolfowitz, on 13 May 2004:

Senator Reed: Mr Secretary, do you think crouching naked for 45 minutes is humane?

Mr Wolfowitz: Not naked, absolutely not.

Senator Reed: So if he is dressed up that is fine? [. . .] Sensory deprivation, which would be a bag over your head for 72 hours. Do you think that is humane? [. . .]

Mr Wolfowitz: Let me come back to what you said, the work of this government . . .

Senator Reed: No, no. Answer the question, Mr Secretary. Is that humane?

Mr Wolfowitz: I don't know whether it means a bag over your head for 72 hours, Senator. I don't know.

Senator Reed: Mr Secretary, you're dissembling, non-responsive. Anybody would say putting a bag over someone's head for 72 hours, which is . . .

Mr Wolfowitz: It strikes me as not humane, Senator.
Senator Reed: Thank you very much Mr Secretary.[23]

*

The materials released by the White House raised a great number of questions. Were these the only techniques approved? Were other techniques approved for use by the CIA or other agencies? How are the approved techniques to be squared with the accounts given by released Guantánamo detainees? The accounts by the British detainees, if accurate, describe practices that go beyond what is permitted under international law and even beyond Rumsfeld's revised standards. Tarek Dergoul has reported being poked, kicked, punched, shaved, exposed to intense heat and cold, deprived of sleep, and being kept chained in painful positions. He claims he was threatened with return to an Arab country where he was told he would be subjected to full-blown torture. These are some of the eleven techniques recommended by the Pentagon's Working Group Report of April 2003, but not approved by Rumsfeld. This inevitably raises a question: did interrogators exceed their orders, or was a parallel system of interrogations established which was permitted to apply the eleven techniques?

That question needs to be answered because similar techniques – and others which were even worse – appear to have been used in Afghanistan and in Iraq. The situation in Iraq should have been very different, since the United States accepted that the Geneva Conventions were applicable. But it is plain that the Conventions were not respected in relation to all the detainees. In January 2004, Joseph Darby, a low-ranking American soldier, spilled the beans. An internal inquiry was carried out, but Congress was not informed. Why, asked Senator Robert Byrd, was the report on abuse 'left to languish on the shelf at the Pentagon unread by the top leadership until the media revealed it to the world'?[24] In the spring of 2004 media photographs and reports described pictures of graphic abuse and torture at Abu Ghraib prison, Saddam Hussein's former punishment centre, turned into a US POW camp. They had been taken from the summer of 2003 onwards. The most notorious included a picture of a hooded detainee standing on a box with what appeared to be electrode wires attached to his fingers and genitals. Another showed Private First Class Lynndie England holding a leash tied to the neck of a naked man on the floor. Others showed a terrified detainee cowering naked before dogs; a hooded detainee apparently handcuffed in an awkward position on top of two boxes in a prison hallway; a soldier kneeling on naked detainees; a hooded detainee collapsed over railings to which he was handcuffed; and two soldiers posing over the body of Manadel al-Jamadi, a detainee who had allegedly been beaten to death by the CIA or civilian interrogators in the prison's showers. Would the US accept the treatment of its nationals in this way, under any circumstances?

Also in the spring of 2004, a Red Cross report condemning the treatment of Iraqi prisoners was leaked. This described violations of the Geneva Conventions which had been documented or observed while the International Committee of the Red Cross (ICRC) had been visiting Iraqi prisoners of war, civilian internees and other persons protected by the Geneva Conventions, between March and November 2003. The leaked extracts described brutality causing death or serious injury, physical or psychological coercion during interrogation, prolonged solitary confinement in cells devoid of daylight, and excessive and disproportionate use of force. The ICRC report described the ill-treatment as 'systematic . . . with regard to persons arrested in connection with suspected security offences or deemed to have an "intelligence" value'.[25] In some cases, wrote the ICRC, the treatment 'was tantamount to torture'.

The rules governing interrogations in Iraq have been less easy to identify. Until August 2003 the rules set out in *FM 34–52* applied. At the end of August, Major General Geoffrey Miller, who was head of detention operations at Guantánamo, visited Iraq. According to Lieutenant General Keith Alexander, a Deputy Chief of Staff for US Intelligence, Miller's mission was 'to help get the most that we could out of human intelligence operations in Iraq as a whole'.[26] He visited Abu Ghraib. By 9 September Miller had completed a review and recommended a new interrogation policy that 'borrowed heavily' from the approved Guantánamo procedures.[27] On 14 September Lt. Gen. Ricardo Sanchez, the ground commander in Iraq, authorized rules which allowed the harsh procedures *not* permitted at Guantánamo, including sleep deprivation and stress (crouching) positions for up to an hour. Military lawyers objected, and a month later – on 12 October – Sanchez restricted the policy. The new procedures were claimed to be consistent with Geneva. Nevertheless, as the *New York Times* described, troubling practices were tolerated, including forced nudity, slapping, handcuffing, hooding and intimidation with dogs. The picture which emerges from the documents, interviews and congressional testimony 'points to a broader pattern of misconduct and knowledge about it stretching up the chain of command'.[28] It was only in May 2004, after the press got hold of the details of the procedures, that coercive practices were reported to have been ended. Whether that included any CIA interrogations which may have been taking place is not known.

*

As the media got hold of the material, the Bush Administration came under increased pressure to explain its commitment to international rules, and the Geneva Conventions in particular. President Bush's General Counsel, Alberto Gonzales (who has been nominated as Attorney General in the second George W. Bush Administration), made it clear that the Administration had never authorized torture, but he left open the possibility that agencies other than the Department of Defense might have engaged in interrogation by reference to different rules. During his press conference on 22 June 2004 he was asked whether interrogation went beyond the twenty-four methods approved for Guantánamo, either through a 'special access programme' or through another government agency. 'We're not going to comment on anything beyond what is accepted [by the] Department of Defense,' he responded, adding that there was a directive throughout the entire government that every agency was to follow the law and could not engage in torture. But whose definition of the law? And torture defined by whom? By Beaver or Bybee? By the Working Group? When he was asked whether the CIA was subject to the twenty-four categories of interrogation technique, he responded: 'I'm not going to get into questions related to the CIA.' When pushed, he responded: 'I'm not going to get into discussions about the CIA, except to repeat what I just said, and that is that the techniques that they used that have been approved – they've been approved and vetted by the Department of Justice – are lawful and do not constitute torture.' This fell far short of the denial that the thirty-five techniques recommended by the Working Group Report – which adopted the Department of Justice's approach – might actually be in use by some other agency, including the CIA.

Gonzales did disavow some of the earlier memoranda that had been drafted, including Bybee's memo of 1 August 2002. 'Unnecessary, overbroad discussions in some of these memos that address abstract legal theories, or discussions subject to misinterpretation, but not relied upon by decision-makers', he said, 'are under review.' To the best of his knowledge, he added, the memos did not make it into the hands of soldiers in the field or to the President. They did 'not reflect the policies that the Administration ultimately adopted'. But that disavowal did not extend to the memoranda's findings on international law, which were incorporated more or less unchanged into the April 2003 Working Group Report, which remained in effect.

*

Over time a great deal more information will emerge. But even at this stage it seems pretty clear that the legal minds which created Bush's doctrine of pre-emption in the use of force and established the procedures at the Guantánamo detention camp led directly to an environment in which the monstrous images from Abu Ghraib could be created. Disdain for global rules underpins the whole enterprise. The international rules on torture, the treatment of prisoners of war and human rights norms do not apply, or they add nothing to US law, or they are not enforceable. To the seventeen or twenty-four or thirty-five techniques of interrogation there can be added these three techniques for avoiding international legal obligations. In this way the rules put in place by the US after the horrors of the Second World War are side-stepped, and the 'war on terror' is brought into disrepute.

What I find most remarkable is that such a scheme could have been put in place for the treatment of foreigners, of non-Americans, where respect for the international rules was bound to be raised. It is clear that many American military lawyers and legal advisers in the US State Department were horrified by what was happening. Some took active steps to stop the new rules and practices from being adopted. When their efforts failed they alerted others, with leaks to the press, for which we must be thankful. Temporarily, however, it was the Yoos and the Bybees and the Gonzales of the Administration that prevailed. They seem never to have asked themselves, as David Scheffer has put it, '"Would we tolerate such treatment of US prisoners?" If the answer is no, then the subject is closed.'[29] Nor, it seems, did they detain themselves for very long in deliberating whether their duty, as lawyers, was to ensure respect for the international rules or, rather, to provide legal cover for their political masters.

IO

Tough Guys and Lawyers

'Making the world a safer place for hypocrisy . . .'
Thomas Wolfe, *Look Homeward, Angel* (1929)

In the early summer of 1999, a few weeks after the House of Lords gave its third and final judgment in the Pinochet case, I was in Tehran. A professor at the University's Law School invited me to give an early evening lecture to his graduate students, on an international law topic of my choosing. I opted for the Pinochet judgment, although with some trepidation. The professor did not dissuade me. I assumed that the Court's decision not to recognize Pinochet's claim to immunity would be taken as a further example of the colonialist/imperialist tendency endemic in British culture, including its legal culture, and an inability to refrain from meddling in the internal affairs of Chile, another state.

The safest approach, I thought, would be to describe the case, say what happened and leave it at that. Don't give my own views on the rights and wrongs of the judgment. Don't provide a lecture on the triumph of international law. Just say what happened, take the questions. That is what I did, to a room overflowing with several hundred of Tehran's finest law students, at least half of whom were wearing chadors.

They listened attentively, and during my lecture numerous hands were raised to make requests for clarification. I was not quite sure what to expect once I had finished, after about forty minutes of storytelling without analysis or critique. The response came as a surprise. Many, many hands were raised. The discussion ran for more than two hours. It could have continued for much longer. Even from the early questions it became clear that a great number of people in the room were knowledgeable about every twist and turn in Pinochet's case, from the minutiae of the Convention against Torture to the role of Amnesty International. From the comments it was also clear that the decision to strike out the claim to immunity was viewed as the right decision. Surprise or criticism was directed not at the House of Lords but at me: why the reticence about the decision, why was I not more positive, why did I not embrace the case as a great moment for international law and the cause of human rights? In private discussions after the event many of the students were even more open. 'You have understood, I hope, why so many of us in that room, at this University, in this city, would follow a case like Pinochet' was the way one student put it.

This is not what I had expected in Tehran. It was striking that international law had provided a common language to explore complex moral and political issues faced by just about every country in the world: how to balance power and law, how to make political leaders globally accountable for their local actions. Given the political and religious divides, the surprise in Tehran was that the Convention against Torture and its application by the House of Lords was not taken as imperialist law: there will always be room for disagreement as to what a particular rule of international law may require a state to do, but there is general acceptance that the Convention's requirements are 'law', that they encapsulate common values and agreement, at least to the extent that that is possible, and that they set the outer limits within which the legitimacy and propriety of state actions and individual behaviour are to be addressed. Treaties like the Convention against Torture and judgments like that of the House of Lords in the Pinochet case provide hope to a great number of people around the world. That is a crucial difference between the world as it was in the 1930s and the world as it is today.

*

Of course law students are not governments, and knowledge of international law is not the same thing as compliance. Not everybody takes a rosy view of the onward march of international law or the international organizations that are charged with promulgating and enforcing them. That was horrifically demonstrated in the summer of 2003, when the United Nations headquarters in Baghdad was bombed and the organization's representative in Iraq, Sergio de Mello, was murdered along with many other UN workers. More recently there have been direct attacks in Afghanistan and Iraq on the Red Cross's humanitarian workers, probably the first time that the organization charged with ensuring respect for the Geneva Conventions has found itself treated as being in alliance with an 'occupying power'. These outrageous attacks, like 9/11, violate the most basic precepts of international law, making it clear that global rules are not universally respected. But is the attack from the terrorists the only challenge, or even the greatest challenge? What role now for the self-proclaimed leaders of the civilized world, those countries which promised to deliver the international rule of law?

The legacy of the Atlantic Charter is now in the hands of the Atlantic cowboys. It is difficult to imagine George W. Bush and Tony Blair coming together to produce a document of the kind that Roosevelt and Churchill sprang on the world in the summer of 1941, when the threat to the two countries was of a wholly different order. Sixty years on, an American President can show contempt for international obligations, in actions and in words: 'I don't care what the international lawyers say.' His British counterpart pays lip-service to international law, and then proceeds to override the views of those government advisers who actually know something about the subject. He feels able to proclaim, as he did in his speech in March 2004, the need for global rules, as though the achievements of the past sixty years count for nought. What is left of the transatlantic commitment to international law? What place now for the three pillars of the global legal order: prohibiting the use of force, promoting fundamental human rights, and promulgating fair economic liberalization?

To be sure, the commitment to international economic law remains strong. Trade and investment is the 'pathway to promote prosperity, the rule of law and liberty', President Bush's Trade Representative reminded us in October 2002. Where the rules promote the US's economic interests, respect for treaty commitments is undiminished, even if there is the odd wobble. There is no suggestion here that treaties are not legally binding and constraining. When it comes to economic globalization, it seems to be accepted that international judges and arbitrators are entitled to oversee the enforcement of international laws which protect commercial interests. Even if political leaders sometimes find it difficult to explain that tough decisions have to be taken because of international obligations, there is yet no sign of reneging on those international commitments. That may change as the economic obligations are increasingly melded with other social values, such as human rights and environmental standards, and as the US finds itself on the receiving end of a growing number of international claims which threaten domestic jobs or local environmental rules. When international economic laws come to be seen as allowing the values of others to be imposed upon the US, rather than the other way around, the equation may change. For the time being, however, international law continues to be seen as a means of opening overseas markets and protecting America's international investments. This is good international law.

Then there is the other international law, which some in the Bush Administration say is not really law at all. These are the rules that are seen as posing unacceptable constraints on the American way of life: rules which place human rights limits on the conduct of the 'war on terrorism', or which seek to limit the use of energy and combat global warming, or which create international mechanisms to punish perpetrators of the gravest international crimes. To be sure, there is a decent history of considering the rules on human rights and humanitarian law carefully before signing up to them, a reflection of the inherent scepticism accorded to anything international and which has dogged presidents from Wilson to Clinton. The US waited forty years to become a party to the 1948 Genocide Convention and fifteen years to join the 1966 International Covenant on Civil and Political Rights (both accessions taking place under Republican Administrations), and ten years before acceding to the 1984 Convention against Torture. The 1949 Geneva Conventions took just six years to ratify. In each case participation required the support of the Senate and proper congressional scrutiny. But once the US became a party it took its obligations as seriously as any state and much more than most. In each case participation was premised on the belief that the benefits of membership outweighed the disadvantages. The benefits included added protection of American military and business interests. American participation enhanced the acceptability of the rules, and their effectiveness. No one in their right mind would claim that the world is better off with the US playing outside the rules.

So what changed? In the Clinton years, the Breard case on rights of access to consular officials for arrested foreigners made it clear that support for international law was not unbridled.[1] Important domestic constituencies at the federal and state levels imposed constraints. The Law of the Sea Convention remained unratified, although Clinton felt able, at least, to sign the Kyoto Protocol on global warming in 1998 and the Rome Statute of the International Criminal Court in December 2000. The Bush Administration took office with a clear agenda to create an international order which would be friendlier to America's security, prosperity and principles, as the right-leaning Project for the New American Century proposed in its 1997 statement of principles.[2] This was not so much a change of values as a ratcheting up of efforts to tap into the rich seam of scepticism which had lain dormant for much of the twentieth century, slowing but not halting the incoming tide of global commitments. That meant holding back support for unfriendly international laws, or at least making sure that they did not bind America. There was no objection to applying international law to others, as Bush's support for the international criminal proceedings against Slobodan Milošević and Charles Taylor made clear. Early victims included the Kyoto Protocol and the Rome Statute, easy targets since they merely required declarations that the US would not become a party. As we have seen, that was not enough. In the case of the International Criminal Court, the Administration embarked on an unprecedented programme of intimidation of other states to prevent them from joining and sought to immunize its own nationals from the Court's jurisdiction.

A greater problem was posed by those treaties which the US had already joined. The events of 9/11 provided the perfect opportunity to refashion the global legal order. International law became the bogeyman, a constraint on America's ability to defend itself, prosecute the war on terrorism and protect its economic and military interests around the world. The Geneva Conventions? Not applicable. The International Covenant on Civil and Political Rights? Not applicable. The Convention against Torture? Not relevant. The UN Charter's prohibition on the use of force? Allows us to decide unilaterally that Saddam Hussein's Iraq is in material breach of Security Council resolutions. 'What the Administration is trying to do is create a new legal regime' was how the US Deputy Assistant Attorney General John Yoo described the Guantánamo initiative. The words aptly describe the Bush Administration's attitude more generally. Simplistic. Unilateral. Misconceived. Poorly presented. Rushed. It is one thing to re-evaluate the adequacy of international laws in the light of changing circumstances, like new terrorist threats and the proliferation of weapons of mass destruction. It is quite another to impose them on the rest of the world without proper consultation or consideration of the likely consequences. These actions are not without their costs. As legitimacy and moral authority are lost it becomes more difficult to persuade friends and allies to join in on difficult decisions.

How was the Administration able to implement the project to create its new legal regime? To begin with, the Bush Administration's approach to remaking international law had the great merit of not requiring input from other countries. Notwithstanding the fact that treaties were involved, the rewriting of international conventions could be achieved unilaterally. It was a domestic project initiated by the widespread dissemination of a great deal of misinformation, beginning well before 9/11. The ICC is a perfect example of the way in which the Administration could trash an international treaty by arguing that it posed a threat to American sovereignty on grounds which bore little relation to what the treaty actually said. It was as though there were two statutes: Secretary Rumsfeld's 'thing called the ICC' and the real ICC. The same approach was applied to other international instruments which were no longer perceived to serve American interests.

Misstating what international law requires is not in itself sufficient. America is a nation of rules and lawyers. Lawyers had to be found who could be relied upon to provide the right legal advice and opinions. The relevant government departments – State, Justice, Defense – have large numbers of extraordinarily able lawyers on hand to advise on America's obligations under international law. They know the rules, as well as their strengths and weaknesses. They understand how treaties are interpreted, how a unilateral interpretation by the US in one context can come back to haunt it in another, how the benefits and protections granted by treaties are based on the fundamental principle of reciprocity. They also appreciate how allies and other states will react to interpretations that bear no relation to the plain meaning of the treaties or the intent of the drafters. The problem with these lawyers was that they could not be relied upon to follow political instructions and come up with the right opinions. Colin Powell's unsuccessful attempt to ensure full respect for the Geneva Conventions at Guantánamo reflected a classical approach. It was the right advice, but, following a decision taken at the highest levels of the White House, it was not adopted.

Instead, a decision was taken to follow the advice of political appointees, many of whom had no real background in international law or were closely associated with a group of American academics known to be hostile to international law. This included appointees such as the General Counsel at the White House – he who had found the Geneva Conventions 'quaint' – and numerous appointees at the Justice Department's Office of Legal Counsel. Some of their legal advice has made its way into the public domain. The 'Torture Memos' which emerged against the background of the scandals at Abu Ghraib prison and elsewhere revealed what many outsiders feared: the advice from some of the most senior appointees was partial, poorly researched, misleading, and disconnected from general agreement on the standards imposed by the 1984 Convention against Torture and other treaties. In some cases it was plain wrong. US Assistant Attorney General Jay Bybee's memorandum of 1 October 2002 should be compulsory reading for every student of international law. It makes for a mildly entertaining read, until you pause to reflect that this atrocious legal advice could provide legal cover for actions which may have contributed to the mistreatment of large numbers of people, and perhaps even deaths in custody.[3] According to the Red Cross, there is evidence that many of those who were involved in the consequences of the Administration's effort to remake the global rules were innocent of any wrongdoing, unfortunates caught up in the relentless logic of the 'war on terror'. The enforcement of international law can turn on the advice of a single lawyer. Good faith efforts aside, the principle of individual criminal responsibility bears equally on those whose legal advice allows the state to act.

How did the Administration get away with it? No doubt there are several explanations. The US Congress did not engage with the issues until late in the day. Most of the US media took its eye off the ball and some engaged in the kind of post-9/11 coverage that made it impossible to give rules which might constrain American actions a decent hearing. The *New York Times* and the *Washington Post* have now accepted their shortcomings in reporting preparations for the war in Iraq. Equally, between 9/11 and the emergence of the scandals at Abu Ghraib there was a noticeable reluctance on the part of the press and TV to investigate critically the Administration's misuses of legal arguments to justify everything from the indefinite detention of foreigners at Guantánamo to the legal basis for the war in Iraq. Outside small circulation publications like the *New York Review of Books* and *The Nation* magazine these issues were simply not considered to be newsworthy.

Beyond a limited number of NGOs like Human Rights Watch and the Lawyers' Committee for Human Rights there was no powerful constituency to defend the international rule of law. In the aftermath of 9/11 a great number of academic international lawyers – but by no means all – who might have spoken out about what was happening maintained a discreet and regrettable silence. The airwaves were generously available to international lawyers willing to defend the Administration's acts. Those who were willing to speak out found that even serious newspapers like the *New York Times* would not publish their letters.[4] This contrasted sharply with most other countries in Europe and elsewhere, like Britain and Spain, where constituencies for the international rule of law had little difficulty in finding space to air their views. The reasons for these differences are complex, but the point is a simple one: until the revelations at Abu Ghraib there was virtually no informed public dissent against the Administration's efforts to rewrite international law into irrelevance. In a climate in which the President could declare that those who were not with the US were against it, the proponents of the global rules were easily marginalized and mostly silenced. It took Abu Ghraib to end America's collective amnesia and re-ignite serious investigative journalism from CBS's *60 Minutes* television programme, *Newsweek* magazine and the *Washington Post*. By then the damage had been done, both to the US's reputation and to international law.

*

In its effort to remake the global rules America did not act alone. Over the past four years it has been able to count on support from Britain and from a small number of other countries. The terrorist attacks of 9/11 brought Blair and Bush together to give rise to one of the great enigmas of modern British political life: why did Tony Blair lend British support to the war on Iraq? Blair's support for that war and the 'war on terrorism', as well as the implicit support for the regime which was put in place at Guantánamo, provided oxygen and international legitimacy to acts of dubious legality and effectiveness, which had virtually no hard international support.

It is not as though Blair and Bush set off from the same starting point, at least as far as attitudes to international law were concerned. In the months after Bush assumed the Presidency the two governments were poles apart on important international legal issues of the day. Blair's support for the Kyoto Protocol was strong, and the two countries went through a bruising trade war in the run-up to the British general election in May 2001. Blair's professional training as a barrister meant he was comfortable with international rules. After first being elected in 1997 the new Labour government had taken steps to incorporate the European Convention on Human Rights into English law (as the Human Rights Act 1998). This made the treaty directly enforceable in cases before the English courts and, in effect, gave Britain a written quasi-constitution. Under Blair's leadership Britain was shifted away from a more sceptical stance into being one of the strongest proponents of the International Criminal Court. The Labour government allowed the Pinochet case to go much further than the Conservative party would have allowed. There was decent support for the treaty rules of the European Community, a departure from the internecine strife and eurosclerosis which had characterized John Major's Conservative government throughout the 1990s. The intervention in Kosovo provided the only real hint that the rules of international law might need to be revisited, but this would be in order to promote respect for human rights.

September 11 and its aftermath shattered the Labour government's internationalist credentials, as well as Britain's. The Bush Administration's early announcements about the creation of Camp Delta at Guantánamo Bay and the special military tribunals, together with the declaration that the Geneva Conventions were not applicable to foreign detainees in the war on terrorism, were met with a silence that must have sent a strong message to Washington. Yet, in the 'war on terrorism', Britain was the only one of the forty-five members of the Council of Europe to pass its own anti-terror legislation, requiring it to derogate from the European Convention on Human Rights to authorize the indefinite detention without charge or trial of non-nationals who could not be deported. In December 2004 the judges of the House of Lords ruled by an overwhelming majority that the law – Part 4 of the Anti-Terrorism, Crime and Security Act 2001 – was discriminatory and in violation of Britain's international legal obligations. The Law Lords were devastating in their critique of the government's actions. 'The real threat to the life of the nation', wrote Lord Hoffmann, 'comes not from terrorism but from laws such as these.' Lord Scott described the law's power to allow indefinite imprisonment on the basis of a denunciation on grounds that are not disclosed, and made by a person whose identity cannot be disclosed, as 'the stuff of nightmares'. Lord Bingham, presiding, reaffirmed the central importance of Britain's international legal obligations, placing them at the heart of this landmark judgment.[5] In the context of legal proceedings before the Special Immigration Appeals Commission created by the 2001 law, the British government indicated that it could rely on evidence obtained from detainees at Guantánamo, even if it had been obtained as a result of torture.

In the run-up to the war on Iraq, Blair even expressed a willingness to override the UN Charter, suggesting that he might ignore any unreasonable French veto of a Security Council resolution authorizing force against Saddam Hussein's regime. On the legality of the war, he and his Attorney General dismissed the views of Foreign Office legal advisers – and almost all international lawyers in Britain – that the use of force was not authorized by the Security Council. In so doing he ignored the language and negotiating history of Security Council resolution 1441 which did not suit his interests. The Attorney General accorded to the Prime Minister the right to decide unilaterally and on the basis of an unspecified standard that Iraq was in material breach of resolution 1441 so as to justify the use of force. In taking that decision the Prime Minister did not even receive the benefit of up-to-date advice from the Joint Intelligence Committee.[6] At around the same time Britain entered into an agreement with the US, acceding to a request not to transfer Americans to the International Criminal Court. And in July 2004 – after the Abu Ghraib scandal – Britain was virtually alone amongst Security Council members in ignoring UN Secretary General Kofi Annan's exhortation not to support American efforts to give immunity from the ICC to UN peacekeepers. The Americans' proposal failed.

Why has Britain associated itself so closely with an Administration that has such scant regard for the international rule of law? That is a difficult question that only Blair himself can answer. If an illegal war in Iraq had made the world a safer place then arguably it might be justified. But there is little evidence that the world is a safer place, and a great deal more evidence that the Iraq War has provided a major distraction to the very real challenge posed by global terrorism and al-Qaeda. Nor can it be said that the Middle East is more stable or peaceful, or that the enraging of the populations of many parts of that region and elsewhere in the world has been quelled; or that the existence of the detention camp at Guantánamo Bay and the failure to apply human rights and humanitarian law is the best way to win hearts and minds or persuade the occupied of your humanitarian intentions.

Has Britain's support for the US brought other benefits to the international community? There is no evidence to suggest that Blair's support reduced the Bush Administration's hostility to the Kyoto Protocol or the ICC, or enhanced its willingness to engage in new arms control agreements which will play a vital part in limiting the proliferation of weapons of mass destruction, or gave the UK a stronger hand in its dealings over British nationals at Guantánamo Bay. There is clear evidence, however, that the violations of human rights and humanitarian law engendered by the 'war on terrorism' have undermined respect for human rights in other parts of the world. 'If the US can do it, and if Britain turns a blind eye, then why should we not be able to act in the same way?' is a familiar refrain. If America can propose a doctrine of pre-emption, then why not also Russia after the Beslan school atrocity in September 2004?[7]

The only plausible answer is that the Prime Minister believed that solidarity and self-interest required him to place Britain alongside the US, more or less whatever the US chose to do. History will tell whether that was the right choice. In the meantime Britain's stock as a law-abiding global citizen has taken a beating. Its authority and leadership role are seriously degraded. Many British and American diplomats have expressed disquiet, recognizing that their job has been made that much more difficult by the events of the past three years. Some Foreign Office and State Department personnel have resigned.

The views of some of the diplomats from other states who received Britain's assurances when Security Council resolution 1441 was being negotiated are unprintable.

It could be argued, I suppose, that Britain is following the US because it has taken a considered decision that the wholesale reconstruction of the international legal order is justified. But so far I have seen no hint that that is in fact the case, with the exception of a somewhat emotive speech by the Prime Minister which suggested he was out of his depth on what the law actually required or permitted.

*

How might the American effort to remake the global rules be justified? Three arguments are put forward.

The first is the argument that the International Rules are Inadequate. Existing international rules, it is claimed, are not up to the task of meeting present challenges, in particular global terrorism and the protection of human rights around the world. This was the main thrust of Blair's Sedgefield speech in March 2004, following earlier speeches at the Labour party conference and in Chicago in 1999. 'We need global rules', he declared, to defend our security and to spread 'our values'. In seeking to justify his actions against Iraq he asked:

It may well be that under international law as presently constituted, a regime can systematically brutalize and oppress its people and there is nothing anyone can do, when dialogue, diplomacy and even sanctions fail, unless it comes within the definition of a humanitarian catastrophe (though the 300,000 remains in mass graves already found in Iraq might be thought by some to be something of a catastrophe). This may be the law, but should it be?[8]

The question hints at an underlying recognition that the war may not have been as legal as the Prime Minister would have liked. It also suggests that international law as it stands may be part of the problem, not the solution. I disagree. The speech disingenuously conflates three issues – the violation of fundamental human rights, threats from WMD, and terrorism – which are distinct. Two of the three – human rights and terrorism – were not raised by the Iraqi situation, at least as it was argued by the British government in the period up to March 2003. In assessing the adequacy of international law, that has to be kept in mind. Iraq is not a good case for revisiting broader issues about the inadequacy of the international legal order in dealing with repressive regimes. It is a good case, however, to revisit the processes by which governments assess and act upon intelligence material which cannot be made public. The public is entitled to be reassured that the process of assessment is sound and is motivated by the application of the proper criteria. This is where the recent Iraqi conflict has caused potentially great harm, since the presentation of the evidence in Britain and the US has undermined public confidence in the assessment of the threat. The most important challenge is to restore public trust in governmental decision-making. Complaining about the inadequacies of the legal order is a distraction from the more pressing issues.

A second argument is that America's Constitution Trumps (or Ignores) International Law Because it is Undemocratic. On this view international law can be ignored because international rules are inherently undemocratic, at least by reference to certain approaches to principles of American constitutional theory. This is an old argument, a recent version of which has been put forward by Professor Jed Rubenfeld of Yale Law School.[9] He recognizes the irony of the current situation: that the US is responsible for the creation of the international law system it now resists. But, he says, it was a system which was essentially seen as transmitting American principles to the rest of the world, which would recognize international law as law America already had: the principal organs of US foreign policy 'emphatically resisted the idea that international law could be a means of changing internal US law'. This was because 'from an American point of view, if the law is to be democratic, the law and the courts that interpret it must retain strong connections to the nation's democratic political systems'. So, as the rules of international law took on a life of their own and became more powerful, and as they diverged from American national law, the US moved away from its historical commitment to international rules.

I agree that international law is not sufficiently democratic, at the global level or even in terms of regional arrangements like the European Union. The difficulty is that the international legal order we have – and the principle that treaties create binding obligations under international law – is long-established and accepted, including by the US. The argument applies the old canard of American exceptionalism, that 'international law is only for others'. Applied generally this would mean, in effect, that every state would be free to apply or ignore international law as it wished. There would be no international law. This goes against the basic principle that a state is not entitled to rely on its own internal constitutional law to justify international wrongdoing. When the US raised this argument in the Breard case the International Court quickly dismissed it.[10] But the problem with the argument is not just that it flies in the face of established practice long supported by the US. The real problem is that it does not adequately explain the US's selective application of international rules: if the Geneva Conventions, the Convention against Torture and the International Covenant on Civil and Political Rights do not impose obligations which require compliance at Guantánamo and elsewhere, how does Rubenfeld explain support for international economic obligations such as the WTO, NAFTA and foreign investment agreements, which plainly impose internal obligations on the US? Fine constitutional theory provides neither description nor explanation. Nor does it explain the selectivity of American demands that international legal rules (like the Geneva Conventions) be adhered to strictly by other states.

The third argument is the most brutal: Power Trumps. This posits that the US has abandoned international law because it is powerful and can afford to do so. Robert Kagan is a proponent of the view that a state's support for international law is directly related to its relative strength or weakness in the global system. When the US was weak – in the eighteenth and nineteenth centuries – it practised the strategies of weakness, including greater support for international rules. As it has become more powerful it has started to behave as powerful nations do, tilting towards unilateralism and away from international law: '[t]oday's transatlantic problem, in short, is not a George Bush problem. It is a power problem. US military strength has produced a propensity to use that strength.'[11] By contrast, Kagan argues, Europeans hanker for an idealized vision of a world of sovereign states who share essential common values and who function 'within an accepted framework of international law that they have the capacity and the will to enforce by mutual consent'. Kagan does not believe that such a situation exists or has existed since 1914. The logic of his argument leads inexorably to the question that was posed by Sir Michael Howerd, the distinguished military historian, a year after 9/11: 'If the Americans do not badge themselves as sheriff and hunt down the bad guys, who will?' This gives rise to the proposition, which Howerd identifies in political thinkers like Phillip Bobbitt and Robert Cooper, that what is now needed is a total paradigm shift in world order – with all that implies for international law – so that power brings with it the responsibility to rescue populations from starvation, to enforce human rights and ensure that no state provides a safe haven for terrorists. Howerd paraphrases their thinking, although he does not share it:

If this means the assertion of hegemonial [*sic*] or imperial rule, so be it. There are worse things than empires. After half a century the White Man's Burden must be taken up again.[12]

There are many problems with this argument, not least the fact that it is unlikely to find favour with many states or any significant proportion of the world's population. But the insurmountable difficulty is that it provides only a partial response to the current situation. It assumes that the US can go it alone – and it cannot, as Iraq has shown. American unilateralism is not isolationism: the US's exposure to the world is premised on economic objectives, amongst others, not military objectives. The use of military power is a means to an end, not the end itself. The business community will be the first to say that commerce cannot be dictated by brute force. You cannot intimidate consumers into buying American goods, or manufacturing cheaper products for import into the US, or supplying oil and other strategically significant products. Military and economic considerations cannot be separated, any more than free trade and environmental objectives can be disconnected. Once that is recognized, and you accept that some of your foreign policy objectives are premised on the application of global rules, the marginalization of international law becomes more difficult to justify. Moreover, if Iraq and the 'war on terrorism' have shown anything it is that the US is highly dependent on alliances and coalitions whose members require something in return. That something in return is usually some form of international agreement, whether an over-extensive Article 98(2) agreement to immunize Americans from the reaches of the ICC, or rights to access the territorial waters of third states, or trade and investment agreements which will encourage trade and other commercial exchanges. There are no free lunches. Whichever way you look at it, the United States needs international agreements.

*

This is the reason, I believe, that the present effort by the US and Britain to remake the global rules will not succeed. It does not mean that new circumstances – failed states, terrorism and the emergence of non-state actors in particular – do not require the existing global rules to be continually assessed, and to be modified where necessary to ensure that states feel that their vital needs are being met. Nor does it mean that some of the global rules are not in need of a thorough over-haul, to make them more efficient and accountable to parliaments and to the people. But change is a process which inevitably requires co-operation and a broad degree of support. It cannot be imposed at gun-point.

In this globalizing, interdependent world it is hopeless to conceive of a return to nature, to a pre-regulatory environment in which each state is free to act as it wishes, unfettered by international obligations. Nor is it realistic to give concrete effect to any sort of *à la carte* multilateralism, in which states are able to pick and choose those areas of international law they like and those they don't. The lessons from the World Trade Organization and elsewhere make it clear that different social objectives are interdependent.

There are usually good reasons why international laws have been adopted. For the most part they work reasonably well. Imperfect as some of the international rules may be, they reflect minimum standards of acceptable behaviour and, to the extent they can be ascertained, common values. They provide an independent standard for judging the legitimacy of international actions. I do not believe that idealized notions of the sovereign state, or 9/11, or events in Iraq, have funda-mentally changed the basic assumptions or created a new paradigm.

Finally, whatever the superficial attractions of the claim that America is against international rules (or doesn't need them) and that Europe and the others are for them (because they need them), the approach is unsustainable. It does not reflect the complex realities of the modern world, and the price a country pays when it opts out. Nor does it reflect America's distinguished history of commitment to inter-national law, aptly reflected in US Supreme Court Justice Story's 1814 opinion (in the context of the war of 1812 against Great Britain) that the President 'cannot lawfully exercise powers or authorize proceed-ings which the civilized world repudiates and disclaims'.[13] In the US, recent decisions of the Supreme Court on the 'war on terrorism' confirm that the values reflected in human rights law and humanitarian law continue to have support at the highest levels of the American judiciary. Recent hearings in the Senate have shown broad recognition for the basic humanitarian principles of the Geneva Conventions. The Kyoto Protocol and the International Criminal Court will outlive the Bush Administration. Chile's Supreme Court confirmed the approach taken by the House of Lords in the Pinochet case. And the US federal courts have given effect to rulings of the International Court of Justice in the Breard case and related judgments. In Britain, respect for international rules is now a political issue, as is the nature and extent of Britain's support for the US.

The rules of international law will turn out to be more robust than the policies of the Bush Administration. Tough guys are not enough in international relations. In the twenty-first century you need rules, and proper lawyers too.[14]

Appendix I

Atlantic Charter (1941)

14 August 1941

The President of the United States of America and the Prime Minister, Mr. Churchill, representing His Majesty's Government in the United Kingdom, being met together, deem it right to make known certain common principles in the national policies of their respective countries on which they base their hopes for a better future for the world.

First, their countries seek no aggrandizement, territorial or other;

Second, they desire to see no territorial changes that do not accord with the freely expressed wishes of the peoples concerned;

Third, they respect the right of all peoples to choose the form of government under which they will live; and they wish to see sovereign rights and self government restored to those who have been forcibly deprived of them;

Fourth, they will endeavor, with due respect for their existing obligations, to further the enjoyment by all States, great or small, victor or vanquished, of access, on equal terms, to the trade and to the raw materials of the world which are needed for their economic prosperity;

Fifth, they desire to bring about the fullest collaboration between all nations in the economic field with the object of securing, for all, improved labor standards, economic advancement and social security;

Sixth, after the final destruction of the Nazi tyranny, they hope to see established a peace which will afford to all nations the means of dwelling in safety within their own boundaries, and which will afford assurance that all the men in all lands may live out their lives in freedom from fear and want;

Seventh, such a peace should enable all men to traverse the high seas and oceans without hindrance;

Eighth, they believe that all of the nations of the world, for realistic as well as spiritual reasons must come to the abandonment of the use of force.

Since no future peace can be maintained if land, sea or air armaments continue to be employed by nations which threaten, or may threaten, aggression outside of their frontiers, they believe, pending the establishment of a wider and permanent system of general security, that the disarmament of such nations is essential. They will likewise aid and encourage all other practicable measure which will lighten for peace-loving peoples the crushing burden of armaments.

Franklin D. Roosevelt

Winston S. Churchill

Appendix II

Charter of the United Nations
(1945, extracts)

Preamble

We the Peoples of the United Nations

Determined

> to save succeeding generations from the scourge of war, which twice in our lifetime has brought untold sorrow to mankind, and

> to reaffirm faith in fundamental human rights, in the dignity and worth of the human person, in the equal rights of men and women and of nations large and small, and

> to establish conditions under which justice and respect for the obligations arising from treaties and other sources of international law can be maintained, and

> to promote social progress and better standards of life in larger freedom,

And for these Ends

> to practice tolerance and live together in peace with one another as good neighbors, and

> to unite our strength to maintain international peace and security, and

> to ensure by the acceptance of principles and the institution of methods, that armed force shall not be used, save in the common interest, and

> to employ international machinery for the promotion of the economic and social advancement of all peoples,

Have Resolved to Combine our Efforts to Accomplish these Aims

> Accordingly, our respective Governments, through representatives assembled in the city of San Francisco, who have exhibited their full

powers found to be in good and due form, have agreed to the present Charter of the United Nations and do hereby establish an international organization to be known as the United Nations.

CHAPTER I

Purposes and Principles

Article 1

The Purposes of the United Nations are:

1. To maintain international peace and security, and to that end: to take effective collective measures for the prevention and removal of threats to the peace, and for the suppression of acts of aggression or other breaches of the peace, and to bring about by peaceful means, and in conformity with the principles of justice and international law, adjustment or settlement of international disputes or situations which might lead to a breach of the peace;

2. To develop friendly relations among nations based on respect for the principle of equal rights and self-determination of peoples, and to take other appropriate measures to strengthen universal peace;

3. To achieve international cooperation in solving international problems of an economic, social, cultural, or humanitarian character, and in promoting and encouraging respect for human rights and for fundamental freedoms for all without distinction as to race, sex, language, or religion; and

4. To be a center for harmonizing the actions of nations in the attainment of these common ends.

Article 2

The Organization and its Members, in pursuit of the Purposes stated in Article 1, shall act in accordance with the following Principles.

1. The Organization is based on the principle of the sovereign equality of all its Members.

2. All Members, in order to ensure to all of them the rights and benefits resulting from membership, shall fulfill in good faith the obligations assumed by them in accordance with the present Charter.

3. All Members shall settle their international disputes by peaceful means in such a manner that international peace and security, and justice, are not endangered.

4. All Members shall refrain in their international relations from the threat or use of force against the territorial integrity or political independence of any state, or in any other manner inconsistent with the Purposes of the United Nations.

5. All Members shall give the United Nations every assistance in any action it takes in accordance with the present Charter, and shall refrain from giving assistance to any state against which the United Nations is taking preventive or enforcement action.

6. The Organization shall ensure that states which are not Members of the United Nations act in accordance with these Principles so far as may be necessary for the maintenance of international peace and security.

7. Nothing contained in the present Charter shall authorize the United Nations to intervene in matters which are essentially within the domestic jurisdiction of any state or shall require the Members to submit such matters to settlement under the present Charter; but this principle shall not prejudice the application of enforcement measures under Chapter VII.

[. . .]

CHAPTER VII

Action with respect to threats to the peace, breaches of the peace, and acts of aggression

Article 39

The Security Council shall determine the existence of any threat to the peace, breach of the peace, or act of aggression and shall make recommendations, or decide what measures shall be taken in accordance with Articles 41 and 42, to maintain or restore international peace and security.

[. . .]

Article 41

The Security Council may decide what measures not involving the use of armed force are to be employed to give effect to its decisions, and it may call upon the Members of the United Nations to apply such measures. These may include complete or partial interruption of economic relations and of rail, sea, air, postal, telegraphic, radio, and other means of communication, and the severance of diplomatic relations.

Article 42

Should the Security Council consider that measures provided for in Article 41 would be inadequate or have proved to be inadequate, it may take such action by air, sea, or land forces as may be necessary to maintain or restore international peace and security. Such action may include demonstrations, blockade, and other operations by air, sea, or land forces of Members of the United Nations.

[. . .]

Article 51

Nothing in the present Charter shall impair the inherent right of individual or collective self-defense if an armed attack occurs against a Member of the United Nations, until the Security Council has taken measures necessary to maintain international peace and security. Measures taken by Members in the exercise of this right of self-defense shall be immediately reported to the Security Council and shall not in any way affect the authority and responsibility of the Security Council under the present Charter to take at any time such action as it deems necessary in order to maintain or restore international peace and security.

[. . .]

Appendix III

Universal Declaration of Human Rights
(1948, extracts)

10 December 1948

Preamble

Whereas recognition of the inherent dignity and of the equal and inalienable rights of all members of the human family is the foundation of freedom, justice and peace in the world,

Whereas disregard and contempt for human rights have resulted in barbarous acts which have outraged the conscience of mankind, and the advent of a world in which human beings shall enjoy freedom of speech and belief and freedom from fear and want has been proclaimed as the highest aspiration of the common people,

Whereas it is essential, if man is not to be compelled to have recourse, as a last resort, to rebellion against tyranny and oppression, that human rights should be protected by the rule of law,

Whereas it is essential to promote the development of friendly relations between nations,

Whereas the peoples of the United Nations have in the Charter reaffirmed their faith in fundamental human rights, in the dignity and worth of the human person and in the equal rights of men and women and have determined to promote social progress and better standards of life in larger freedom,

Whereas Member States have pledged themselves to achieve, in co-operation with the United Nations, the promotion of universal respect for and observance of human rights and fundamental freedoms,

Whereas a common understanding of these rights and freedoms is of the greatest importance for the full realization of this pledge,

Now, therefore, the General Assembly proclaims this Universal Declaration of Human Rights as a common standard of achievement for all peoples and all

246

nations, to the end that every individual and every organ of society, keeping this Declaration constantly in mind, shall strive by teaching and education to promote respect for these rights and freedoms and by progressive measures, national and international, to secure their universal and effective recognition and observance, both among the peoples of Member States themselves and among the peoples of territories under their jurisdiction.

Article 1

All human beings are born free and equal in dignity and rights. They are endowed with reason and conscience and should act towards one another in a spirit of brotherhood.

Article 2

Everyone is entitled to all the rights and freedoms set forth in this Declaration, without distinction of any kind, such as race, colour, sex, language, religion, political or other opinion, national or social origin, property, birth or other status. Furthermore, no distinction shall be made on the basis of the political, jurisdictional or international status of the country or territory to which a person belongs, whether it be independent, trust, non-self-governing or under any other limitation of sovereignty.

Article 3

Everyone has the right to life, liberty and security of person.

Article 4

No one shall be held in slavery or servitude; slavery and the slave trade shall be prohibited in all their forms.

Article 5

No one shall be subjected to torture or to cruel, inhuman or degrading treatment or punishment.

Article 6

Everyone has the right to recognition everywhere as a person before the law.

Article 7

All are equal before the law and are entitled without any discrimination to equal protection of the law. All are entitled to equal protection against any discrimination in violation of this Declaration and against any incitement to such discrimination.

Article 8

Everyone has the right to an effective remedy by the competent national tribunals for acts violating the fundamental rights granted him by the constitution or by law.

Article 9

No one shall be subjected to arbitrary arrest, detention or exile.

Article 10

Everyone is entitled in full equality to a fair and public hearing by an independent and impartial tribunal, in the determination of his rights and obligations and of any criminal charge against him.

Article 11

(1) Everyone charged with a penal offence has the right to be presumed innocent until proved guilty according to law in a public trial at which he has had all the guarantees necessary for his defence.

(2) No one shall be held guilty of any penal offence on account of any act or omission which did not constitute a penal offence, under national or international law, at the time when it was committed. Nor shall a heavier penalty be imposed than the one that was applicable at the time the penal offence was committed.

Article 12

No one shall be subjected to arbitrary interference with his privacy, family, home or correspondence, nor to attacks upon his honour and reputation. Everyone has the right to the protection of the law against such interference or attacks.

[. . .]

Article 29

(1) Everyone has duties to the community in which alone the free and full development of his personality is possible.

(2) In the exercise of his rights and freedoms, everyone shall be subject only to such limitations as are determined by law solely for the purpose of securing due recognition and respect for the rights and freedoms of others and of meeting the just requirements of morality, public order and the general welfare in a democratic society.

(3) These rights and freedoms may in no case be exercised contrary to the purposes and principles of the United Nations.

[. . .]

Appendix IV

Geneva Convention III relative to the Treatment of Prisoners of War (1949, extracts) and Geneva Protocol I (1977, extract)

GENEVA CONVENTION III

Article 1

The High Contracting Parties undertake to respect and to ensure respect for the present Convention in all circumstances.

[...]

Article 3

In the case of armed conflict not of an international character occurring in the territory of one of the High Contracting Parties, each party to the conflict shall be bound to apply, as a minimum, the following provisions:

1. Persons taking no active part in the hostilities, including members of armed forces who have laid down their arms and those placed *hors de combat* by sickness, wounds, detention, or any other cause, shall in all circumstances be treated humanely, without any adverse distinction founded on race, colour, religion or faith, sex, birth or wealth, or any other similar criteria.

To this end the following acts are and shall remain prohibited at any time and in any place whatsoever with respect to the above-mentioned persons:
(a) violence to life and person, in particular murder of all kinds, mutilation, cruel treatment and torture;
(b) taking of hostages;
(c) outrages upon personal dignity, in particular, humiliating and degrading treatment;
(d) the passing of sentences and the carrying out of executions without previous judgment pronounced by a regularly constituted court affording all the judicial guarantees which are recognized as indispensable by civilized peoples.

2. The wounded and sick shall be collected and cared for.

An impartial humanitarian body, such as the International Committee of the Red Cross, may offer its services to the Parties to the conflict.

The Parties to the conflict should further endeavour to bring into force, by means of special agreements, all or part of the other provisions of the present Convention.

The application of the preceding provisions shall not affect the legal status of the Parties to the conflict.

Article 4

A. Prisoners of war, in the sense of the present Convention, are persons belonging to one of the following categories, who have fallen into the power of the enemy:

1. Members of the armed forces of a Party to the conflict as well as members of militias or volunteer corps forming part of such armed forces.

2. Members of other militias and members of other volunteer corps, including those of organized resistance movements, belonging to a Party to the conflict and operating in or outside their own territory, even if this territory is occupied, provided that such militias or volunteer corps, including such organized resistance movements, fulfil the following conditions:
(a) That of being commanded by a person responsible for his subordinates;
(b) That of having a fixed distinctive sign recognizable at a distance;
(c) That of carrying arms openly;
(d) That of conducting their operations in accordance with the laws and customs of war.

3. Members of regular armed forces who profess allegiance to a government or an authority not recognized by the Detaining Power.

4. Persons who accompany the armed forces without actually being members thereof, such as civilian members of military aircraft crews, war correspondents, supply contractors, members of labour units or of services responsible for the welfare of the armed forces, provided that they have received authorization from the armed forces which they accompany, who shall provide them for that purpose with an identity card similar to the annexed model.

5. Members of crews, including masters, pilots and apprentices, of the merchant marine and the crews of civil aircraft of the Parties to the conflict, who do not benefit by more favourable treatment under any other provisions of international law.

6. Inhabitants of a non-occupied territory, who on the approach of the enemy

spontaneously take up arms to resist the invading forces, without having had time to form themselves into regular armed units, provided they carry arms openly and respect the laws and customs of war.

[...]

Article 5

The present Convention shall apply to the persons referred to in Article 4 from the time they fall into the power of the enemy and until their final release and repatriation.

Should any doubt arise as to whether persons, having committed a belligerent act and having fallen into the hands of the enemy, belong to any of the categories enumerated in Article 4, such persons shall enjoy the protection of the present Convention until such time as their status has been determined by a competent tribunal.

[...]

Article 13

Prisoners of war must at all times be humanely treated. Any unlawful act or omission by the Detaining Power causing death or seriously endangering the health of a prisoner of war in its custody is prohibited, and will be regarded as a serious breach of the present Convention. In particular, no prisoner of war may be subjected to physical mutilation or to medical or scientific experiments of any kind which are not justified by the medical, dental or hospital treatment of the prisoner concerned and carried out in his interest.

Likewise, prisoners of war must at all times be protected, particularly against acts of violence or intimidation and against insults and public curiosity.

Measures of reprisal against prisoners of war are prohibited.

[...]

Article 17

Every prisoner of war, when questioned on the subject, is bound to give only his surname, first names and rank, date of birth, and army, regimental, personal or serial number, or failing this, equivalent information. If he wilfully infringes this rule, he may render himself liable to a restriction of the privileges accorded to his rank or status.

Each Party to a conflict is required to furnish the persons under its jurisdiction who are liable to become prisoners of war, with an identity card showing the owner's surname, first names, rank, army, regimental, personal or serial number or equivalent information, and date of birth. The identity card may, furthermore, bear the signature or the fingerprints, or both, of the owner, and may bear, as well, any other information the Party to the conflict may wish to add concerning persons belonging to its armed forces. As far as possible the card shall measure 6.5 x 10 cm. and shall be issued in duplicate. The identity card shall be shown by the prisoner of war upon demand, but may in no case be taken away from him.

No physical or mental torture, nor any other form of coercion, may be inflicted on prisoners of war to secure from them information of any kind whatever. Prisoners of war who refuse to answer may not be threatened, insulted, or exposed to any unpleasant or disadvantageous treatment of any kind.

Prisoners of war who, owing to their physical or mental condition, are unable to state their identity, shall be handed over to the medical service. The identity of such prisoners shall be established by all possible means, subject to the provisions of the preceding paragraph.

The questioning of prisoners of war shall be carried out in a language which they understand.

[. . .]

Article 129

The High Contracting Parties undertake to enact any legislation necessary to provide effective penal sanctions for persons committing, or ordering to be committed, any of the grave breaches of the present Convention defined in the following Article.

Each High Contracting Party shall be under the obligation to search for persons alleged to have committed, or to have ordered to be committed, such grave breaches, and shall bring such persons, regardless of their nationality, before its own courts. It may also, if it prefers, and in accordance with the provisions of its own legislation, hand such persons over for trial to another High Contracting Party concerned, provided such High Contracting Party has made out a prima facie case.

Each High Contracting Party shall take measures necessary for the suppression of all acts contrary to the provisions of the present Convention other than the grave breaches defined in the following Article.

In all circumstances, the accused persons shall benefit by safeguards of proper trial and defence, which shall not be less favourable than those provided by Article 105 and those following of the present Convention.

Article 130

Grave breaches to which the preceding Article relates shall be those involving any of the following acts, if committed against persons or property protected by the Convention: wilful killing, torture or inhuman treatment, including biological experiments, wilfully causing great suffering or serious injury to body or health, compelling a prisoner of war to serve in the forces of the hostile Power, or wilfully depriving a prisoner of war of the rights of fair and regular trial prescribed in this Convention.

[...]

PROTOCOL I
ADDITIONAL TO THE GENEVA CONVENTIONS, 1977

Section III
Treatment of Persons in the Power of a Party to the Conflict

Article 72 – Field of application

The provisions of this Section are additional to the rules concerning humanitarian protection of civilians and civilian objects in the power of a Party to the conflict contained in the Fourth Convention, particularly Parts I and III thereof, as well as to other applicable rules of international law relating to the protection of fundamental human rights during international armed conflict.

[...]

Article 75 – Fundamental guarantees

1. In so far as they are affected by a situation referred to in Article 1 of this Protocol, persons who are in the power of a Party to the conflict and who do not benefit from more favourable treatment under the Conventions or under this Protocol shall be treated humanely in all circumstances and shall enjoy, as a minimum, the protection provided by this Article without any adverse distinction based upon race, colour, sex, language, religion or belief, political

or other opinion, national or social origin, wealth, birth or other status, or on any other similar criteria. Each Party shall respect the person, honour, convictions and religious practices of all such persons.

2. The following acts are and shall remain prohibited at any time and in any place whatsoever, whether committed by civilian or by military agents:

(a) violence to the life, health, or physical or mental well-being of persons, in particular:
(i) murder;
(ii) torture of all kinds, whether physical or mental;
(iii) corporal punishment; and
(iv) mutilation;

(b) outrages upon personal dignity, in particular humiliating and degrading treatment, enforced prostitution and any form of indecent assault;

(c) the taking of hostages;

(d) collective punishments; and

(e) threats to commit any of the foregoing acts.

3. Any person arrested, detained or interned for actions related to the armed conflict shall be informed promptly, in a language he understands, of the reasons why these measures have been taken. Except in cases of arrest or detention for penal offences, such persons shall be released with the minimum delay possible and in any event as soon as the circumstances justifying the arrest, detention or internment have ceased to exist.

4. No sentence may be passed and no penalty may be executed on a person found guilty of a penal offence related to the armed conflict except pursuant to a conviction pronounced by an impartial and regularly constituted court respecting the generally recognized principles of regular judicial procedure, which include the following:

(a) the procedure shall provide for an accused to be informed without delay of the particulars of the offence alleged against him and shall afford the accused before and during his trial all necessary rights and means of defence;

(b) no one shall be convicted of an offence except on the basis of individual penal responsibility;

(c) no one shall be accused or convicted of a criminal offence on account of any act or omission which did not constitute a criminal offence under the national or international law to which he was subject at the time when it was committed; nor shall a heavier penalty be imposed than that which was applicable at the time when the criminal offence was committed; if, after the commission of the offence, provision is made by law for the imposition of a lighter penalty, the offender shall benefit thereby;

(d) anyone charged with an offence is presumed innocent until proved guilty according to law;

(e) anyone charged with an offence shall have the right to be tried in his presence;

(f) no one shall be compelled to testify against himself or to confess guilt;

(g) anyone charged with an offence shall have the right to examine, or have examined, the witnesses against him and to obtain the attendance and examination of witnesses on his behalf under the same conditions as witnesses against him;

(h) no one shall be prosecuted or punished by the same Party for an offence in respect of which a final judgement acquitting or convicting that person has been previously pronounced under the same law and judicial procedure;

(i) anyone prosecuted for an offence shall have the right to have the judgement pronounced publicly; and

(j) a convicted person shall be advised on conviction of his judicial and other remedies and of the time-limits within which they may be exercised.

[. . .]

8. No provision of this Article may be construed as limiting or infringing any other more favourable provision granting greater protection, under any applicable rules of international law, to persons covered by paragraph 1.

[. . .]

Appendix V

Convention against Torture and Other Cruel,
Inhuman or Degrading Treatment or Punishment
(1984, extracts)

The States Parties to this Convention,

Considering that, in accordance with the principles proclaimed in the Charter of the United Nations, recognition of the equal and inalienable rights of all members of the human family is the foundation of freedom, justice and peace in the world,

Recognizing that those rights derive from the inherent dignity of the human person,

Considering the obligation of States under the Charter, in particular Article 55, to promote universal respect for, and observance of, human rights and fundamental freedoms,

Having regard to article 5 of the Universal Declaration of Human Rights and article 7 of the International Covenant on Civil and Political Rights, both of which provide that no one may be subjected to torture or to cruel, inhuman or degrading treatment or punishment,

Having regard also to the Declaration on the Protection of All Persons from Being Subjected to Torture and Other Cruel, Inhuman or Degrading Treatment or Punishment, adopted by the General Assembly on 9 December 1975,

Desiring to make more effective the struggle against torture and other cruel, inhuman or degrading treatment or punishment throughout the world,

Have agreed as follows:

Part I

Article 1

1. For the purposes of this Convention, the term 'torture' means any act by which severe pain or suffering, whether physical or mental, is intentionally inflicted on a person for such purposes as obtaining from him or a third person information or a confession, punishing him for an act he or a third person has committed or is suspected of having committed, or intimidating or coercing him or a third person, or for any reason based on discrimination of any kind, when such pain or suffering is inflicted by or at the instigation of or with the consent or acquiescence of a public official or other person acting in an official capacity. It does not include pain or suffering arising only from, inherent in or incidental to lawful sanctions.

2. This article is without prejudice to any international instrument or national legislation which does or may contain provisions of wider application.

Article 2

1. Each State Party shall take effective legislative, administrative, judicial or other measures to prevent acts of torture in any territory under its jurisdiction.

2. No exceptional circumstances whatsoever, whether a state of war or a threat of war, internal political instability or any other public emergency, may be invoked as a justification of torture.

3. An order from a superior officer or a public authority may not be invoked as a justification of torture.

Article 3

1. No State Party shall expel, return ('refouler') or extradite a person to another State where there are substantial grounds for believing that he would be in danger of being subjected to torture.

2. For the purpose of determining whether there are such grounds, the competent authorities shall take into account all relevant considerations including, where applicable, the existence in the State concerned of a consistent pattern of gross, flagrant or mass violations of human rights.

Article 4

1. Each State Party shall ensure that all acts of torture are offences under its criminal law. The same shall apply to an attempt to commit torture and to an act by any person which constitutes complicity or participation in torture.

2. Each State Party shall make these offences punishable by appropriate penalties which take into account their grave nature.

Article 5

1. Each State Party shall take such measures as may be necessary to establish its jurisdiction over the offences referred to in article 4 in the following cases:
   (a) When the offences are committed in any territory under its jurisdiction or on board a ship or aircraft registered in that State;
   (b) When the alleged offender is a national of that State;
   (c) When the victim was a national of that State if that State considers it appropriate.

2. Each State Party shall likewise take such measures as may be necessary to establish its jurisdiction over such offences in cases where the alleged offender is present in any territory under its jurisdiction and it does not extradite him pursuant to article 8 to any of the States mentioned in paragraph 1 of this article.

3. This Convention does not exclude any criminal jurisdiction exercised in accordance with internal law.

Article 6

1. Upon being satisfied, after an examination of information available to it, that the circumstances so warrant, any State Party in whose territory a person alleged to have committed any offence referred to in article 4 is present, shall take him into custody or take other legal measures to ensure his presence. The custody and other legal measures shall be as provided in the law of that State but may be continued only for such time as is necessary to enable any criminal or extradition proceedings to be instituted.

2. Such State shall immediately make a preliminary inquiry into the facts.

3. Any person in custody pursuant to paragraph 1 of this article shall be assisted in communicating immediately with the nearest appropriate representative of

the State of which he is a national, or, if he is a stateless person, to the representative of the State where he usually resides.

4. When a State, pursuant to this article, has taken a person into custody, it shall immediately notify the States referred to in article 5, paragraph 1, of the fact that such person is in custody and of the circumstances which warrant his detention. The State which makes the preliminary inquiry contemplated in paragraph 2 of this article shall promptly report its findings to the said State and shall indicate whether it intends to exercise jurisdiction.

Article 7

1. The State Party in territory under whose jurisdiction a person alleged to have committed any offence referred to in article 4 is found shall in the cases contemplated in article 5, if it does not extradite him, submit the case to its competent authorities for the purpose of prosecution.

2. These authorities shall take their decision in the same manner as in the case of any ordinary offence of a serious nature under the law of that State. In the cases referred to in article 5, paragraph 2, the standards of evidence required for prosecution and conviction shall in no way be less stringent than those which apply in the cases referred to in article 5, paragraph 1.

3. Any person regarding whom proceedings are brought in connection with any of the offences referred to in article 4 shall be guaranteed fair treatment at all stages of the proceedings.

Article 8

1. The offences referred to in article 4 shall be deemed to be included as extraditable offences in any extradition treaty existing between States Parties. States Parties undertake to include such offences as extraditable offences in every extradition treaty to be concluded between them.

2. If a State Party which makes extradition conditional on the existence of a treaty receives a request for extradition from another State Party with which it has no extradition treaty, it may consider this Convention as the legal basis for extradition in respect of such offences. Extradition shall be subject to the other conditions provided by the law of the requested State.

3. States Parties which do not make extradition conditional on the existence of a treaty shall recognize such offences as extraditable offences between themselves subject to the conditions provided by the law of the requested State.

4. Such offences shall be treated, for the purpose of extradition between States Parties, as if they had been committed not only in the place in which they occurred but also in the territories of the States required to establish their jurisdiction in accordance with article 5, paragraph 1.

[. . .]

Appendix VI

Rome Statute of the International Criminal Court
(1998, extracts)

Preamble

The States Parties to this Statute,

Conscious that all peoples are united by common bonds, their cultures pieced together in a shared heritage, and concerned that this delicate mosaic may be shattered at any time,

Mindful that during this century millions of children, women and men have been victims of unimaginable atrocities that deeply shock the conscience of humanity,

Recognizing that such grave crimes threaten the peace, security and well-being of the world,

Affirming that the most serious crimes of concern to the international community as a whole must not go unpunished and that their effective prosecution must be ensured by taking measures at the national level and by enhancing international cooperation,

Determined to put an end to impunity for the perpetrators of these crimes and thus to contribute to the prevention of such crimes,

Recalling that it is the duty of every State to exercise its criminal jurisdiction over those responsible for international crimes,

Reaffirming the Purposes and Principles of the Charter of the United Nations, and in particular that all States shall refrain from the threat or use of force against the territorial integrity or political independence of any State, or in any other manner inconsistent with the Purposes of the United Nations,

Emphasizing in this connection that nothing in this Statute shall be taken as authorizing any State Party to intervene in an armed conflict or in the internal affairs of any State,

Determined to these ends and for the sake of present and future generations, to establish an independent permanent International Criminal Court in relationship with the United Nations system, with jurisdiction over the most serious crimes of concern to the international community as a whole,

Emphasizing that the International Criminal Court established under this Statute shall be complementary to national criminal jurisdictions,

Resolved to guarantee lasting respect for and the enforcement of international justice,

Have agreed as follows

Article 1

The Court

An International Criminal Court ('the Court') is hereby established. It shall be a permanent institution and shall have the power to exercise its jurisdiction over persons for the most serious crimes of international concern, as referred to in this Statute, and shall be complementary to national criminal jurisdictions. The jurisdiction and functioning of the Court shall be governed by the provisions of this Statute.

[. . .]

Article 5

Crimes within the jurisdiction of the Court

1. The jurisdiction of the Court shall be limited to the most serious crimes of concern to the international community as a whole. The Court has jurisdiction in accordance with this Statute with respect to the following crimes:
    (a) The crime of genocide;
    (b) Crimes against humanity;
    (c) War crimes;
    (d) The crime of aggression.

2. The Court shall exercise jurisdiction over the crime of aggression once a provision is adopted in accordance with articles 121 and 123 defining the crime and setting out the conditions under which the Court shall exercise jurisdiction with respect to this crime. Such a provision shall be consistent with the relevant provisions of the Charter of the United Nations.

Article 6

Genocide

For the purpose of this Statute, 'genocide' means any of the following acts committed with intent to destroy, in whole or in part, a national, ethnical, racial or religious group, as such:
(a) Killing members of the group;
(b) Causing serious bodily or mental harm to members of the group;
(c) Deliberately inflicting on the group conditions of life calculated to bring about its physical destruction in whole or in part;
(d) Imposing measures intended to prevent births within the group;
(e) Forcibly transferring children of the group to another group.

Article 7

Crimes against humanity

1. For the purpose of this Statute, 'crime against humanity' means any of the following acts when committed as part of a widespread or systematic attack directed against any civilian population, with knowledge of the attack:
   (a) Murder;
   (b) Extermination;
   (c) Enslavement;
   (d) Deportation or forcible transfer of population;
   (e) Imprisonment or other severe deprivation of physical liberty in violation of fundamental rules of international law;
   (f) Torture;
   (g) Rape, sexual slavery, enforced prostitution, forced pregnancy, enforced sterilization, or any other form of sexual violence of comparable gravity;
   (h) Persecution against any identifiable group or collectivity on political, racial, national, ethnic, cultural, religious, gender as defined in paragraph 3, or other grounds that are universally recognized as impermissible under international law, in connection with any act referred to in this paragraph or any crime within the jurisdiction of the Court;
   (i) Enforced disappearance of persons;
   (j) The crime of apartheid;
   (k) Other inhumane acts of a similar character intentionally causing great suffering, or serious injury to body or to mental or physical health.

2. For the purpose of paragraph 1:
   (a) 'Attack directed against any civilian population' means a course of conduct involving the multiple commission of acts referred to in paragraph 1

against any civilian population, pursuant to or in furtherance of a State or organizational policy to commit such attack;

(b) 'Extermination' includes the intentional infliction of conditions of life, *inter alia* the deprivation of access to food and medicine, calculated to bring about the destruction of part of a population;

(c) 'Enslavement' means the exercise of any or all of the powers attaching to the right of ownership over a person and includes the exercise of such power in the course of trafficking in persons, in particular women and children;

(d) 'Deportation or forcible transfer of population' means forced displacement of the persons concerned by expulsion or other coercive acts from the area in which they are lawfully present, without grounds permitted under international law;

(e) 'Torture' means the intentional infliction of severe pain or suffering, whether physical or mental, upon a person in the custody or under the control of the accused; except that torture shall not include pain or suffering arising only from, inherent in or incidental to, lawful sanctions;

(f) 'Forced pregnancy' means the unlawful confinement of a woman forcibly made pregnant, with the intent of affecting the ethnic composition of any population or carrying out other grave violations of international law. This definition shall not in any way be interpreted as affecting national laws relating to pregnancy;

(g) 'Persecution' means the intentional and severe deprivation of fundamental rights contrary to international law by reason of the identity of the group or collectivity;

(h) 'The crime of apartheid' means inhumane acts of a character similar to those referred to in paragraph 1, committed in the context of an institutionalized regime of systematic oppression and domination by one racial group over any other racial group or groups and committed with the intention of maintaining that regime;

(i) 'Enforced disappearance of persons' means the arrest, detention or abduction of persons by, or with the authorization, support or acquiescence of, a State or a political organization, followed by a refusal to acknowledge that deprivation of freedom or to give information on the fate or whereabouts of those persons, with the intention of removing them from the protection of the law for a prolonged period of time.

3. For the purpose of this Statute, it is understood that the term 'gender' refers to the two sexes, male and female, within the context of society. The term 'gender' does not indicate any meaning different from the above.

Article 8

War crimes

1. The Court shall have jurisdiction in respect of war crimes in particular when committed as part of a plan or policy or as part of a large-scale commission of such crimes.

2. For the purpose of this Statute, 'war crimes' means:

(a) Grave breaches of the Geneva Conventions of 12 August 1949, namely, any of the following acts against persons or property protected under the provisions of the relevant Geneva Convention:
  (i) Wilful killing;
  (ii) Torture or inhuman treatment, including biological experiments;
  (iii) Wilfully causing great suffering, or serious injury to body or health;
  (iv) Extensive destruction and appropriation of property, not justified by military necessity and carried out unlawfully and wantonly;
  (v) Compelling a prisoner of war or other protected person to serve in the forces of a hostile Power;
  (vi) Wilfully depriving a prisoner of war or other protected person of the rights of fair and regular trial;
  (vii) Unlawful deportation or transfer or unlawful confinement;
  (viii) Taking of hostages.

(b) Other serious violations of the laws and customs applicable in international armed conflict, within the established framework of international law, namely, any of the following acts:
  (i) Intentionally directing attacks against the civilian population as such or against individual civilians not taking direct part in hostilities;
  (ii) Intentionally directing attacks against civilian objects, that is, objects which are not military objectives;
  (iii) Intentionally directing attacks against personnel, installations, material, units or vehicles involved in a humanitarian assistance or peacekeeping mission in accordance with the Charter of the United Nations, as long as they are entitled to the protection given to civilians or civilian objects under the international law of armed conflict;
  (iv) Intentionally launching an attack in the knowledge that such attack will cause incidental loss of life or injury to civilians or damage to civilian objects or widespread, long-term and severe damage to the natural environment which would be clearly excessive in relation to the concrete and direct overall military advantage anticipated;
  (v) Attacking or bombarding, by whatever means, towns, villages,

dwellings or buildings which are undefended and which are not military objectives;

(vi) Killing or wounding a combatant who, having laid down his arms or having no longer means of defence, has surrendered at discretion;

(vii) Making improper use of a flag of truce, of the flag or of the military insignia and uniform of the enemy or of the United Nations, as well as of the distinctive emblems of the Geneva Conventions, resulting in death or serious personal injury;

(viii) The transfer, directly or indirectly, by the Occupying Power of parts of its own civilian population into the territory it occupies, or the deportation or transfer of all or parts of the population of the occupied territory within or outside this territory;

(ix) Intentionally directing attacks against buildings dedicated to religion, education, art, science or charitable purposes, historic monuments, hospitals and places where the sick and wounded are collected, provided they are not military objectives;

(x) Subjecting persons who are in the power of an adverse party to physical mutilation or to medical or scientific experiments of any kind which are neither justified by the medical, dental or hospital treatment of the person concerned nor carried out in his or her interest, and which cause death to or seriously endanger the health of such person or persons;

(xi) Killing or wounding treacherously individuals belonging to the hostile nation or army;

(xii) Declaring that no quarter will be given;

(xiii) Destroying or seizing the enemy's property unless such destruction or seizure be imperatively demanded by the necessities of war;

(xiv) Declaring abolished, suspended or inadmissible in a court of law the rights and actions of the nationals of the hostile party;

(xv) Compelling the nationals of the hostile party to take part in the operations of war directed against their own country, even if they were in the belligerent's service before the commencement of the war;

(xvi) Pillaging a town or place, even when taken by assault;

(xvii) Employing poison or poisoned weapons;

(xviii) Employing asphyxiating, poisonous or other gases, and all analogous liquids, materials or devices;

(xix) Employing bullets which expand or flatten easily in the human body, such as bullets with a hard envelope which does not entirely cover the core or is pierced with incisions;

(xx) Employing weapons, projectiles and material and methods of warfare which are of a nature to cause superfluous injury or unnecessary suffering or which are inherently indiscriminate in violation of the international law of armed conflict, provided that such weapons, projectiles and material and methods of warfare are the subject of a comprehensive prohibition and are included in an annex to this Statute, by an amendment in accordance with the relevant provisions set forth in articles 121 and 123;

(xxi) Committing outrages upon personal dignity, in particular humiliating and degrading treatment;

(xxii) Committing rape, sexual slavery, enforced prostitution, forced pregnancy, as defined in article 7, paragraph 2 (f), enforced sterilization, or any other form of sexual violence also constituting a grave breach of the Geneva Conventions;

(xxiii) Utilizing the presence of a civilian or other protected person to render certain points, areas or military forces immune from military operations;

(xxiv) Intentionally directing attacks against buildings, material, medical units and transport, and personnel using the distinctive emblems of the Geneva Conventions in conformity with international law;

(xxv) Intentionally using starvation of civilians as a method of warfare by depriving them of objects indispensable to their survival, including wilfully impeding relief supplies as provided for under the Geneva Conventions;

(xxvi) Conscripting or enlisting children under the age of fifteen years into the national armed forces or using them to participate actively in hostilities.

(c) In the case of an armed conflict not of an international character, serious violations of article 3 common to the four Geneva Conventions of 12 August 1949, namely, any of the following acts committed against persons taking no active part in the hostilities, including members of armed forces who have laid down their arms and those placed *hors de combat* by sickness, wounds, detention or any other cause:

(i) Violence to life and person, in particular murder of all kinds, mutilation, cruel treatment and torture;

(ii) Committing outrages upon personal dignity, in particular humiliating and degrading treatment;

(iii) Taking of hostages;

(iv) The passing of sentences and the carrying out of executions without previous judgement pronounced by a regularly constituted court, affording all judicial guarantees which are generally recognized as indispensable.

(d) Paragraph 2 (c) applies to armed conflicts not of an international character and thus does not apply to situations of internal disturbances and tensions, such as riots, isolated and sporadic acts of violence or other acts of a similar nature.

(e) Other serious violations of the laws and customs applicable in armed conflicts not of an international character, within the established framework of international law, namely, any of the following acts:

(i) Intentionally directing attacks against the civilian population as such or against individual civilians not taking direct part in hostilities;

(ii) Intentionally directing attacks against buildings, material, medical units and transport, and personnel using the distinctive emblems of the Geneva Conventions in conformity with international law;

(iii) Intentionally directing attacks against personnel, installations, material, units or vehicles involved in a humanitarian assistance or peacekeeping mission in accordance with the Charter of the United Nations, as long as they are entitled to the protection given to civilians or civilian objects under the international law of armed conflict;

(iv) Intentionally directing attacks against buildings dedicated to religion, education, art, science or charitable purposes, historic monuments, hospitals and places where the sick and wounded are collected, provided they are not military objectives;

(v) Pillaging a town or place, even when taken by assault;

(vi) Committing rape, sexual slavery, enforced prostitution, forced pregnancy, as defined in article 7, paragraph 2 (f), enforced sterilization, and any other form of sexual violence also constituting a serious violation of article 3 common to the four Geneva Conventions;

(vii) Conscripting or enlisting children under the age of fifteen years into armed forces or groups or using them to participate actively in hostilities;

(viii) Ordering the displacement of the civilian population for reasons related to the conflict, unless the security of the civilians involved or imperative military reasons so demand;

(ix) Killing or wounding treacherously a combatant adversary;

(x) Declaring that no quarter will be given;

(xi) Subjecting persons who are in the power of another party to the conflict to physical mutilation or to medical or scientific experiments of any kind which are neither justified by the medical, dental or hospital treatment of the person concerned nor carried out in his or her interest, and which cause death to or seriously endanger the health of such person or persons;

(xii) Destroying or seizing the property of an adversary unless such destruction or seizure be imperatively demanded by the necessities of the conflict;

(f) Paragraph 2 (e) applies to armed conflicts not of an international character and thus does not apply to situations of internal disturbances and tensions, such as riots, isolated and sporadic acts of violence or other acts of a similar nature. It applies to armed conflicts that take place in the territory of a State when there is protracted armed conflict between governmental authorities and organized armed groups or between such groups.

3. Nothing in paragraph 2 (c) and (e) shall affect the responsibility of a Government to maintain or re-establish law and order in the State or to defend the unity and territorial integrity of the State, by all legitimate means.

[. . .]

Article 12

Preconditions to the exercise of jurisdiction

1. A State which becomes a Party to this Statute thereby accepts the jurisdiction of the Court with respect to the crimes referred to in article 5.

2. In the case of article 13, paragraph (a) or (c), the Court may exercise its jurisdiction if one or more of the following States are Parties to this Statute or have accepted the jurisdiction of the Court in accordance with paragraph 3:
   (a) The State on the territory of which the conduct in question occurred or, if the crime was committed on board a vessel or aircraft, the State of registration of that vessel or aircraft;
   (b) The State of which the person accused of the crime is a national.

[. . .]

Article 17

Issues of admissibility

1. Having regard to paragraph 10 of the Preamble and article 1, the Court shall determine that a case is inadmissible where:
   (a) The case is being investigated or prosecuted by a State which has jurisdiction over it, unless the State is unwilling or unable genuinely to carry out the investigation or prosecution;
   (b) The case has been investigated by a State which has jurisdiction over it and the State has decided not to prosecute the person concerned, unless the decision resulted from the unwillingness or inability of the State genuinely to prosecute;
   (c) The person concerned has already been tried for conduct which is the subject of the complaint, and a trial by the Court is not permitted under article 20, paragraph 3;

(d) The case is not of sufficient gravity to justify further action by the Court.

[. . .]

Article 98

Cooperation with respect to waiver of immunity and consent to surrender

[. . .]

2. The Court may not proceed with a request for surrender which would require the requested State to act inconsistently with its obligations under international agreements pursuant to which the consent of a sending State is required to surrender a person of that State to the Court, unless the Court can first obtain the cooperation of the sending State for the giving of consent for the surrender.

Appendix VII

The North American Free Trade Agreement
(1994, extracts)

Chapter Eleven: Investment
Section A – Investment

Article 1101: Scope and Coverage

1. This Chapter applies to measures adopted or maintained by a Party relating to:

(a) investors of another Party;
(b) investments of investors of another Party in the territory of the Party; and
(c) with respect to Articles 1106 and 1114, all investments in the territory of the Party.

[. . .]

Article 1102: National Treatment

1. Each Party shall accord to investors of another Party treatment no less favorable than that it accords, in like circumstances, to its own investors with respect to the establishment, acquisition, expansion, management, conduct, operation, and sale or other disposition of investments.

2. Each Party shall accord to investments of investors of another Party treatment no less favorable than that it accords, in like circumstances, to investments of its own investors with respect to the establishment, acquisition, expansion, management, conduct, operation, and sale or other disposition of investments.

3. The treatment accorded by a Party under paragraphs 1 and 2 means, with

respect to a state or province, treatment no less favorable than the most favorable treatment accorded, in like circumstances, by that state or province to investors, and to investments of investors, of the Party of which it forms a part.

4. For greater certainty, no Party may:

(a) impose on an investor of another Party a requirement that a minimum level of equity in an enterprise in the territory of the Party be held by its nationals, other than nominal qualifying shares for directors or incorporators of corporations; or

(b) require an investor of another Party, by reason of its nationality, to sell or otherwise dispose of an investment in the territory of the Party.

Article 1103: Most-Favored-Nation Treatment

1. Each Party shall accord to investors of another Party treatment no less favorable than that it accords, in like circumstances, to investors of any other Party or of a non-Party with respect to the establishment, acquisition, expansion, management, conduct, operation, and sale or other disposition of investments.

2. Each Party shall accord to investments of investors of another Party treatment no less favorable than that it accords, in like circumstances, to investments of investors of any other Party or of a non-Party with respect to the establishment, acquisition, expansion, management, conduct, operation, and sale or other disposition of investments.

Article 1104: Standard of Treatment

Each Party shall accord to investors of another Party and to investments of investors of another Party the better of the treatment required by Articles 1102 and 1103.

[. . .]

Article 1105: Minimum Standard of Treatment

1. Each Party shall accord to investments of investors of another Party treatment in accordance with international law, including fair and equitable treatment and full protection and security.

[. . .]

Article 1110: Expropriation and Compensation

1. No Party may directly or indirectly nationalize or expropriate an investment of an investor of another Party in its territory or take a measure tantamount to nationalization or expropriation of such an investment ('expropriation'), except:

  (a) for a public purpose;
  (b) on a non-discriminatory basis;
  (c) in accordance with due process of law and Article 1105(1); and
  (d) on payment of compensation in accordance with paragraphs 2 through 6.

2. Compensation shall be equivalent to the fair market value of the expropriated investment immediately before the expropriation took place ('date of expropriation'), and shall not reflect any change in value occurring because the intended expropriation had become known earlier. Valuation criteria shall include going concern value, asset value including declared tax value of tangible property, and other criteria, as appropriate, to determine fair market value.

3. Compensation shall be paid without delay and be fully realizable.

[. . .]

Appendix VIII

The Agreement establishing the World Trade
Organization (1994, extracts)

General Agreement on Tariffs and Trade 1994

Article I (1) General Most-Favoured Nation Treatment

With respect to customs duties and charges of any kind imposed on or in connection with importation or exportation or imposed on the international transfer of payments for imports or exports, and with respect to the method of levying such duties and charges, and with respect to all rules and formalities in connection with importation and exportation, and with respect to all matters referred to in paragraphs 2 and 4 of Article III, any advantage, favour, privilege or immunity granted by any contracting party to any product originating in or destined for any other country shall be accorded immediately and unconditionally to the like product originating in or destined for the territories of all other contracting parties.

[. . .]

Article III(1) National Treatment

The contracting parties recognize that internal taxes and other internal charges, and laws, regulations and requirements affecting the internal sale, offering for sale, purchase, transportation, distribution or use of products, and internal quantitative regulations requiring the mixture, processing or use of products in specified amounts or proportions, should not be applied to imported or domestic products so as to afford protection to domestic production.

[. . .]

Article XI(1) General Elimination of Quantitative Restrictions

No prohibitions or restrictions other than duties, taxes or other charges, whether made effective through quotas, import or export licences or other measures, shall be instituted or maintained by any contracting party on the importation of any product of the territory of any other contracting party or on the exportation or sale for export of any product destined for the territory of any other contracting party.

[. . .]

Article XX General Exceptions

Subject to the requirement that such measures are not applied in a manner which would constitute a means of arbitrary or unjustifiable discrimination between countries where the same conditions prevail, or a disguised restriction on international trade, nothing in this Agreement shall be construed to prevent the adoption or enforcement by any contracting party of measures:

(a) necessary to protect public morals;

(b) necessary to protect human, animal or plant life or health;

(c) relating to the importation or exportation of gold or silver;

(d) necessary to secure compliance with laws or regulations which are not inconsistent with the provisions of this Agreement, including those relating to customs enforcement, the enforcement of monopolies operated under paragraph 4 of Article II and Article XVII, the protection of patents, trade marks and copyrights, and the prevention of deceptive practices;

(e) relating to the products of prison labour;

(f) imposed for the protection of national treasures of artistic, historic or archaeological value;

(g) relating to the conservation of exhaustible natural resources if such measures are made effective in conjunction with restrictions on domestic production or consumption; [. . .]

Appendix IX

UN *Framework Convention on Climate Change (1992, extracts) and the Kyoto Protocol (1997, extracts)*

UN FRAMEWORK CONVENTION ON CLIMATE CHANGE (1992)

[...]

Article 2 Objectives

The ultimate objective of this Convention and any related legal instruments that the Conference of the Parties may adopt is to achieve, in accordance with the relevant provisions of the Convention, stabilization of greenhouse gas concentrations in the atmosphere at a level that would prevent dangerous anthropogenic interference with the climate system. Such a level should be achieved within a time-frame sufficient to allow ecosystems to adapt naturally to climate change, to ensure that food production is not threatened and to enable economic development to proceed in a sustainable manner.

Article 3 Principles

In their actions to achieve the objective of the Convention and to implement its provisions, the Parties shall be guided, *inter alia*, by the following:

1. The Parties should protect the climate system for the benefit of present and future generations of humankind, on the basis of equity and in accordance with their common but differentiated responsibilities and respective capabilities. Accordingly, the developed country Parties should take the lead in combating climate change and the adverse effects thereof.

2. The specific needs and special circumstances of developing country Parties, especially those that are particularly vulnerable to the adverse effects of climate change, and of those Parties, especially developing country Parties, that would have to bear a disproportionate or abnormal burden under the Convention, should be given full consideration.

3. The Parties should take precautionary measures to anticipate, prevent or minimize the causes of climate change and mitigate its adverse effects. Where there are threats of serious or irreversible damage, lack of full scientific certainty should not be used as a reason for postponing such measures, taking into account that policies and measures to deal with climate change should be cost-effective so as to ensure global benefits at the lowest possible cost. To achieve this, such policies and measures should take into account different socio-economic contexts, be comprehensive, cover all relevant sources, sinks and reservoirs of greenhouse gases and adaptation, and comprise all economic sectors. Efforts to address climate change may be carried out co-operatively by interested Parties.

4. The Parties have a right to, and should, promote sustainable development. Policies and measures to protect the climate system against human-induced change should be appropriate for the specific conditions of each Party and should be integrated with national development programmes, taking into account that economic development is essential for adopting measures to address climate change.

5. The Parties should cooperate to promote a supportive and open international economic system that would lead to sustainable economic growth and development in all Parties, particularly developing country Parties, thus enabling them better to address the problems of climate change. Measures taken to combat climate change, including unilateral ones, should not constitute a means of arbitrary or unjustifiable discrimination or a disguised restriction on international trade.

Article 4 Commitments

1. All Parties, taking into account their common but differentiated responsibilities and their specific national and regional development priorities, objectives and circumstances, shall:

(a) Develop, periodically update, publish and make available to the Conference of the Parties, in accordance with Article 12, national inventories of anthropogenic emissions by sources and removals by sinks of all greenhouse gases not controlled by the Montreal Protocol, using comparable methodologies to be agreed upon by the Conference of the Parties;

(b) Formulate, implement, publish and regularly update national and, where appropriate, regional programmes containing measures to mitigate climate change by addressing anthropogenic emissions by sources and removals by sinks of all greenhouse gases not controlled by the Montreal

Protocol, and measures to facilitate adequate adaptation to climate change;

(c) Promote and cooperate in the development, application and diffusion, including transfer, of technologies, practices and processes that control, reduce or prevent anthropogenic emissions of greenhouse gases not controlled by the Montreal Protocol in all relevant sectors, including the energy, transport, industry, agriculture, forestry and waste management sectors;

(d) Promote sustainable management, and promote and cooperate in the conservation and enhancement, as appropriate, of sinks and reservoirs of all greenhouse gases not controlled by the Montreal Protocol, including biomass, forests and oceans as well as other terrestrial, coastal and marine ecosystems;

(e) Cooperate in preparing for adaptation to the impacts of climate change; develop and elaborate appropriate and integrated plans for coastal zone management, water resources and agriculture, and for the protection and rehabilitation of areas, particularly in Africa, affected by drought and desertification, as well as floods;

(f) Take climate change considerations into account, to the extent feasible, in their relevant social, economic and environmental policies and actions, and employ appropriate methods, for example impact assessments, formulated and determined nationally, with a view to minimizing adverse effects on the economy, on public health and on the quality of the environment, of projects or measures undertaken by them to mitigate or adapt to climate change;

(g) Promote and cooperate in scientific, technological, technical, socio-economic and other research, systematic observation and development of data archives related to the climate system and intended to further the understanding and to reduce or eliminate the remaining uncertainties regarding the causes, effects, magnitude and timing of climate change and the economic and social consequences of various response strategies;

(h) Promote and cooperate in the full, open and prompt exchange of relevant scientific, technological, technical, socio-economic and legal information related to the climate system and climate change, and to the economic and social consequences of various response strategies;

(i) Promote and cooperate in education, training and public awareness related to climate change and encourage the widest participation in this process, including that of non-governmental organizations; and

(j) Communicate to the Conference of the Parties information related to implementation, in accordance with Article 12.

2. The developed country Parties and other Parties included in Annex I commit themselves specifically as provided for in the following:

(a) Each of these Parties shall adopt national policies and take corresponding measures on the mitigation of climate change, by limiting its anthropogenic emissions of greenhouse gases and protecting and enhancing its greenhouse gas sinks and reservoirs. These policies and measures will demonstrate that developed countries are taking the lead in modifying longer-term trends in anthropogenic emissions consistent with the objective of the Convention, recognizing that the return by the end of the present decade to earlier levels of anthropogenic emissions of carbon dioxide and other greenhouse gases not controlled by the Montreal Protocol would contribute to such modification, and taking into account the differences in these Parties' starting points and approaches, economic structures and resource bases, the need to maintain strong and sustainable economic growth, available technologies and other individual circumstances, as well as the need for equitable and appropriate contributions by each of these Parties to the global effort regarding that objective. These Parties may implement such policies and measures jointly with other Parties and may assist other Parties in contributing to the achievement of the objective of the Convention and, in particular, that of this subparagraph;

(b) In order to promote progress to this end, each of these Parties shall communicate, within six months of the entry into force of the Convention for it and periodically thereafter, and in accordance with Article 12, detailed information on its policies and measures referred to in subparagraph (a) above, as well as on its resulting projected anthropogenic emissions by sources and removals by sinks of greenhouse gases not controlled by the Montreal Protocol for the period referred to in subparagraph (a), with the aim of returning individually or jointly to their 1990 levels these anthropogenic emissions of carbon dioxide and other greenhouse gases not controlled by the Montreal Protocol. This information will be reviewed by the Conference of the Parties, at its first session and periodically thereafter, in accordance with Article 7;

[. . .]

KYOTO PROTOCOL TO THE UNITED NATIONS FRAMEWORK CONVENTION ON CLIMATE CHANGE (1997)

[. . .]

Article 2

1. Each Party included in Annex I,[1] in achieving its quantified emission limitation and reduction commitments under Article 3, in order to promote sustainable development, shall:

(a) Implement and/or further elaborate policies and measures in accordance with its national circumstances, such as:

(i) Enhancement of energy efficiency in relevant sectors of the national economy;

(ii) Protection and enhancement of sinks and reservoirs of greenhouse gases not controlled by the Montreal Protocol, taking into account its commitments under relevant international environmental agreements; promotion of sustainable forest management practices, afforestation and reforestation;

(iii) Promotion of sustainable forms of agriculture in light of climate change considerations;

(iv) Research on, and promotion, development and increased use of, new and renewable forms of energy, of carbon dioxide sequestration technologies and of advanced and innovative environmentally sound technologies;

(v) Progressive reduction or phasing out of market imperfections, fiscal incentives, tax and duty exemptions and subsidies in all greenhouse gas emitting sectors that run counter to the objective of the Convention and application of market instruments;

(vi) Encouragement of appropriate reforms in relevant sectors aimed at promoting policies and measures which limit or reduce emissions of greenhouse gases not controlled by the Montreal Protocol;

(vii) Measures to limit and/or reduce emissions of greenhouse gases not controlled by the Montreal Protocol in the transport sector;

(viii) Limitation and/or reduction of methane emissions through recovery

---

[1] Annex I to the 1992 UN Framework Convention on Climate Change lists: Australia, Austria, Belarus, Belgium, Bulgaria, Canada, Czechoslovakia, Denmark, European Economic Community, Estonia, Finland, France, Germany, Greece, Hungary, Iceland, Ireland, Italy, Japan, Latvia, Lithuania, Luxembourg, Netherlands, New Zealand, Norway, Poland, Portugal, Romania, Russian Federation, Spain, Sweden, Switzerland, Turkey, Ukraine, United Kingdom of Great Britain and Northern Ireland, United States of America.

and use in waste management, as well as in the production, transport and distribution of energy;

[. . .]

Article 3

1. The Parties included in Annex I shall, individually or jointly, ensure that their aggregate anthropogenic carbon dioxide equivalent emissions of the greenhouse gases listed in Annex A do not exceed their assigned amounts, calculated pursuant to their quantified emission limitation and reduction commitments inscribed in Annex B and in accordance with the provisions of this Article, with a view to reducing their overall emissions of such gases by at least 5 per cent below 1990 levels in the commitment period 2008 to 2012.

2. Each Party included in Annex I shall, by 2005, have made demonstrable progress in achieving its commitments under this Protocol.

3. The net changes in greenhouse gas emissions by sources and removals by sinks resulting from direct human-induced land-use change and forestry activities, limited to afforestation, reforestation and deforestation since 1990, measured as verifiable changes in carbon stocks in each commitment period, shall be used to meet the commitments under this Article of each Party included in Annex I. The greenhouse gas emissions by sources and removals by sinks associated with those activities shall be reported in a transparent and verifiable manner and reviewed in accordance with Articles 7 and 8.

[. . .]

Annex B
Party Quantified emission limitation or reduction commitment

(percentage of base year or period)

Australia 108	Liechtenstein 92
Austria 92	Lithuania* 92
Belgium 92	Luxembourg 92
Bulgaria* 92	Monaco 92
Canada 94	Netherlands 92
Croatia*95	New Zealand 100
Czech Republic* 92	Norway 101
Denmark 92	Poland* 94
Estonia* 92	Portugal 92
European Community 92	Romania* 92
Finland 92	Russian Federation* 100
France 92	Slovakia* 92
Germany 92	Slovenia* 92
Greece 92	Spain 92
Hungary* 94	Sweden 92
Iceland 110	Switzerland 92
Ireland 92	Ukraine* 100
Italy 92	United Kingdom of Great Britain
Japan 94	and Northern Ireland 92
Latvia* 92	United States of America 93

* Countries that are undergoing the process of transition to a market economy.

Notes

Preface

1. *Breard v. Commonwealth, 248 Va. 68, 445 S.E. 2d 670 (1994)*, cert. denied, *513 U.S. 971 (1994)*.
2. See the *Case Concerning the Vienna Convention on Consular Relations (Paraguay v. United States)*, Order of 9 April 1998, ICJ Reports (1998), p. 248.
3. *Richmond Times Dispatch*, 10 April 1998, p. A1.
4. *Richmond Times Dispatch*, 7 April 1998, p. B5.
5. In 1980 the International Court of Justice ruled that the Islamic Republic of Iran's decision to continue the subjection of the premises of the US Embassy to occupation by militants and of the Embassy Staff to detention as hostages gave rise to repeated and multiple breaches of various conventions, including the 1963 Convention on Consular Relations: <http://www.icjcij.org/icjwww/icases/iusir/iusir_ijudgment/iusir_iJudgment_19800524.pdf>
6. See letters, *Los Angeles Times*, 21 April 1998, p. B6.
7. The Privy Council ruled that Thomas and Hilaire had a general right 'not to have the outcome of any pending appellate or other legal process pre-empted by executive action', and those processes included mechanisms before international human rights bodies. See the majority judgment of Lord Browne-Wilkinson, Lord Steyn and Lord Millett, Privy Council Appeal No. 60 of 1998, Judgment delivered on 17 March 1999. The case was decided shortly before the main judgment of the House of Lords in the Pinochet case and gave an early indication to attentive readers of the likely outcome of that case: see Chapter 2.

1 International Law: a Short and Recent History

1. 'PM warns of continuing global terror threat', 5 March 2004. <http://www.number-10.gov.uk/output/Page5461.asp>
2. D. R. Thorpe, *Eden: The Life and Times of Anthony Eden, First Earl of Avon, 1897–1977* (Pimlico, 2004), p. 478. See also Clare Dyer, 'Remember

Suez?', *The Guardian*, 9 March 2004; Jesse Norman, 'Tell us the reason why', *The Spectator*, 1 November 2003.

3. 'All the Many Tony's', *Financial Times*, 3–4 April 2004, p. W5.

4. For a useful historical summary, see Malcolm Shaw, *International Law*, 5th edn (Cambridge University Press, 2003), pp. 13–41.

5. The traditional sources of international legal obligation are set out in Article 38 of the Statute of the International Court of Justice. This Article directs the Court to apply:

> a. international conventions, general or particular, establishing rules recognized by the contesting states
>
> b. international custom as evidence of a general practice accepted as law
>
> c. the general principles of law recognized by *civilized nations* [my italics]
>
> d. subject to Art 59, judicial decisions and teachings . . .

6. 'International law governs relations between independent States. The rules of law binding upon States therefore emanate from their own free will as expressed in conventions or by usages generally accepted as expressing principles of law and established in order to regulate the relations between these co-existing independent communities or with a view to the achievement of common aims. Restrictions upon the independence of States cannot therefore be presumed.' *SS Lotus (Turkey v. France)*, Permanent Court of International Justice, Series A-No.10, 1927.

7. Nelson Mandela, *Long Walk to Freedom* (Abacus, 1994), p. 110.

8. J. Q. Barrett (ed.), *That Man: An Insider's Portrait of Franklin D. Roosevelt* (Oxford University Press, 2003), p. 110.

9. <http://www.udhr.org/history/frbioer.htm>

10. Federal News Service, 4 November 1988.

11. See ICJ, Advisory Opinion on Legal Consequences of the Construction of a Wall in the Occupied Palestinian Territory, 9 July 2004, <http://www.icj-cij.org/icjwww/idocket/imwp/imwpframe.htm>

12. T. M. Franck, 'The emerging right to democratic governance', *American Journal of International Law*, vol. 86 (1992), pp. 46–91.

13. 'Treaties are "law" only for U.S. domestic purposes. In their international operation, treaties are simply "political", and not legally binding': the Federalist Society at <http://www.fed-soc.org/Publications/practicegroup-newsletters/internationalnews/ino20101.htm>, 25 September 1997. He has also written that 'There may be good and sufficient reasons to abide by the provisions of a treaty, and in most cases one would expect to do so because of the mutuality of benefits that treaties provide, but not because the United States is "legally" obligated to do so.' John Bolton, 'Is There Really "Law" in International Affairs?', *Transnational Law and Contemporary Problems*, vol. 10, Spring 2000.

14. *San Francisco Chronicle*, 10 August 2001, p. A25.

15. 'PM warns of continuing global terror threat', speech, 5 March 2004, available at <http://www.number-10.gov.uk/output/Page5461.asp>

2 Pinochet in London

1. *Financial Times*, 19 October 1998, p. 24.

2. See Hugh O'Shaughnessy, *Pinochet: The Politics of Terror* (Latin America Bureau, 2000), p. 64.

3. As quoted in John Dinges, *The Condor Years* (The New Press, 2004), p. 67.

4. See O'Shaughnessy, op. cit., at p. 65.

5. See Dinges, op. cit., p. 15.

6. Jon Lee Anderson, 'The Dictator', *New Yorker*, 19 October 1998, p. 55.

7. The issue of the arrest warrant was the culmination of a chain of events dating back some years: see Dinges, op. cit., pp. 23–33.

8. <http://news.bbc.co.uk/1/hi/uk_politics/195821.stm>

9. *Hatch v. Baez* (1876) 7 Hun. 596.

10. *Re. Ugarte; R v. Evans and others, ex parte Pinochet Ugarte*, Queen's Bench Division, 28 October 1998 (Lord Bingham CJ, Collins J, Richards J).

11. *Financial Times*, USA edition, 22 September 1998, first section, p. 1.

12. Case for the Appellants (Crown Prosecution Service), November 1998, para. 36, in R. Brody and M. Ratner, *The Pinochet Papers* (Kluwer Law International, 2000), p. 113.

13. Case for the Respondent, para. 52 (November 1998), in ibid., p. 121.

14. *R v. Bow Street Metropolitan Stipendiary Magistrate, ex parte Pinochet Ugarte* (No. 2) (House of Lords), 25 November 1998 [2000] 1 AC 61 at 84.

15. Ibid., at 98.

16. Ibid., at 115.

17. <http://news.bbc.co.uk/1/hi/uk/221718.htm>

18. *Financial Times*, 26 November 1998, London edition, p. 6.

19. BBC Worldwide Monitoring, 25 November 1998, source RNE, Radio 1, Madrid, 1449 GMT.

20. *Daily Mail*, 26 November 1998, p. 9.

21. *The Guardian*, 26 November 1998, p. 24.

22. *Chattanooga Times* (Tennessee), 26 November 1998, p. 354.

23. See Dinges, op. cit., at p. 39.

24. *The Guardian*, 26 November. 1998, p. 4.

25. 'In one way it was a sort of a storm in a teacup, because obviously it was a misjudgement on my part when I decided that there didn't seem to be anything wrong in my sitting in that case. It was slightly more complicated than

it was presented as being and I probably didn't have time to talk to my colleagues about it. Anyway they afterwards thought I'd made a mistake and so there it is.' *Hampstead & Highgate Express*, 18 June 2004, p. 17.

26. This second requirement is referred to as *opinio juris*; it describes the belief that action is required as a matter of law.

27. *New York Times*, 2 July 1999, Section A, p. 16.

28. *R v. Bow Street Metropolitan Stipendiary Magistrate, ex parte Pinochet Ugarte (No. 3)*, 24 March 1999 [2000] 1 AC 147 at 205.

29. Hugh O'Shaughnessy, 'Secret UK deal freed Pinochet', *The Observer*, 7 January 2001.

30. See 'Comments of Spanish Doctors on British Medical Report', 18 February 2000, reproduced in Brody and Ratner, *The Pinochet Papers*, op. cit., p. 461.

31. Decision of 2 March 2000, para. 28.

32. Margaret Thatcher, *Statecraft* (HarperCollins, 2003), pp. 269 and 271.

33. In *Arrest Warrant Case* of 11 April 2000 (*Democratic Republic of Congo v. Belgium*) the Court ruled that Belgium had violated the DRC's rights under international law by allowing a Belgian criminal prosecutor to issue an indictment against the serving Foreign Minister of the Democratic Republic of Congo: see judgment of 14 February 2002, <http://www.icj-cij.org/icjwww/idocket/iCOBE/icobejudgment/icobe_ijudgment_20020214.PDF>

34. Special Court of Sierra Leone, Decision on Immunity from Jurisdiction, *Prosecutor v. Charles Ghankay Taylor*, Case No. SCSL-2003-01-I, at <http://www.sc-sl.org/>

35. Henry Kissinger, *Does America Need a Foreign Policy?* (Simon & Schuster, 2001), p. 277.

36. National Security Archive, Telcon: 9/16/73 (Home) 1150.

37. George Kennan, *American Diplomacy* (University of Chicago Press, 1984), p. 95.

3 A New International Court

1. <http://www/amicc.org/Rumsfeld6_21_02.pdf> On the emerging system of international criminal justice, see P. Sands (ed.), *From Nuremberg to The Hague: the Future of International Criminal Justice* (Cambridge University Press, 2003); and M. Lattimer and P. Sands (eds), *Justice for Crimes Against Humanity* (Hart Publishing, 2003).

2. Article 18, Vienna Convention on the Law of Treaties states that:
A State is obliged to refrain from acts which would defeat the object and purpose of a treaty when:
(a) it has signed the treaty or has exchanged instruments constituting the

treaty subject to ratification, acceptance or approval, until it shall have made its intention clear not to become a party to the treaty; or

(b) it has expressed its consent to be bound by the treaty, pending the entry into force of the treaty and provided that such entry into force is not unduly delayed.

3. Statement issued by the US Department of Defense, Washington, DC, 6 May 2002, distributed by the Office of International Information Programs, US Department of State, at <http://usinfo.state.gov>

4. National Security Strategy of the United States of America, September 2002, p. 31.

5. For a general account see Margaret Macmillan, *Peacemakers: The Paris Conference of 1919 and its Attempt to End War* (John Murray, 2001).

6. John F. Barnett (ed.), *That Man: An Insider's Portrait of Franklin D. Roosevelt* (Oxford University Press, 2003), p. 170.

7. On the ICTY see Gary Jonathan Bass, *Stay the Hand of Vengeance* (Princeton University Press, 2000), pp. 206–75.

8. See, for example, *Jane's Security Review*, 2 April 2001, 'Milosevic behind bars: anatomy of an arrest', at <http://www.janes.com/security/international_security/news/jir/jir010402_1_n.shtml>

9. See D. N. Sharp, 'Prosecutions, Development and Justice: The Trial of Hissène Habré', *Harvard Human Rights Journal*, vol. 13 [2003], p. 147.

10. Quoted by John Bolton in his remarks to the Federalist Society, Washington, DC, 14 November 2002.

11. The idea has been so summarized by one of the authors of the proposal: see James Crawford, 'The drafting of the Rome Statute', in P. Sands (ed.), op. cit., p. 137.

12. Ibid., p. 124.

13. See Bart Brown, 'The Statute of the International Criminal Court: Past, Present and Future', in *The United States and the International Criminal Courts*, American Academy of Arts and Sciences, September 2000, p. 13.

14. See Chapter 2, note 29.

15. *Sunday Telegraph*, 29 February 2004, p. 24.

16. Antony Barnett and Martin Bright, 'War chief reveals legal crisis', *The Observer*, 7 March 2004.

17. See Marc Grossman, Under Secretary for Political Affairs, remarks to the Center for Strategic and International Studies, Washington, DC, 6 May 2002 (when the US announced that it had 'unsigned' the ICC treaty). Available at <http://www.state.gov/p/9949.htm>

18. See the speech of John Bolton, Under Secretary of Arms Control and International Security, to the Federalist Society, 14 November 2002.

19. Ibid.

20. Statement by Donald Rumsfeld, 6 May 2002 at <http://www.defenselink. mil/news/May2002/b05062002_bt233_02.html>

21. Title II of Public Law 107–206 (22 USC 7421 et seq.).

22. Security Council resolution 1497, 1 August 2003, at para. 7.

23. Security Council resolution 1502, 26 August 2003, preamble.

24. The other non-NATO allies are Australia, Japan, Argentina, the Republic of Korea and New Zealand. Taiwan is also excluded.

25. BBC Monitoring International Reports, 28 August 2002.

26. Such as the 1961 Vienna Convention on Diplomatic Relations.

27. The international agreements on the stationing of troops are known as 'Status of Forces Agreements'. They set out the detailed rules and conditions governing the treatment of foreign troops who are stationed abroad. The United Kingdom has such an agreement with the United States.

28. Donald Rumsfeld, statement on the International Criminal Court, briefing at the Foreign Press Center, 22 June 2002.

29. CARICOM Press Release 95/2003, 4 July 1998.

30. *Washington Post*, 10 June 2003, p. A17.

31. The concerns were raised by Lincoln P. Bloomfield Jr, Assistant Secretary of State for Political-Military Affairs, in remarks to Parliamentarians for Global Action, New York, 12 September 2003.

32.<http://www.humanrightsfirst.org/international_justice/Art98_061403.pdf>

33. 'Annan Slams War Crimes Exemption', BBC News, 17 June 2004.

34. The treaty was presented to Parliament in May 2003, 'Extradition Treaty between the Government of Great Britain and Northern Ireland and the Government of the United States of America', May 2003. For further information, see Statewatch Briefing No. 17, 'The New UK–US Extradition Treaty', Ben Hayes, July 2003.

35. Letter of 31 March 2003 from David Blunkett to John Ashcroft; see David Hencke and Rob Evans, *The Guardian*, 2 March 2004, p. 10.

4 Global Warming: Throwing Precaution to the Wind

1. Quoted in Peter Stothard, *30 Days: A Month at the Heart of Blair's War* (HarperCollins, 2003), p. 70.

2. *The Independent*, 7 March 2004.

3. See the *Catholic Encyclopedia*, <http://www.newadvent.org/cathen/ 01246b.htm>

4. <http://nmml.afsc.noaa.gov/AlaskaEcosystems/nfshome/nfslifehistory.htm>

5. Since 1982 and the UN Convention on the Law of the Sea, sovereignty has been extended over waters up to twelve miles off the coast.

6. For general background see *Oppenheim's International Law*, 9th edn, (Longman, 1991), pp. 720–22.

7. See the 1991 edition of the Love To Know Encyclopedia Free Online at <http://63.1911encyclopedia.org/S/SE/SEAL_FISHERIES.htm> based on the 11th edition of the *Encyclopaedia Britannica*.

8. *Pacific Fur Seal Arbitration (Great Britain v. United States)* 1 Moore's Int. Arb. Awards, 15 August 1893, 755, at 811.

9. Ibid., p. 853.

10. Quoted in Remarks of the Honourable Russell Train, World Heritage Convention, 30th Anniversary, Venice, 16 November 2002, at <http://whc.unesco.org/venice2002/speeches/pdf/train.pdf>

11. Intergovernmental Panel on Climate Change report, *Climate Change: the IPCC Scientific Assessment* (1990).

12. The 'business-as-usual' scenario assumed a continued reliance on coal and oil, modest improvements in energy efficiency, limited controls on emissions of carbon dioxide, continued deforestation, uncontrolled emissions of methane and nitrous oxide from agricultural sources, and a reduction of CFCs in line with the 1987 Montreal Protocol.

13. Ironically, Vanuatu's head of delegation, Robert van Lierop, is a New York attorney as American as apple pie. I always suspected that the combination of a darker skin and a foreign name, together with the fact that few people know what citizens of Vanuatu actually look like, meant that few took his nationality into consideration during the delicate negotiations of chairmanship. Of course, van Lierop's commitment to Vanuatu's interests cannot be questioned, and I saw first-hand everything he was able to achieve for Vanuatu and AOSIS. But in general it is an unfortunate reality of international diplomacy in a decentralized system that many small countries do not always have the resources to represent themselves at all meetings. It is not uncommon to see hired negotiators (such as myself) sitting behind the nameplates of developing countries.

14. See, for example, *Vellore Citizens' Welfare Forum v. Union of India & Others* [1996] ICHRL 62 (28 August 1996).

15. *Climate Change (1992)*, the Supplementary Report to the IPCC Scientific Assessment Working Group; see also 1992 IPCC Supplement.

16. For an overview of the Protocol, see Philippe Sands, *Principles of International Environmental Law* (Cambridge University Press, 2nd edn, 2003), p. 368.

17. Farhana Yamin, 'The Kyoto Protocol: Origins, Assessment and Future Challenges', *Review of European Community and International Environmental Law* (RECIEL), July 1998, vol. 7, issue 2, pp. 113–27.

18. Climate Research Unit at the University of East Anglia, <http://www.cru.uea.ac.uk/tiempo/flooro/briefing/vietnam/intro4.htm>

19. <http://www.eia.doe.gov/oiaf/1605/ggrpt/summary/overview.html>

20. White House press release, Statement by the President, *Federal Document Clearing House Transcripts*, 10 December 1997.

21. Other signatories to the letter included former UN Ambassador Jeanne Kirkpatrick and former Secretary of State Lawrence Eagleburger; see *National Journal*'s Daily Energy Briefing, 27 January 1998.

22. Quoted in Bill McKibben, 'Crossing the Red Line', *New York Review of Books*, vol. LI, no. 10, p. 32.

23. IPCC Third Assessment Report, *Climate Change 2001* (2001).

24. Sir David King, 'Global Warming: the imperatives for action from the science of climate change', Plenary address to the American Association for the Advancement of Science, British Embassy, Washington, DC, 13 February 2004. <http://www.britainusa.com/science/articles_show.asp?SarticleType=1&Article_ID=4786&i=>

25. Sir David wrote that 'In my view, climate change is the most severe problem we are facing today, more serious even than the threat of terrorism.' According to the BBC, 'The government feared his comments could undermine relations with the US on terror and a Downing Street official wrote to Sir David asking him to tone down his remarks.' BBC News Online, <http://news.bbc.co.uk/1/hi/uk_politics/3584679.stm>

26. Bjorn Lomberg, *The Skeptical Environmentalist* (Cambridge University Press, 2001), pp. 317–18.

27. <http://www.cru.uea.ac.uk/tiempo/flooro/briefing/vietnam/intro4.htm>

28. *Washington Times*, 12 June 2001, page A1.

29. United States Environmental Protection Agency, list of state action plans on global warming. <http://yosemite.epa.gov/globalwarming/ghg.nsf/actions/StateActionPlans?Open>

30. See Jeffrey E. Garten, 'A Foreign Policy Harmful to Business', *Business Week*, 14 October 2002, p. 72.

31. House of Lords Science and Technology Committee, 3rd Report of Session 2003–2004, 'Science and Treaties', 30 June 2004, HL Paper 110–1.

32. Mark Townsend and Gaby Hinsliff, 'US must act over climate, says Queen', *The Observer*, 31 October 2004.

5 Good Trade, Bad Trade, Cheap Shrimp

1. Robert Zoellick, 'Globalization, Trade and Economic Security', remarks at the National Press Club, October 2002, p. 7. His speeches can be found on the website of the Office of the United States Trade Representative, <http://www.ustr.gov>

2. In the *New York Times*, 26 March 2004, p. C5.

3. *Financial Times*, 19 June 2004, London edition, p. 12. See also 'Cultivating Poverty: the Impact of US Cotton Subsidies on Africa', Oxfam, September 2002.

4. See the President's statement on steel, on 4 December 2003, at <http://www.whitehouse.gov/news/releases/2003/12/20031204-5.html>

5. *United States – Definitive Safeguard Measures on Imports of Certain Steel Products*, AB-2003-3, Report of the Appellate Body of the WTO. Under WTO law the value of the sanctions which the EU was entitled to impose were equivalent to the economic harm it had suffered as a result of the unlawful US measures.

6. See 'President announces temporary safeguard for steel industry', statement by the President, 5 March 2002, <http://www.whitehouse.gov/news/releases/2002/03/20020305-6.html>

7. See Andreas Lowenfeld, *International Economic Law* (Oxford University Press, 2002), pp. 22–3.

8. The GATT entered into force on 1 January 1948. The twenty-three founding members were: Australia, Belgium, Brazil, Burma, Canada, Ceylon, Chile, China, Cuba, Czechoslovakia, France, India, Lebanon, Luxembourg, the Netherlands, New Zealand, Norway, Pakistan, Southern Rhodesia, Syria, South Africa, United Kingdom and the United States.

9. Estonia, Latvia, Lithuania, Poland, Czech Republic, Slovakia, Hungary, Slovenia, Malta and Cyprus.

10. See *Ireland v. United Kingdom*, case concerning the MOX plant, oral pleadings, 12 June 2003, p. 3, at <http://www.pca-cpa.org/PDF/MOX%20-%20Day%20Three.pdf>

11. Adam Smith, *The Wealth of Nations* (1776), Book 4, Chapter 2 (Modern Library Edition, Random House, 1937), p. 414.

12. *Integrating Intellectual Property Rights and Development Policy*, Report of the Commission on Intellectual Property Rights, September 2002.

13. Naomi Klein, *No Logo* (Flamingo, 2000), p. 447.

14. The first tuna/dolphin case was brought by Mexico against the US. As a result of pressure from domestic environmental groups, the US had passed the Marine Mammal Protection Act (1972), which banned the sale of any tuna caught by purse seine fishing, a method which killed large numbers of dolphins. A GATT panel ruled against section 101(a)(2) of the Marine Mammal Protection Act, but the decision was never adopted by the GATT and so the ruling never actually took effect (GATT, United States – Restrictions on Imports of Tuna (DS21/R), report of the panel, 3 September 1991). The GATT panel interpreted Article 3, which prohibited discrimination between different goods on the basis of *where* they are produced, also to prohibit discrimination as to *how* they are produced.

The relevant provisions of the Marine Mammal Protection Act were eventually removed by the Clinton Administration, following a settlement between Mexico and the US. For more background see Philippe Sands, *Principles of International Environmental Law* (Cambridge University Press, 2003), pp. 953–61.

15. See, for example, the *Friends of the Earth Trade Activists Guide*, 2001.

16. In the end Mexico and the US compromised on language which left open the possibility that unilateral measures might in certain circumstances be justified.

17. See *Appellate Body Report on US Gasoline* (Appellate Body Report, United States, Standards for Reformulated and Conventional Gasoline WT/DS2/AB/R, adopted 20 May 1996 DSR 1996: 1, 3), p. 17.

18. See *United States – Import Prohibition of Certain Shrimp and Shrimp Products*, WTO case Nos. 58 (and 61). Ruling adopted on 6 November 1998.

19. Elizabeth Olson quotes Chris McGinn of the Washington-based Public Citizen's Global Trade Watch: 'WTO allows companies to try and trump the democratic process in the United States . . . It gives them an additional appeal process once a law is passed to try and undo hard-fought consumer, environmental or health legislation.' Elizabeth Olson, 'Critics Say World Trade Group Disregards Environment', *New York Times*, 16 May 1998. Martin Crutsinger also quotes McGinn: 'This is one more attack by the WTO on environmental law. The WTO favors trade over all other values . . . This puts the United States in the position of changing US law or facing economic sanctions.' Martin Crutsinger, Economics Writer, 'WTO Rules Against US in Turtle Case', Associated Press, 14 March 1998.

20. Appellate Body Report, *United States – Import Prohibition of Certain Shrimp and Shrimp Products*, Recourse to Article 21.5 of the DSU by Malaysia, GATT Doc. WT/DS58/AB/RW (22 October 2001).

21. *Daily Mail*, 12 April 2001, p. 45.

22. *Sun-Sentinel* (Fort Lauderdale, Florida), 12 November 2003, Broward metro edition.

23. *Case concerning military and paramilitary activities in and against Nicaragua (Nicaragua v. United States of America)*, 26 November 1984, International Court of Justice (General List No. 70). The Contras, opposition groups to the Sandinista government in Nicaragua, were considered terrorists. The US government, through the CIA, supplied covert support to the Contras. In 1984 Nicaragua filed a case against the US in the International Court of Justice, which – in effect – found the US responsible for providing assistance to the rebel groups. The ICJ called on the US to 'cease and to

refrain' from activities which were 'in breach of its obligations under customary international law not to use force against another state'. The ICJ's judgment is available at <http://www.icj-cij.org>

24. See Noreena Hertz, *The Silent Takeover* (William Heinemann, 2001), p. 80.

25. 'Globalization, Trade and Economic Security', remarks at the National Press Club, October 2002.

26. 'A Time to Choose: Trade and the American Nation', speech to the Heritage Foundation, 29 June 2001.

27. See Jed Rubenfeld, 'The Two World Orders', *Wilson Quarterly*, Autumn 2003.

6 A Safer World, for Investors

1. The ICJ eventually ruled that Albania should pay the United Kingdom compensation of £843,947: *The Corfu Channel (United Kingdom v. Albania)*, Merits, 9 April 1945, Judgment of 15 December 1949.

2. 'President outlines steps to help Iraq achieve democracy and freedom', remarks by the President on Iraq and the war on terror, at United States Army War College, Carlisle, Pennsylvania, 24 May 2004. Available online at <http://www.whitehouse.you/news/releases/2004/05/ 20040524-10.html>

3. Article 1 of the First Protocol to the ECHR provides:

'Every natural or legal person is entitled to the peaceful enjoyment of his possessions. No one shall be deprived of his possessions except in the public interest and subject to the conditions provided for by law and by the general principles of international law.

The preceding provisions shall not, however, in any way impair the right of a State to enforce such laws as it deems necessary to control the use of property in accordance with the general interest or to secure the payment of taxes or other contributions or penalties.'

4. White House press release, 6 May 2003.

5. *Ethyl Corporation v. Canada*, Jurisdiction, UNCITRAL, 24 June 1998 (NAFTA).

6. Anthony De Palma, 'NAFTA's Powerful Little Secret. Obscure Tribunals Settle Disputes, but Go too Far, Critics Say', *New York Times*, 11 March 2001, Section 3, p. 1.

7. V. V. Veeder, 'The Lena Goldfields Arbitration: the Historical Roots of Three Ideas', *International and Comparative Law Quarterly*, 47 (1998), p. 747.

8. 23 November 1926 (Van Vollenhoven, Presiding Commissioner). See the report in *International Law Reports*, vol. 3, p. 223.

9. See Carrie E. Donovan, 'The Law of the Sea Treaty', in *Just the Facts*, No. 4, 2 April 2004, Heritage Foundation.

10. See <http://www.bushcountry.org>

11. ICSID Case No. ARB/96/1, 17 February 2000, 15 *ICSID Review – Foreign Investment Law Journal*, 169 (2000), available at <http://www.worldbank.org/icsid/cases/santaelena_award.pdf>

12. Ibid., Santa Elena award, paras. 71–2.

13. *Metalclad Corporation v. The United Mexican States*, ICSID Case No. ARB (AB)/97/1, 25 August 2000, 40 *International Legal Materials* 35 (2001).

14. In the European Community context this is known as the principle of 'subsidiarity', which determines the most appropriate level of government at which a decision should be made. The principle of subsidiarity was inserted into the EC Treaty by the Maastricht Treaty on European Union (1992), where it stated (Article 3b): 'In areas which do not fall within its exclusive competence, the Community shall take action, in accordance with the principle of subsidiarity, only if and insofar as the objective of the proposed action cannot be sufficiently achieved by the Member States and can, therefore, by reason of the scale or effects of the proposed action, be better achieved by the Community.'

15. The case was brought under the ICSID additional facility, which allows ICSID to hear conciliation and arbitration proceedings where either the state party or the home state of the foreign national is not an ICSID party.

16. *Metalclad v. Mexico*, 16 *ICSID Review – Foreign Investment Law Journal* at 195.

17. Naomi Klein, 'Time to Fight Free Trade Laws that Benefit Multinationals', *Guardian Weekly*, 15 March 2001.

18. Lori Wallach, 'Trade Pacts Accused of Subverting US Policies', *Los Angeles Times*, 28 February 1999.

19. Ibid.

20. Canadian Department of Foreign Affairs and Trade <http://www.dfait-maeci.gc.ca/tna-nac/NAFTA-Interr.en.asp>

21. A. Liptak, 'Review of US Rulings by NAFTA Tribunals Stir US Worries', *New York Times*, 18 April 2004.

22. Ibid.

23. See Vicki Been, 'Does an International Regulatory Takings Doctrine Make Sense?', *New York University Environmental Law Journal*, vol. 11 (2003), p. 49; at <http://www.law.nyu.edu/journals/envtllaw/issues/vol11/1/been.pdf>

7 Guantánamo: the Legal Black Hole

1. See *BBC News*, 29 January 2002; and *Washington Post*, 28 January 2002.

2. *The Guardian*, 18 July 2003.

3. *The Oxford Companion to Law* defines *habeas corpus* as a prerogative writ for securing the liberty of the subject, affording an effective means of securing release from unjustifiable custody. The writ is older than the Magna Carta and was established by the seventeenth century as the appropriate process for checking illegal imprisonment. The writ is today available as a remedy in most cases of unlawful deprivation of personal liberty, civil or criminal, enabling the court to inquire into the justification for the detention.

4. See Lord Scarman in *R v. Home Secretary ex parte Khawaja* [1984] 1 AC 74, 110, citing the classic dissenting judgment of Lord Atkin in *Liversidge v. Anderson* (1942) AC 206, 245.

5. As required by Article 4(A)(2)(b) of the Geneva Convention III (1949). In February 2002 the US modified its position and distinguished between al-Qaeda and Taliban detainees. Anyone detained in the course of an armed conflict is presumed to be a Prisoner of War (POW) until a competent court or tribunal determines otherwise. The Geneva Convention is widely regarded as an accurate statement of customary international law, which are unwritten rules binding on all. The Office of the White House Press Secretary issued a fact sheet on 7 February 2002 about the status of the detainees in Guantánamo, setting out US policy as follows:

– The United States is treating and will continue to treat all of the individuals detained at Guantánamo humanely and to the extent appropriate and consistent with military necessity, in a manner consistent with the principles of the Third Geneva Convention of 1949.

– The President has determined that the Geneva Convention applies to the Taliban detainees, but not to the al-Qaeda detainees.

– Al-Qaeda is not a state party to the Geneva Conventions; it is a foreign terrorist group. As such, its members are not entitled to Prisoner of War (POW) status.

– Although we never recognized the Taliban as the legitimate Afghan government, Afghanistan is a party to the Convention, and the President has determined that the Taliban are covered by the Convention. Under the terms of the Geneva Convention, however, the Taliban detainees do not qualify as POWs.

– Therefore, neither the Taliban nor al-Qaeda detainees are entitled to POW status.

– Even though the detainees are not entitled to POW privileges, they will be provided many POW privileges as a matter of policy.

This case can be found at <http://www.whitehouse.gov/news/releases/2002/02/20020207-13.html>

On 7 May 2003, the Office of the Press Secretary issued a further statement on the Geneva Convention, stating that the Taliban have not effectively distinguished themselves from the civilian population of Afghanistan, nor have they conducted their operations in accordance with the laws and customs of war, but rather they have provided support to the unlawful terrorist objectives of al-Qaeda. Al-Qaeda is an international terrorist organization and therefore cannot be considered a state party to the Geneva Convention. As a result of this, its members are not covered by the Geneva Convention, and are not entitled to POW status. <http://www.whitehouse.gov/news/releases/2003/05/20030507-18.html>

6. Case Nos. 03-334 and 03-343 (Supreme Court of the United States), *Rasul et al. v. George Bush et al.*, and *Al Odah et al. v. George Bush et al.*, Brief for the Respondents, October 2003.

7. Reprinted in A. Roberts and R. Guelff, *Documents on the Laws of War*, 3rd edn (Oxford University Press, 2000), p. 55.

8. See ibid., p. 53.

9. 'The French have reinforc'd their scatter'd men:

Then every soldier kill his prisoners!' (*Henry V*, Act IV, scene vi)

10. See the Annex to The Hague Convention II, Respecting the Laws and Customs of War on Land (1899).

11. Ibid., Article 1.

12. There was, however, a hint in that direction: the population of an occupied territory which took up arms spontaneously was entitled to be treated as belligerent and to have prisoner of war status: see Article 2.

13. Article 9.

14. Judgment of the International Military Tribunal at Nuremberg, 1 October 1946, *American Journal of International Law*, 41 (1947), pp. 172, 229.

15. The point has been made forcefully by George Aldrich, who served as one of the US negotiators of Geneva Protocol I: see 'The Taliban, Al-Qaeda, and the Determination of Illegal Combatants', Heft 4 (2002), 202 at 205. <http://www.icrc.org/Web/Eng/siteengo.nsf/o/C82A7582AE20DCD1C12 56D34004AEA41/$File/George+Aldrich_3_final.pdf?OpenElement>

16. The Red Cross indicated that 'There are divergent views between the United States and the ICRC on the procedures which apply on how to determine that the persons detained are not entitled to prisoner of war status', *Washington Times*, 9 February 2002. It is worth pointing out that the Red Cross almost never makes public any differences of view it may have with a state.

17. Geneva Protocol I, Article 44(4).

18. *US Army's Operational Law Handbook*, JA 422, sections 18–20, cited in A. Roberts, 'Counter-Terrorism, Armed Force and the Laws of War', *Survival*, vol. 44, no. 1, Spring 2002, pp. 7–32, note 46 and accompanying text.

19. Forty-eight states voted in favour, eight abstentions, two not present.

20. <http://www.unhchr.ch/udhr/miscinfo/carta.htm> Mrs Eleanor Roosevelt was personally dedicated to the task of preparing this Declaration and chaired the Human Rights Commission in its first years. She famously proclaimed: 'The destiny of human rights is in the hands of all our citizens in all our communities.'

21. Quoted in Mary Ann Glendon, *A World Made New* (Random House, 2001), p. 166.

22. In its General Comment No. 31 (The Nature of the General Legal Obligation Imposed on States Parties to the Covenant) the UN Human Rights Committee stated: 'States Parties are required by article 2, paragraph 1, to respect and to ensure the Covenant rights to all persons who may be within their territory and to all persons subject to their jurisdiction. This means that a State Party must respect and ensure the rights laid down in the Covenant to anyone within the power or effective control of that State Party, even if not situated within the territory of the State Party.' (UN Doc. CCPR/C/21/Rev.1/Add.13 (2004))

23. The term 'war on terror' was first used by President Bush on 20 September 2001; <http://www.whitehouse.gov/news/releases/2001/09/20010920-8.html> On 24 September 2001 Bush used the term 'war on terrorism': <http://www. whitehouse.gov/news/releases/2001/09/2001024-4.html>

24. Quoted in the *Sydney Morning Herald*, 17 May 2002: see also *ex parte Abbassi*, note 55 below.

25. Memorandum of Colin Powell, 26 January 2001, United States Department of State: available at MSN NBC news, <http://msnbc.msn. com/id/4999363 1/site/newsweek>; memorandum of William H. Taft IV to Counsel to the President, 2 February 2002, <http://www.fas.org/sgp/othergov/taft.pdf>

26. For example, the 1997 Convention for the Suppression of Terrorist Bombings criminalizes terrorist bombings. Article 2(1) states: 'any person commits an offence within the meaning of this convention if that person unlawfully and intentionally delivers, places, discharges or detonates an explosive or other lethal device in, into or against a place of public use, a state or government facility, a public transport system or an infrastructure facility'. Security Council Resolution 1373 (adopted on 28 September 2001) called on states to co-operate in criminalizing a range of activities which could support terrorist attacks.

27. Clive Stafford-Smith, *The Observer*, 22 February 2004: 'Martin Mubanga is one of four apparently condemned to remain indefinitely in Guantánamo. The US pretends he was captured in Afghanistan. He was seized in Zambia. Another British citizen in Cuba, Richard Belmar, was arrested by the Pakistani authorities for overstaying his visa.' Moazzam Begg was not in Afghanistan, but 'abducted from Pakistan', and 'after a year in a windowless cell in Kandahar, he was shackled and taken to Guantánamo'. Jamie Fellner, director of Human Rights Watch's US Programme claimed that at least six suspected al-Qaeda members were picked up in Bosnia-Herzegovina: 'US Courts Abandon Guantánamo Detainees' (21 March 2003 <http://www.hrw.org/editorials/2003/uso32103.htm>). Holding detainees in foreign countries may have certain consequences: 'We don't kick the [expletive] out of them. We send them to other countries so they can kick the [expletive] out of them', unnamed official interviewed by the *Washington Post*, 26 December 2002.

28. <http://www.fas.org/sgp/news/2001/11/bush111301.html> accessed 14 November 2003. The US Department of Defense issued procedural and other rules and instructions on 21 March 2002 and 30 April 2003.

29. President George W. Bush has called the detainees 'bad people' and Secretary of Defense Donald Rumsfeld has labelled them 'hard-core, well-trained terrorists'; 'United States: Guantánamo Two Years On; US Detentions Undermine the Rule of Law', 9 January 2004, Human Rights Watch at <http://hrw.org/english/docs/2004/01/09/usdom6917_txt.htm>

30. This is Lord Steyn's description, in a public lecture given in November 2003. He added the following explanation: 'It derives from the jumps of the kangaroo, and conveys the idea of a preordained arbitrary rush to judgment by an irregular tribunal which makes a mockery of justice.'

31. 'US: New Military Commissions Threaten Rights Credibility', New York, 15 November 2001. Human Rights Watch called on President Bush to rescind his Executive Order permitting the trial of non-citizens by special military commissions; see <http://www.hrw.org/press/2001/11/miltribs1115.htm> accessed 26 February 2004. Elizabeth Andersen, Executive Director of Human Rights Watch, Europe and Central Asia Division, has expressed similar concerns with the UK's Anti-Terrorism, Crime and Security Bill.

32. William F. Schulz, Executive Director, Amnesty International USA, 'Presidential Order on Military Tribunals Threatens Fundamental Principles of Justice', 15 November 2001; at <http://www.amnestyusa.org/news/2001/usa11152001.html>

33. Lawyers' Committee for Human Rights, *Assessing the New Norms: Liberty and Security for the Post September 11 United States* (2003), p. 58.

34. *Johnson v. Eisentrager*, 339 U.S. 763 (1950) (the Supreme Court ruled thus at p. 790).

35. Statement of Daniel Fisk, in *Guantánamo Bay Gazette*, 28 February 2003, p. 3; at <http://www.nsgtmo.navy.mil/gazette/Gazette%20Online%20%20PDF%20Archive/030228.pdf> accessed 17 November 2003.

36. Interview by Bob Edwards with Michael O'Hanlon, Senior Fellow, Brookings Institution, National Public Radio, 28 December 2001; at <http://www.brook.edu/dybdocroot/views/interviews/ohanlon/20011228.htm>

37. Shafiq Rasul, Asif Iqbal, Ruhal Ahmed. For more details, see <http://news.bbc.co.uk/1/hi/uk/3089395.stm>

38. *BBC News*, world edition, 10 October 2003.

39. *The Observer*, 14 March 2004, p. 1.

40. *The Observer*, 16 May 2004, p. 8.

41. Lawyers' Committee for Human Rights, 2003 Report, at p. 54.

42. *Foreign and Commonwealth Office News*, edited transcript of an interview given by the Foreign Secretary to BBC Radio 4, 15 January 2002.

43. *Financial Times*, 15 January 2002 (London edition).

44. *Daily Telegraph*, 17 January 2002.

45. *Financial Times*, 21 January 2002 (London edition).

46. *Washington Times*, 18 January 2002.

47. Memorandum of 7 February 2002, recently declassified; *Washington Post*, 23 June 2004, p. A1.

48. Statement by Kim Gordon-Bates, *Daily Telegraph*, 17 January 2002.

49. *Rasul v. Bush*, No. 03-334 S.C. U.S., 25 October 2002.

50. *Al Odah v. Bush*, No. 03-343 S.C. U.S., 14 January 2004.

51. *Johnson v. Eisentrager*, 339 U.S. 763 (1950).

52. The rules are reproduced in volume 37 of the *International and Comparative Law Quarterly* (1988) at p. 1006.

53. See Hansard, 16 December 1999, statement of Baroness Scotland of Asthal.

54. It has subsequently been reported that it was around this time – April 2002 – that Blair and Bush were reaching agreement on the use of force in Iraq: see John Kampfner, *Blair's Wars* (Free Press, 2003), p. 191.

55. *Abbassi v. Secretary of State for Foreign and Commonwealth Affairs*, 6 November 2002, *International Legal Materials*, 42 (2003), p. 358, at para. 57.

56. *Oppenheim v. Cattermole* [1976] AC 249, see Lord Cross at 277G.

57. Letter from the IACHR to the US, 12 March 2001.

58. *Liversidge v. Anderson* (1942) AC 206, at 244.

59. See note 55 above, at paragraphs 64, 66 and 107.

60. *The Guardian*, 25 January 2002.

61. Reported in *Evening Standard*, 22 October 2003; Hansard, col. 632 (22 October 2003), reply in House of Commons to Mr A. J. Beith (Berwick-upon-Tweed).

62. See Lord Brennan QC, 'Camp Delta is a legal black hole for the US', *Financial Times*, 24 November 2003.

63. Chris Mullin, Minister of State at the Foreign and Commonwealth Office, quoted in *The Guardian*, 9 July 2003.

64. Press Association, 9 July 2003.

65. *Financial Times*, 10 July 2003.

66. In October 2002 the Attorney General appeared before the English Court of Appeal to challenge the decision of a lower court that the indefinite detention of suspected terrorists who were non-nationals but resident in the United Kingdom violated English law because it was discriminatory on grounds of nationality (equally dangerous British nationals could not be detained under these or similar conditions). Although his application before the Court of Appeal was successful, on 16 December 2004 the Appellate Committee of the House of Lords ruled that the detentions were discriminatory and contrary to the United Kingdom's international treaty obligations. Lord Bingham set out the rationale for his judgment: 'What cannot be justified here is the decision to detain one group of suspected international terrorists, defined by nationality or immigration status, and not another.' See *A and others v. Secretary of State for the Home Department*, 16 December 2004, at para. 68.

67. See written answer of Baroness Scotland, Hansard, HL 2060, col. WA71 (28 April 2004). The government conceded that the means by which evidence was obtained could go to its reliability and weight.

68. Lord Steyn, 'Guantánamo Bay: The Legal Black Hole', Twenty-Seventh F. A. Mann Lecture, British Institute of International and Comparative Law and Herbert Smith, Lincoln's Inn Old Hall, 25 November 2003.

69. Nicholas Watt, 'Bush aids Blair by halting trial of Britons in Guantánamo Bay', *The Guardian*, 19 July 2003, p. 8.

70. *BBC News*, 21 July 2003; available at <http://news.bbc.co.uk/1/hi/uk-politics/3082773.stm>

71. Julian Borger, 'Britons held in Cuba will not be executed', *The Guardian*, 23 July 2003, p. 1.

72. Nicholas Watt, 'US ready to make new offer on Guantánamo Bay Britons', *The Guardian*, 13 August 2003, p. 7.

73. Clare Dyer, 'Democracies must respect terror suspects' rights says Attorney General', *The Guardian*, 18 September 2003, p. 7.

74. Charles Levendosky, 'Isolation and despair in a legal limbo: Guantánamo', *International Herald Tribune*, 15 October 2003, p. 9.

75. 'President Bush discusses Iraq policy at Whitehall Palace in London', remarks by the President at Whitehall Palace, London, Office of the Press Secretary, 9 November 2003; available at <http://www.whitehouse.gov/news/releases/2003/11/20031119-1.html>

76. David Rose, 'How We Survived Jail Hell', *The Observer*, 14 March 2004.

77. *BBC News*, 25 June 2004; available at <http://news.bbc.co.uk/1/hi/uk-politics/3837823.stm>

78. Press Association, 26 June 2004.

79. *Rasul et al. v. Bush*, No. 03-334, and 03-343, 28 June 2004.

80. See Tim Golden, 'Threats and responses : tough justice', *New York Times*, 25 October 2004, p. 1.

81. *Sadim Ahmed Hamdan v. Donald H. Rumsfeld*, Civil Action No. 04-1519, US District Court for the District of Columbia, Judge Robertson, 8 November 2004.

82. Separate Opinion of President Schwebel, Case concerning Vienna Convention on Consular Relations (*Paraguay v. US*), ICJ Order of 9 April 1998.

8 Kicking Ass in Iraq

1. John Bolton, '"Legitimacy" in International Affairs: The American Perspective in Theory and Practice', remarks to the Federalist Society, Washington, DC, 13 November 2003.

2. Quoted in Richard Clarke, *Against All Enemies* (Free Press, 2004), p. 24.

3. Anne-Marie Slaughter, 'Good Reasons for Going Around the UN', *New York Times*, 18 March 2003, Section A, p. 33.

4. See *American Society of International Law Newsletter*, March/April 2004, p. 1.

5. *The Times*, 1 March 2004, p. 4; *Daily Telegraph*, 1 March 2004, p. 9.

6. *BBC News*, 8 November 2004; Stephen Wall, 'The US can only be constrained by international law', *The Independent*, 9 November 2004, p. 31.

7. See the Covenant of the League of Nations, Articles 12, 13 and 15.

8. Ibid., Article 15(7).

9. On 'anticipatory self-defence', see the author's Memorandum to the House of Commons Select Committee on Foreign Affairs, 1 June 2004.

10. T. Franck, *Recourse to Force: State Action Against Threats and Armed Attacks* (Cambridge University Press, 2002), p. 50.

11. The National Security Strategy of the United States, September 2002, at p. 15; available at <http://www.whitehouse.gov/nsc/nss.html>

12. Speech by Tony Blair at Sedgefield, County Durham, 5 March 2004.

13. In 1966 Article 42 had provided the basis for the Security Council's authorization for Britain to use force against tankers discharging oil from Rhodesia.

14. Resolution 678 does not mention Article 42, which has led to different

views as to whether that provision was indeed the legal basis on which force was authorized. Although that seems to be the more compelling view, there is some academic support for the view that the Council was acting on the basis of Articles 42 and 51 of the Charter; see B. Simma, *The Charter of the United Nations: A Commentary* (Oxford University Press, 1995), p. 635.

15. Quoted in T. Franck, op. cit., p. 167, note 3.

16. Ibid., pp. 167–8.

17. Security Council resolution 1244 (10 June 1999); see also G. Simpson, *Great Powers and Outlaw States: Unequal Sovereigns in the International Legal Order* (Cambridge University Press, 2004).

18. *Sunday Telegraph*, 29 February 2004, p. 24.

19. At a meeting in London in November 2003, Richard Perle, then a member of the US Defense Policy Board advising Donald Rumsfeld, surprised his audience with the claim that 'international law . . . would have required us to leave Saddam Hussein alone'; *The Guardian*, 20 November 2003.

20. See Robert Cooper, *The Breaking of Nations: Order and Chaos in the Twenty-First Century* (Atlantic Books, 2003), p. 155, where he discusses Robert Kagan's argument in *Paradise and Power* (Atlantic Books, 2003).

21. *BBC News*, World edition, 12 January 2004.

22. John Kampfner, *Blair's Wars* (Free Press, 2003), p. 156.

23. *New York Times*, 6 April 2002, Section A, p. 9.

24. Gaby Hinsliff, 'Blair in firing line on Iraq leak', *The Observer*, 19 September 2004, p. 4.

25. Cited in Andrew Gilligan, 'Why did the Attorney General change his advice?', *The Spectator*, 6 March 2004, p. 12.

26. Kampfner, op. cit., p. 168.

27. Margaret Thatcher, *The Downing Street Years* (HarperCollins, 1993), p. 331.

28. Statement to House of Commons, 25 February 2003, Hansard, HC, vol. 400, col. 125.

29. Speech at Sedgefield, County Durham, 5 March 2004, op. cit.

30. BBC Radio 4, *Today* programme, 26 February 2004,('I had to make sure that we didn't promise a misuse of aid in a way that would be illegal.') <http://news. bbc.co.uk/l/hi/uk_politics/3489372.stm>

31. Brian Brady, 'Secrets and lies', *Scotland on Sunday*, 29 February 2004, p. 13. On 27 February 2004, Mexico's UN Ambassador, Enrique Berruga, stated that Mexico had sent a diplomatic note to the British government in December 2003 asking whether Britain and the US had been bugging diplomatic calls. Asked if Mexico was worried Britain might have been spying, he replied: 'Yes, based upon what was released out of this (Gun) trial': *The Guardian*, 28 February 2004.

32. Kampfner, op. cit., p. 276.

33. Available at <http://www.number-10.gov.uk/output/Page3250.asp>

34. 'Iraq's Weapons of Mass Destruction: The Assessment of the British Government', September 2002, p. 17; at <http://www.number-10.gov.uk/files/pdf/iraqdossier.pdf>

35. The Report of the Butler Inquiry concluded that the Joint Intelligence Committee should not have included the '45-minute' report in its assessment and in the government's dossier without stating what it was believed to refer to: *Review of Intelligence on Weapons of Mass Destruction*, 14 July 2004, para. 511. The '45'-minute claim was subsequently withdrawn: Marie Woolf, 'The 45-minute claim was false', *The Independent*, 13 October 2004.

36. National Security Strategy of the United States (September 2002), p. 15; see also note 10 above.

37. Hansard, HL, vol. 646, col. WA3 (17 March 2003).

38. These are reflected in Articles 31 and 32 of the 1969 Vienna Convention on the Law of Treaties, which embody customary international law.

39. Colin Powell, *A Soldier's Way* (Arrow Books, 1995), p. 490.

40. General Sir Peter de la Billiere, *Storm Command* (HarperCollins, 1995), p. 304, cited by Lord Alexander of the Weedon in 'Iraq: Pax Americana and the Law', Tom Sargant memorial annual lecture, 14 October 2003.

41. John Major, speaking at Texas A&M University 10th anniversary celebrations of the liberation of Kuwait, 23 February 2001, cited in Lord Alexander of the Weedon, 'Iraq: Pax Americana and the Law', op. cit., 14 October 2003.

42. V. Lowe, 'The Iraq Crisis: What Now?', vol. 52, *International and Comparative Law Quarterly* (2003), p. 859 at 865. The Attorney General has also sought to derive support for the 'revival' argument from the practice of the Security Council. He has referred to actions taken by the coalition in 1993 and 1998 following determinations by the Security Council that Iraq was in violation of its obligations under various resolutions. Three points may be made in response. First, the actions taken in 1993 and 1998 were of a far more limited character and scope than those taken in March 2003. Second, the respective actions have to be taken in the context of the particular facts which existed, including the statements made by the presidency and members of the Security Council, reflecting the assent of that body. Third, and most importantly, the 1993 and 1998 actions were not accompanied by any equivalent to resolution 1441, which envisaged a particular 'mechanism of controls and assessment' to be applied by the Council in relation to any Iraqi non-compliance.

43. 'Legal authority for the possible use of force against Iraq', 1998 *Proceedings of the 92nd Annual Meeting of the American Society of*

International Law, pp. 136–50 (see in particular the comments of Michael Matheson, Principal Deputy Legal Adviser, US State Department).

44. US Explanation of Vote, given by US Permanent Representative to the United Nations, John Negroponte:<http://www.un.org/webcast/usa110802.htm> See also the opinion by Rabinder Singh, QC, and Charlotte Kilroy, 15 November 2002, available at <http://www.publicinterestlawyers.co.uk/legaldocs/OPINION2.doc>

45. Quoted by Lord Thomas of Gresford during the debate in the House of Lords, 17 March 2003, Hansard, cols. 78 and 79.

46. Ibid.

47. Lord Alexander of the Weedon, 'Iraq: Pax Americana and the Law', op. cit.

48. Kofi Annan is quoted by Lord Brennan as having stated that 'The members of the Security Council now face a great choice. If they fail to agree on a common position, and action is taken without the authority of the Security Council, the legitimacy and support for any such action will be seriously impaired.' Hansard, House of Lords, 17 March 2003, col. 85.

49. The Report of the Butler Review (Stationery Office, 14 July 2004), para. 266; also available online at <http://www.butlerreview.org.uk/report>

50. Ibid., para. 267.

51. Memorandum from Sir David Manning to the Prime Minister, 18 March 2003, in *The Observer*, 19 September 2004, p. 4.

52. Ministerial Code of Conduct, para. 22.

53. Robin Cook, *The Point of Departure* (Pocket Books, 2004) p. 135.

54. *The Observer*, 7 March 2004, p. 1.

55. Ibid., p. 2.

56. The Report of the Butler Review, op. cit., para. 472.

57. Paragraph 23 of the Code states: 'When advice from the law officer is included in correspondence between Ministers, or in papers for the Cabinet or Ministerial Committees, the conclusions may if necessary be summarized but, if this is done, the complete text of the advice should be attached.'

58. Ms Short did resign a few weeks later, however. In 1991 she had resigned from the Labour Shadow Cabinet in opposition to the first Gulf War, even though it had been authorized by the Security Council and was plainly legal.

59. J. Kampfner, 'The law chief who bowed to Blair', *New Statesman*, 22 November 2004, p. 9.

60. *New Statesman*, 29 November 2004.

61. Felicity Barringer, 'The Struggle for Iraq: United Nations; Annan tells General Assembly that UN must correct its weaknesses', *New York Times*, 23 September 2003, p. 13. Also Secretary General's Address to the General

Assembly available at <http://www.un.org/webcast/ga/58/ statements/sg2eng 030923.htm>

62. See note 19.

9 Terrorists and Torturers

1. Convention against Torture and Other Cruel, Inhuman or Degrading Treatment or Punishment (1984), Article 16.

2. Ibid., Article 2(2).

3. The International Convention for the Suppression of Terrorist Bombings (1997), Article 14.

4. Supreme Court of Israel, judgment concerning the legality of the General Security Service's interrogation methods, 6 September 1999, reproduced in *International Legal Materials*, vol. 38 (1999), 1471.

5. US Army *Field Manual* (1987), sections 34–52, Chapter 1.

6. See US Department of Defense, News Release No. 596-04, 22 June 2004.

7. Joint Task Force 170-SJA, Memorandum to Commander, Joint Task Force 170, 11 October 2002.

8. Memorandum from the Office of the Deputy Assistant Attorney General to Alberto Gonzales, Counsel to the President, 1 August 2002. This and other memoranda are reproduced in R. Greenberg and J. Dratel, *The Torture Papers: The Road to Abu Ghraib* (Cambridge University Press, forthcoming, 2005).

9. Memorandum from Assistant Attorney General for Alberto Gonzales, Counsel to the President, Re: Standards for the Conduct for Interrogation under 18 USC 2340–2340A, 1 August 2002.

10. David Johnston and James Risen, 'US memo provided basis for CIA coercion', *New York Times*, 28 June 2004, p. 6.

11. Memorandum from Alberto Gonzales, Counsel to the President, 1 August 2002, US Department of Justice, Office of Legal Counsel, p. 46; also available at <http://www.washingtonpost.com/wp_srv/nation/documents/ dojinterrogationmemo20020801/.pdf>

12. Ibid.

13. Ibid., p. 41.

14. Ibid., p. 45.

15. Quoted in Edward Alden, 'Dismay at attempt to find legal justification for torture', *Financial Times*, 10 June 2004, p. 7.

16. Joint Task Force-J2, Memorandum for Commander, Joint Task Force 170, 'Request for Approval of Counter-Resistance Strategies', 11 October 2002.

17. Memorandum for Chairman of Joint Chiefs of Staff, on Counter-

Resistance Techniques, 25 October 2002.

18. Memorandum from William J. Haynes, General Counsel Department of Defense, to the Secretary of Defense, 27 November 2002.

19. Jess Bravin, 'Security or Legal Factors Could Trump Restrictions, Memo to Rumsfeld Argued', *Wall Street Journal*, 7 June 2004, section A, p. 1.

20. Ibid.

21. Ibid.

22. Working Group Report on Detainee Interrogations in the Global War on Terrorism: Assessment of Legal, Historical, Policy and Operational Conditions, 6 March 2003, p. 21; available on Center for Constitutional Rights website at <http://www.ccr_ny.org>

23. Hearing of the Senate Armed Services Committee, Federal News Service, 13 May 2004.

24. Guy Dinmore and James Harding, 'Rumsfeld stays vague on what and when', *Financial Times*, 8 May 2004, p. 3.

25. 'Violations were "tantamount to torture"', *The Guardian*, 8 May 2004, p. 4.

26. The White House, press briefing by White House Counsel, Judge Alberto Gonzales, and others, 22 June 2004.

27. Douglas Jehl, 'US Rules on Prisoners Seen as a Back and Forth of Mixed Messages to GIs', *New York Times*, 22 June 2004, section A, p. 7.

28. Ibid.

29. Edward Alden, 'Dismay at attempt to find legal justification for torture', *Financial Times*, 10 June 2004, p. 7.

10 Tough Guys and Lawyers

1. See the discussion in Preface, pp. xiii–xiv.

2. The signatories to the statement of principles included many individuals closely associated with George W. Bush's Administration, including Jeb Bush, Dick Cheney, Paula Dobriansky, Lewis Libby, Donald Rumsfeld and Paul Wolfowitz.

3. The US Army's Report on the investigation of the Abu Ghraib prison concluded that 'the existence of confusing and inconsistent interrogation technique policies contributed to the belief that additional interrogation techniques were condoned in order to gain intelligence'. AR 15– Investigation of the Abu Ghraib Prison and 205th Military Intelligence Brigade, LTG Anthony Jones, August 2004, p. 15.

4. The *New York Times* declined to publish the following letter written by leading American academics: 'Forgotten in the debate over war with Iraq is the effect on our entire structure as a society operating under the rule of

law. That effect could be highly destructive. The United Nations Charter is not just an obsolete inconvenience to those in power, although law is frequently so regarded by politicians. It is the most widely ratified treaty in human history, a binding legal obligation to which the U.S. has committed itself in accordance with its constitutional process. Article VI of that Constitution decrees that treaties are "the supreme Law of the Land" and that the President "shall take care that the Laws be faithfully executed." Charter law does not permit the President to launch this war unless there has first been an armed attack by Iraq against the U.S. (Charter Art. 51) or the Security Council has authorized the use of force (Charter Art. 39). In the case of America's response to al-Qaeda, both of these conditions were arguably met before force was deployed. In respect of the use of force against Iraq, neither condition has been met. These limitations on the right of states to decide for themselves when their national interest required the use of force against others was included in the Charter at our insistence and in reaction against Hitler's claim to have been defending Germany against Czechoslovakia and Poland. Whether these Charter-imposed limitations on the President's right to protect America by making war on Iraq are convenient or reasonable is beside the point. They are the law and there are powerful policy reasons for respecting that law. Indeed they are not only international, but also U.S. constitutional, law. For the President to treat them as dispensable is not only to violate the Charter but also to call into question his commitment to carrying out his constitutional duty to faithfully execute all of the laws, including international law, a costly way to pursue our security. As professors of constitutional and international law we are concerned that if the U.S. rides roughshod over international law today, we will create precedents that will surely come back to haunt us when invoked by our enemies in the years ahead.' The letter was signed by Thomas Franck, New York University (NYU); Philip Alston, NYU; Richard Falk, University of California, Santa Barbara; Balakrishnan Rajagopal, MIT; Jose Alvarez, Columbia University; Hurst Hannum, Tufts University; David Golove, NYU; Norman Dorsen, NYU; Tom Farer, University of Denver.

5. *A and others v. Secretary of State for the Home Department, X and another v. Secretary of State for the Home Department,* Appellate Committee of the House of Lords, 16 December 2004, at paras 97 and 155. In July 2004 the House of Lords and House of Commons Joint Committee on Human Rights had recommended that the powers of indefinite detention under Part 4 of the Anti-Terrorism, Crime and Security Act 2001 should be replaced as a matter of urgency: 18th Report, 21 July 2004, HL 158/HC713. The Committee endorsed a similar conclusion by the Privy Council or Review

Committee (Anti-Terrorism, Crime and Security Act 2001 Review); Report HC 100, 2003–4, 18 December 2003.

6. The Report of the Butler Review (Stationery Office, 14 July 2004), para. 472.

7. In September 2004, Chechen separatists stormed a school in Beslan in the southern Russian province of Northern Ossetia, taking hundreds of children, teachers and parents hostage. The ending of the siege resulted in the deaths of hundreds of hostages and most of the terrorists.

8. Speech by Tony Blair at Sedgefield, County Durham, 5 March 2004.

9. Jed Rubenfeld, 'The Two World Orders', *Wilson Quarterly*, Autumn 2003.

10. See Preface, note 2.

11. Robert Kagan, 'The Power Divide', *Prospect*, 25 July 2002, p. 23.

12. Sir Michael Howerd, 'Smoke on the horizon', *Financial Times*, 7 September 2002, Weekend section, p. 1.

13. 12 U.S. (8 Cranch) 110, 129, 153 (1814).

14. Francis Ford Coppola's film *The Godfather, Part III* (Michael Corleone (Al Pacino): 'I don't need tough guys, I need more lawyers.')

Index

NOTE: Page numbers in bold refer to the Appendices; the Notes are indexed (as 290n) only where there is substantial additional information.